CLARA
AT THE DOOR
WITH A
REVOLVER

Clara Ford, *Toronto World,* December 1, 1894

CAROLYN WHITZMAN

CLARA AT THE DOOR WITH A REVOLVER

*The Scandalous Black Suspect,
the Exemplary White Son, and the
Murder That Shocked Toronto*

on
point
PRESS | a UBC Press imprint
Vancouver . Toronto

© On Point Press, an imprint of UBC Press 2023

32 31 30 29 28 27 26 25 24 23   5 4 3 2 1

Printed in Canada on FSC-certified ancient-forest-free paper (100% postconsumer recycled) that is processed chlorine- and acid-free, with vegetable-based inks.

Library and Archives Canada Cataloguing in Publication

Title: Clara at the door with a revolver : the scandalous Black suspect, the exemplary White son, and the murder that shocked Toronto / Carolyn Whitzman.

Names: Whitzman, Carolyn, author.

Description: Includes bibliographical references and index.

Identifiers: Canadiana (print) 20220411980 | Canadiana (ebook) 20220412030 | ISBN 9780774890618 (softcover) | ISBN 9780774890625 (PDF) | ISBN 9780774890632 (EPUB)

Subjects: LCSH: Ford, Clara, 1864?– | LCSH: Ford, Clara, 1864?– —Trials, litigation, etc. | LCSH: Westwood, Frank, –1894. | LCSH: Murder—Ontario—Toronto—Case studies. | LCSH: Trials (Murder)—Ontario—Toronto. | LCSH: Women, Black—Ontario—Toronto—Social conditions—19th century. | LCSH: Toronto (Ont.)—Race relations—History—19th century. | LCSH: Toronto (Ont.)—Social life and customs—19th century. | LCGFT: Biographies.

Classification: LCC HV6535.C33 T67 2023 | DDC 364.152/3092—dc23

Canadä

UBC Press gratefully acknowledges the financial support for our publishing program of the Government of Canada (through the Canada Book Fund), the Canada Council for the Arts, and the British Columbia Arts Council.

On Point, an imprint of UBC Press
The University of British Columbia
2029 West Mall
Vancouver, BC V6T 1Z2
www.ubcpress.ca

I *am* a woman's rights.
I have as much muscle as any man,
and can do as much work as any man ...
I am as strong as any man that is now.

– SOJOURNER TRUTH'S SPEECH
AT THE WOMEN'S RIGHTS CONVENTION
IN AKRON, OHIO, 1851

CONTENTS

THE FORD-MCKAY FAMILY

Clara Ford: The hero of this story. Born in 1861, she disappears from the historical record in 1898. A mixed-race woman who worked as a tailor, waitress, servant, and dancer.

Flora McKay: Clara's elder daughter. Born in 1879, she disappears from the historical record in 1895. Flora was fourteen at the time of the murder and worked as a servant. She was the chief witness against her mother, refuting Clara's alibi that they'd been to the theatre together the night of the murder.

Jessie McKay: Clara's mother. Born circa 1826, she died in March 1894. A white woman born in Scotland, she worked as a nurse-maid, washerwoman, and housecleaner.

Annie (Mitchell) Ford: Clara's younger daughter. Born in 1887, she disappears from the historical record in 1903. Age seven at the time of the murder, she was in the Girl's Home (an orphanage) during the arrest and trial. She later became a servant.

THE WESTWOOD FAMILY

Frank Westwood: Born in 1876, he was murdered in 1894 at the age of eighteen. The son of a successful businessman, he'd just graduated from high school and started work in a department store owned by a friend of his father.

Benjamin Westwood: Frank's father. A successful businessman, ardent Methodist and prohibitionist, and Liberal politician.

Clara Westwood: Frank's mother.

Willie and Emily Westwood: Frank's younger brother, with whom he shared a room, and his sister, aged sixteen and twelve at the time of their older brother's murder.

Bert and Maggie Westwood: Frank's older brother and sister-in-law. Recently married and the parents of a baby, they lived around the corner from the rest of the family.

THE JOURNALISTS

Hector Charlesworth: Clara's chief journalistic persecutor, he worked for *The World,* the most sensationalist of Toronto's seven newspapers in 1894. His 1925 memoirs are the main source of misinformation on the murder.

Charles Clark: Journalist for *The Telegram* and Clara's chief defender in the media.

John Miller: Journalist for *The Mail* and drinking buddy of Gus Clark.

C.S. Clark: Pseudonymous author of *Of Toronto the Good* (1898), who both exposed and glorified sexual hypocrisy.

THE POLICE DETECTIVES

Charley Slemin: A detective based in Parkdale, his suborning of false testimony during Clara's trial was a major determinant in her acquittal. His partner on the day of Clara's arrest was *George Porter.*

Sergeant Henry Reburn: A senior detective, he secured Clara's confession on the night of her arrest. His superior officer was *Inspector William Stark.*

THE CLARK FAMILY

Gus Clark: The Westwoods' twenty-three-year-old next-door neighbour, Clark was the chief suspect in the murder until he suggested Clara as a suspect. An alcoholic and petty criminal, he was in prison for stealing from his mother at the time of the trial.

John Clark: Gus's father. An inspector at the Customs Office, heavily involved in local Liberal politics and ambitious land schemes, he fathered thirteen children and died in 1889 after a long illness.

Catherine Clark: John's second wife and Gus's mother, she was Clara's friend and landlady from 1888 to 1892. She testified as a character witness for Clara at her trial. By then, she owned the CPR Tavern on Yonge Street in North Toronto.

Carrie and Christian Dorenwend: Gus's sister and brother-in-law. Christian employed Gus in his electric vibrator business and was a witness against Clara at the trial.

Ida Clark: Carrie Dorenwend's younger sister, she shared a room with Clara in 1889–90 and testified as a character witness on her behalf.

CLARA'S CONFIDANTES

Rev. Charles Ingles: He knew Clara for fifteen years, from his time at St. Luke's Anglican Church in uptown Toronto to his tenure at St. Mark's in Parkdale. He testified as a character witness for Clara.

Mary Crosier: The mother of eleven children, with a sickly husband, she was Clara's landlady in 1893 and a close friend. She and her daughters testified against Clara at the trial, saying that they saw her armed, agitated, and halfway to Parkdale the night of the murder.

Chloe Dorsey: Clara's landlady at the time of her arrest. She, her husband, John, and his four brothers were some of the most prominent businesspeople on York Street, the epicentre of Toronto's Black community. Chloe, her daughter Mamie, her lodger Eliza Reed, and three staff at the Grand Opera House provided an alibi for Clara.

Harriet Phyall: As housekeeper at the Magann house close to the Westwoods and Clarks, Harriet employed Flora in Parkdale in the early 1890s and in a downtown boarding house she ran in late 1894. She testified against Clara, saying Flora had been at her house on the night of Frank's shooting, not at the theatre with her mother.

THE LAWYERS AND JUDGES

Colonel George Denison: A prominent Toronto landowner; as police magistrate for Toronto from 1877 to 1921, he was the enemy of Black, Irish Catholic, and labour defendants. He presided over Clara's arraignment. His memoir, along with that of Hector Charlesworth, is one of only two accounts of Clara Ford's trial by someone directly involved.

William Murdoch: A journeyman lawyer, he defended Clara at her arraignment and carried most of the defence at her trial. No relation to Maureen Jennings' fictional detective.

E.F.B. (Ebenezer Forsyth Blackie) Johnston, Queen's Counsel: A show-pony lawyer, and one of the best known of his era, he joined Clara's defence team in January 1895 and is usually given credit for her acquittal.

B.B. (Britton Bath) Osler, Queen's Counsel: The most famous lawyer of the day, he rose to prominence by helping secure the conviction of Louis Riel for treason. He was brought in to lead the Crown's case against Clara after Johnston came on board. The death of his wife on the second day of the trial led to his withdrawal from the case.

Hartley Dewart: An ambitious young Crown, he was involved in the inquest and took over the lead prosecution role after Osler's withdrawal. He later became the leader of the Ontario Liberal Party.

John Alexander Boyd: Chancellor of the High Court of Justice for Ontario and the remarkably incompetent judge in Clara's trial, he referred to himself in the third person as "the Chancellor." His ruling in the *St. Catharine's Milling and Lumber Company* case set back Indigenous land rights claims for nearly a century.

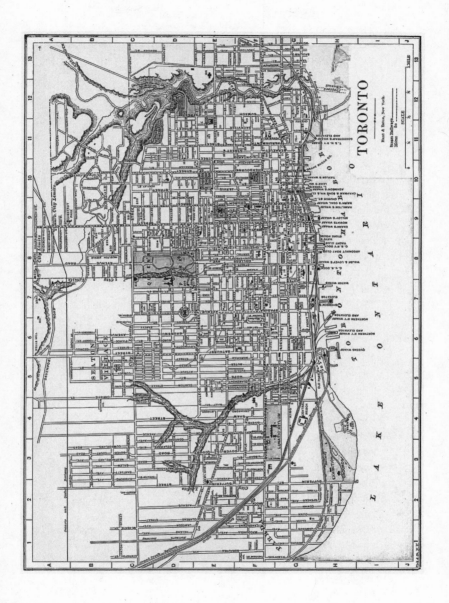

TORONTO

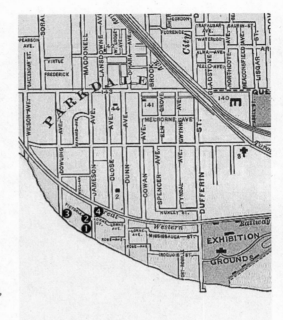

Parkdale neighbourhood, showing (1) the Westwood estate, Lakeside Hall, (2) the Clark estate, (3) the Magann estate, and (4) the train station.

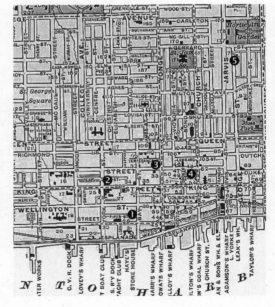

Downtown and the Ward, showing (1) where Frank Westwood worked, (2) Chloe Dorsey's restaurant and lodgings, (3) the Grand Opera House, (4) the courthouse, and (5) Mrs. Phyall's boarding house, where Flora McKay lived and worked.

CLARA
AT THE DOOR
WITH A
REVOLVER

CAKEWALK

Florence Hines, undated (circa 1890–1905)

*S*aturday, *April 21, 1894, Academy of Music, Toronto*
The curtain rises, and a Black woman steps onto centre stage.

Florence Hines is dressed as a man. And not just any man but a young white dandy, arrayed in the latest fashion, with a flask in his pocket, a fedora hat set at a jaunty angle on his head, and a cane in his elegant hand.

Florence begins the show with her latest hit song, "Hi Waiter! A Dozen More Bottles!":

> *Lovely woman was made to be loved,*
> *To be fondled and courted and kissed;*
> *And the fellows who've never made love to a girl,*
> *Well they don't know what fun they have missed.*
> *I'm a fellow, who's up on the times,*
> *Just the boy for a lark or a spree*
> *There's a chap that's dead stuck on women and wine,*
> *You can bet your old boots that it's me.*

Hundreds of audience members raise a cheer for the star of Sam T. Jack's Creole Company.

One of them sits in the fifteen-cent stalls. Thirty-two-year-old Clara Ford, an impoverished Black woman, works as a tailor in the slums of downtown Toronto. Tall and striking, she is well known to the ushers because she, like Florence Hines, is notorious for wearing men's clothes. Her sartorial choices have nearly gotten her arrested more than once, and they've given her a reputation for being eccentric and possibly insane. But whether dressed as a woman or a man, Clara prides herself on looking neat. Her close-fitting hunter green Eton jacket is on its last legs, but there are no loose threads. She holds in her lap a dashing black fedora with ribbon and feather, a new kind of hat that can be worn by both women and men.

Next to Clara is her fourteen-year-old daughter, Flora McKay. Flora works as a servant in a boarding house. Her grey plaid tam-o'-shanter cap pays tribute to her Scottish name and ancestry. Her long curly black hair is held back by a brown comb. Flora is lighter-skinned than her mother and considered conventionally attractive (sexualization begins young for nineteenth-century Black girls). Some people have told her, as though it's praise, that Flora could "pass for white." Both wear black crepe sashes on their arms to signify mourning. Jessie McKay, Clara's mother and Flora's grandmother, died a month ago, after a long illness.

Six months later, in November 1894, Clara Ford will be arrested for the murder of a rich, young white man, Frank Westwood, and will hit levels of fame only dreamed of by Florence Hines. In a year, after giving the performance of her life, she'll be acquitted, even though she confessed to the crime the night she was arrested. Three months after that, she'll step onto a stage as a member of the chorus in Sam T. Jack's Creole Company, and she'll dance the cakewalk.

Clara is about to set impressive precedents. The first woman – and only the second person – to testify on her own behalf in a Canadian trial, she will successfully convince a jury of twelve white men that she was forced into a false confession by the police. During the trial by the media that preceded her day in court, she will become the first person described by a North American newspaper as "homosexual" – in a two-day, multipage spread devoted to her alleged perversions, no less. Clara will triumph over near-universal vilification to become a working-class heroine. An impromptu parade on the streets of downtown Toronto will follow her acquittal. And then she will disappear, and liars will take her reputation and stomp all over it again.

Clara loved the dramatic arts. After a late dinner at her boarding house, she'd disappear into her room to read novels, and on Saturday nights, she and Flora would treat themselves to a show. She sang in a church choir on Sundays until the minister, Charles Ingles, dismissed all women and replaced them with choirboys.

Florence Hines was a role model for Clara. Hines had been a stand-out success since Sam T. Jack's Creole Minstrel Show began touring North America in 1891. Newspapers referred to her as an "excellent male impersonator" and "the greatest living female song and dance artist." Little is known about Hines (including where and when she was born) or her path to becoming "the highest paid Black woman on the stage." We do know that Florence's on-stage performances included flirting with women, which probably reflected her off-stage sexuality. In 1892, she got into an on-stage fight with a fellow performer named Marie Roberts. The *Cincinnati Reporter* said: "The utmost intimacy has existed between the two women for the past year, their marked devotion being not only noticeable but a subject of comment among their associates on the stage."

There was a delicate balance on stage between exploitation and challenging societal stereotypes, as Clara would have known watching the show. Sam T. Jack, the producer of the show, was white. His show was advertised, that spring evening in Toronto, as featuring scantily clad "genuine Creole maidens from the balmy shores of Louisiana." One headline attraction was Mademoiselle Fatima, a supposed "Cairo girl" who'd introduced belly dancing at the Chicago World Exhibition's midway stage in 1891. She, like the rest of the company, was an American-born Black actor playing a role. In many ways, Jack was continuing the tradition of the minstrel show: exoticized and degrading portrayals of Black people as objects to be laid out for the white gaze. What we now call "Orientalism," a fetishization of the Other, could be seen in full glory across North America in the 1890s. The competing travelling attractions at Toronto's two other main theatres that Saturday night were *A Trip to Chinatown* at the Grand Opera House and *The Soudan* at Jacob's and Sparrow's.

But Jack did something that no white producer had done before (at least publicly). He hired Black women and men to write as well as perform their own material. Among the performers Clara watched that night were the Mallory Brothers, who created some of the earliest ragtime music for the troupe. Hines herself would later be considered a pioneering blues singer, an inspiration to artists such as Big Mama Thornton and Bessie Smith. Madame Flowers, another performer in the company, was the great gospel voice of her time. Bob Cole and J.R. Johnston, songwriters and performers in the show, also penned some of the best-selling sheet music of the 1890s. (Their most famous song today, one of the first hit records in 1902, is "Under the Bamboo Tree." It remains popular despite its dated lyrics about Zulus and their ways of expressing attraction.) Inspired by *A Trip to Chinatown,* Cole and Johnston had started work on what would be one of the first full-length Broadway musicals, *A Trip to Coontown.*

On the night that Clara Ford sat in the audience, after Hines sang her song, the corps de ballet performed a cakewalk, set to ragtime music. The cakewalk was the dance craze of the day. In 1892 in New York City, one performance drew over a thousand audience members. J.R. Johnston's brother Charles Johnston and Charles' wife, Dora Dean, were the most famous performers of the cakewalk, and they'd continue to be stars for three more decades.

The cakewalk originated in the plantations of the southern United States, where enslaved Black people developed the satiric dance by mimicking the manners of white slaveholders. In the processional march, dancers throw their heads back in pride, and their exaggerated mincing movements mock stately dances such as the minuet. Occasionally, a performer steps out for a dance specialty.

In film capture of the cakewalk from the first decade of the twentieth century, there are echoes of *Soul Train* a century later.

The cakewalk became a signature dance of the minstrel show, a musical genre where white performers rubbed burnt cork on their faces and "sentimentalized the nightmare life of a plantation." Occasionally, Black men joined minstrel troupes and "blacked up" their own faces, but they had no say over the script or the production.

Sam T. Jack's Creole Company show, which shed the term "minstrel" not long after it began touring, was a step forward. It had the same format as a minstrel show (which would go on to influence the next phase of popular entertainment, vaudeville). In the first act, an interlocutor, or master of ceremonies, began by introducing a circle of performers, who told jokes, performed dances, and sang. The second act, called an olio or entr'acte, usually satirized events of the day and had a "star turn." The third act was a short musical drama. The Creole Company show had the same format, but the interlocutor was a Black woman, Black songwriters published the syncopated rhythms of ragtime under their own names, and it supported a new "a comedic tradition ... that was racially grounded but resisted stereotypes."

Florence Hines was riffing on the tradition of Zip Coon, the Black city slicker who was a staple of the minstrel show, along with his country cousin, Jim Crow. But the lyrics of Hines's songs explicitly mocked rich white "swells" with more money than brains. Hines and other Black performers such as Bob Cole, who played the red-whiskered Willy Wayside, a comedic hobo who was a forerunner of Charlie Chaplin's Little Tramp, were in whiteface. They played recognizably white characters and didn't need to chalk their faces to get the point across. The audience laughed with them, not at them. In Hines's case, satirizing the dominant group involved gender and race subversion.

The social origins of the cakewalk were "black people imitating white people imitating black people imitating white people," a dizzying level of cultural complexity. Perhaps it's better to focus on the fact that the theatre was a relatively safe space in a deeply racist, sexist, homophobic, and transphobic world. It took courage for Florence to wear men's clothes, mock white people, and flirt with women on stage, but she was thriving.

After the show, the performers and many audience members left the theatre and entered a city, Toronto, where they were just as much second-class citizens as their counterparts in the United States, where women got arrested for wearing men's clothes and Black people could not book a hotel room. Outside the theatre was a world where Florence Hines would eventually get sick, disappear from the public eye, and die poor and obscure in the 1920s. But on that Saturday night, in April 1894, the audience had paid to enter her world, and she got to set the rules.

Just over a year later, on a Friday afternoon in May 1895, twelve white jurors entered a world that Clara created, at least for the three and a half hours it took to make them believe her word over the testimony of four white police officers. She made it look easy, like a cakewalk. It wasn't.

It's been well over a century since the murder of Frank Westwood, and since then the trial of Clara Ford, his putative killer, has been written about extensively: first by reporters and participants, then by legal scholars and historians. There has been at least one play and one radio drama, and a book was published in 2005. Clara's story still crops up on websites and in newspaper articles. All of these works rely on the memoirs of Hector Charlesworth, a viciously racist journalist who boasted of publishing fake news to boost his newspaper's circulation. His description of Clara Ford reflects more about him and the moral panics of his time than reality. Yet it's his words, not hers, that have endured.

In this book, I take a different angle. I am less interested in the trial itself than in the intertwined lives that preceded, and produced, the crime. I want to describe Clara's life and circumstances as a working-class Black woman as best I can, to examine her city and society. Clara lived most of her life below the poverty line. Except for a wild six-month period when her name was in newspapers around the world, she led an obscure and purposefully secretive life. Yet newspaper reports reveal more about her circle of friends, her everyday life, and her personality than is available about most other contemporary Black and working-class people. She lived at a time just before the popularization of the gramophone and the cinema, a time when photographs were rare and mainstream newspapers wrote about Black women only when they got into trouble. We can listen to her words (and what other people think of her) in a way that Florence Hines is lost to us.

Clara got stuffed into boxes that didn't fit her – Tragic Mulatto Girl, Angry Black Woman, Temptress, Perverted Monster – to satisfy the bigoted imaginations of white people. No one – reporters, police, or lawyers – cared enough to explore Clara's allegations of sexual assault and racial harassment against Frank Westwood. Toronto police officers had to be spectacularly corrupt and incompetent before a Black woman's word would be believed over theirs. The obvious suspect – a white man with motive, means, opportunity, and a serious criminal record – was shielded by the police and reporters. To me, these are the most interesting aspects of the murder of Frank Westwood.

Where to begin? There are only two facts we can say with certainty about the relationship between Frank Westwood and his accused murderer, Clara Ford. One: this rich white boy and impoverished Black woman were neighbours, for a time, in the Toronto suburb of Parkdale. Two: Frank and Clara didn't get along.

Clara's world was shaped by the rules of the stage she loved. Clara danced the cakewalk with power and elegance. She was, above all, a survivor. She was ferociously intelligent and laugh-out-loud funny, an introverted performer with a strong sense of the absurdity of her own situation. I hope you enjoy her story, wrapped up in a murder mystery that persists to this day.

THE PARKDALE MYSTERY

FRANK B. WESTWOOD.

Frank Westwood

THE
MURDEREE

Lakeside Hall, 1891

On the day he was fatally shot, Frank Westwood woke up feeling a bit under the weather. His father, Benjamin, the managing director of the Toronto branch of a successful fishing-goods manufactory, would spend the day in bed with a bad cold. But Frank, the second son, had recently graduated from high school and had just obtained his first job. There were rules, no less clear for being unspoken.

So Frank got dressed in a three-piece grey suit and starched white collar. After breakfast, he wrapped himself in his warm tan overcoat. The forecast for the day, Saturday, October 6, 1894, was for light showers followed by fair autumn weather. He checked himself in the hall mirror and then walked two blocks up Jameson Avenue to the South Parkdale train station.

Four years earlier, *The Mail* had commissioned a centenary celebration of the establishment of Upper Canada, the British colony that would become the province of Ontario. Frank's father, Benjamin, was one of a hundred notables whose careers and stately homes were illustrated in this memorial volume. Like the four hundred New Yorkers who crowded into Caroline Astor's ballroom in 1892 to signify their election into that city's elite, the inclusion of Westwood and his Parkdale villa, Lakeside Hall, in *Toronto, Old and New* must have given some quiet satisfaction to a self-made man.

The Westwoods had bought Lakeside Hall in the summer of 1889 at a bargain price, after the original developer and another speculator failed to sell the property because of the worldwide banking panic that had occurred that year. Although journalists

would later call it "an isolated mansion," the long, narrow house –
two and a half storeys with four bedrooms on the second floor
and an attic bedroom for the maid – was hardly ostentatious. It
did have a spectacular location. The ground floor's parlour bay
window overlooked a private boathouse on Lake Ontario on the
lakeside boardwalk.

The Westwoods loved boats, as was only fitting for a family
whose livelihood depended on the water. Frank had a canoe and
a third share in a sailboat. Along with his closest friends, he was
a founding member of the Maroons Canoe Club, based at Dean's
Boathouse on Sunnyside Beach, a quarter mile to the west. Frank
spent much of the summer of 1894 messing about in boats, including a camping trip along the Etobicoke River in June, where he
and his chums had, scandalously, been spotted swimming nude.

Benjamin was born in Redditch, northern England, in 1845.
Redditch was known throughout the British Empire for its manufacture of needles and fishing tackle, and Benjamin received a
thorough education in that field as a youth. He moved to Toronto

Benjamin Westwood

in 1867 to establish the Toronto office of the leading English manufacturer of rods, nets, and other fishing necessities, Allcock and Laight. He married Clara Bonnick, another emigrant from northern England, in the Toronto suburb of Yorkville in 1870. After a brief sojourn in the United States – where Benjamin and Clara's oldest child, Charles Herbert (known to family and friends as Bert), was born – the Westwoods returned to Toronto in 1873. By 1894, Benjamin had been the managing partner in the Toronto branch of Allcock, Laight and Westwood for a decade, and their ALW fishing rods would remain a Canadian icon well into the twentieth century. In the terminology of the time, the Westwoods were very comfortable, indeed.

The family expanded. Frank was born in 1876, followed by William two years later. A daughter, Emily, rounded out the family in 1882.

The Westwoods were pious. Benjamin had been a Methodist lay preacher from the age of eighteen and was on the building committee for the impressive Parkdale Methodist Church, which seated 1,600 congregants on its completion in 1890.

The Westwoods were close-knit. Bert Westwood, who was in training to take over the family business, lived with his wife, Maggie; their child, Harry; and Maggie's father, the baby's namesake, Henry Nafe, four blocks from the Westwoods on Maynard Avenue.

On the Saturday in question, the Westwoods planned to have tea the following afternoon, after attending church together, as they always did.

On that drizzly autumn morning, Frank waited for the 8:40 a.m. train to Union Station. It was a short trip – only twelve minutes over three miles.

Before a wave of amalgamations absorbed the suburb of Parkdale in the late 1880s, Toronto had been a trim grid that stretched three miles from south to north and five miles from east to west. But even with suburban expansion and a population of almost two hundred thousand, every street in the city could be walked in a day. Like fortunate suburbanites before and since, the Westwoods had physical proximity to Toronto along with psychological distance.

The photograph of Lakeside Hall that appeared in *Toronto, Old and New* – with the equally impressive Clark residence behind it, a private boathouse in front, and Thornhurst, the substantial home of George Magann, the railway-parts manufacturer, in the distance – gives the impression of a remote country estate. And, indeed, writers in early twentieth-century Toronto promulgated a myth of Parkdale as a wealthy residential suburb with residents such as the Westwoods who exemplified a now-vanished patrician charm. According to a description of Frank's murder written in purple prose in 1926, Parkdale in the 1890s was "graced with stately dwellings, overspreading trees, crystal waters, glimmering lawns, the soft footstep, the gentle voice, the contentment, the prosperity, the peace."

Parkdale had been developed as an exclusive "flowery suburb" of "charming villas," according to one of its earliest promoters. And, indeed, from the first, many company owners were lured to this new suburb just west and upwind of the industrializing city. With an undeveloped lakeshore, it was close to High Park's hills and streams to the west and the grounds of the Toronto Industrial Exhibition to the east. The independent village, then town, of Parkdale promised lower taxes, cleaner water, fresher air, and a morally salubrious atmosphere. According to one journalist, the town fathers "ostracized the saloon keepers, frowned on negro minstrels, erected several churches, established a pound, built a schoolhouse, decorated her dead walls with placards of church meetings, tea-parties, temperance socials, sacred concerns and theological lectures, and became pious in good style."

What does "frowned on negro minstrels" mean in this context? Black Canadians were certainly advocating against the racist stereotypes of the minstrel show. But it's far more likely that Parkdale's political leaders were legislating against working-class entertainments and the people associated with them.

Lakeside Hall had a small shack behind it, where a family of four lived from 1888 to 1892. Three of the Ford-McKay household were Black. Did they belong in the suburb of Parkdale? Some people, including Frank, definitely didn't think so. Not long after the Westwoods had moved to Parkdale, in May 1890, thirteen-year-old Frank and twenty-eight-year-old Clara engaged in a public shouting match on the veranda of the Clarks, the Westwoods' next-door neighbours and Clara's landlords.

Four years later, Frank hadn't forgotten. In late August 1894, the summer before his murder, he leaked a story to *The Telegram* suggesting that the arrest of a male impersonator – Clara Ford – was imminent in Parkdale.

Frank's actions notwithstanding, the forces of exclusivity were losing. Toronto's westward expansion, like that of Canada's, was relentless. In 1879, Parkdale barely had the 250 residents required to incorporate as a village; fifteen years later, the suburb's population approached ten thousand. The men who shared the railway platform with Frank ranged from clerks and salesmen to professionals and business owners.

Parkdale was also home to several large institutions. The Catholic Magdalen Asylum for unwed mothers and other disreputable women sat just north of Queen Street, Parkdale's main commercial strip. Three blocks east of the Westwoods, the Home for Incurables housed three hundred residents. Half a mile farther east was a conglomeration of bogeyman institutions: the Toronto Central Prison, with its associated Mercer Reformatory for Women, and the Ontario Lunatic Asylum. Most frustrating for the Westwoods, the Clarks had recently sold their property to the Salvation Army for a

Home for Wayward Girls. For all of the Westwoods' piety, having this charitable institution next door was too close for comfort.

Across the street from Lakeside Hall, new houses lodged travelling salesmen. These men hopped the train downtown to pick up samples from brokers and then rode west to sell their wares in the agricultural settlements of western Ontario. A third of Parkdale's residents were labourers and engineers, as skilled labourers such as machinists were then known. They walked to huge industrial buildings along the four railway lines that converged between Parkdale and downtown Toronto.

By the time Toronto annexed Parkdale in 1889 and it became St. Alban's Ward, its claim to being the Floral Suburb had been eroded. Parkdale Town Council had once refused to grant liquor licences, but by 1894 Queen Street had four "hotels," taverns with rooms to rent upstairs. A similar attempt to bar industries failed. The Toronto Stove Manufacturing Company on Dufferin Street had one hundred employees, and the Gutta Percha Rubber Company, which manufactured hose and belting just north of Queen Street, was the largest rubber company in Canada. The Canadian Pacific rail yards also employed numerous locals.

The area between Parkdale and downtown, along the rail line Frank took to work, was Canada's growing industrial heartland. The Massey-Harris factory, which had over seven thousand employees constructing agricultural machinery sought around the world, was merely the largest of the smoke-spewing factories fuelling Toronto's rapid growth. Next to the factories and institutions sat the city's main slaughterhouse. From cows to combines, all businesses relied on the trains that blocked off access to Toronto's waterfront.

Parkdale, like most western suburbs in the Northern Hemisphere, was protected from the stench by prevailing winds that blew to the east. Three of four main railroads turned north at the eastern border of Parkdale, leaving the lakeshore and its breezes relatively unspoiled. But the dirty realities of Toronto's industrial wealth were all too proximate to rich Parkdalians, as were the people who worked in those industries.

Residences, industry, institutions, parkland ... There was one more element of Toronto's lakeshore between Parkdale and downtown that would assume increasing importance in Frank's afterlife as a murder victim: national pride and defence. Each autumn for two weeks, three hundred thousand people gathered at the Toronto Industrial Exhibition, just east of Lakeside Hall, to view the "displays of Toronto and Provincial manufacturers, art exhibits, Canada's finest breeds of horses and cattle, and the bountiful array of her horticultural and agricultural products." Adjacent to the Industrial Exhibition was the "New Fort," where Canadian militia stood vigilant against American invasion. Further east, the ruins of the "Old Fort" reminded Torontonians of when the Americans invaded in 1812. This array of buildings symbolized both Toronto's pride in the new Canadian nation and its fear of being overrun by foreigners. Canada would be free from pernicious Yankee influences. It would keep tight control over its religious, linguistic, and racial minorities. It would provide new "virgin lands" for British migrants to exploit, emptied by the displacement and extermination of Indigenous peoples. In 1891, when prominent politician Goldwin Smith spoke at the National Press Club in Toronto on the potential of annexation by the United States or independence from the British Empire, Police Magistrate George Denison rose and shouted: "If ever the time came that either should have to be seriously discussed, I would only argue it ... on horseback with my sword." The New Fort occupied a seemingly impregnable cliff over Lake Ontario, surmounted by a twelve-foot-high fence with barbed wire on top. It stood on guard for Canada First.

Frank was on his way to work as a clerk at Henry Smith's department store, which sold "Family Goods, Musical Goods, Sporting

Goods Etc." and was located across Wellington Street from his father's establishment, one block from Union Station. A clerkship in a thriving business was a good entry-level position, especially during the economic recession of the early 1890s, and, of course, his family connections had helped. Frank kept up the ledgers, addressed correspondence, and assisted Smith as he learned the basics of business and prepared to follow in the footsteps of his father and older brother.

After the shooting, when Henry Smith was approached by reporters to discuss his dying employee, he provided Frank with a typical nineteenth-century boilerplate positive reference: Frank, he said, was "always well behaved ... I know of nothing derogatory to his character. He was punctual and most industrious in performing his duties."

To female employees at Smith's shop, Frank must have appeared handsome, with his sandy blonde hair, striking pale blue eyes, and pouty mouth. Frank was a little young for marriage at eighteen, but his prospects as a future match were certainly good. He was physically fit, conventional in his manners and opinions, and popular with his contemporaries: "a sturdy, fine-looking young fellow, free of all visible vice, and a favourite in the circle where he moves." Defined by the absence of negative rather than the presence of positive qualities, Frank "drank no strong liquors, kept good company, and never stayed out at night later than about 10.30 o'clock."

At lunchtime, Frank only had to walk one block west to encounter a different world from the solid brick commercial establishments of Bay Street. There were four "negro-owned" eating houses on York Street, the centre of Toronto's small Black community since the 1840s. Frank's former neighbour Clara Ford lived above one of those restaurants. York Street and the extension of Bay Street above Queen Street, then called Terauley Street, were the commercial strips of the Ward, Toronto's principal slum. There, you could find tailors and laundries, second-hand and pawnshops, restaurants and taverns that served both the middle class and the working poor. The Ward was where the outsiders – Jews, Blacks, Italians, a smattering of Chinese migrants, and Indigenous people – could be found.

By the 1890s, the Ward, like Parkdale, was under threat from relentless economic expansion. Wooden shacks, including the one in which Clara spent her early years, had been torn down for what would be Toronto's third city hall, under construction at the corner of Queen and Terauley Streets. Two department stores – Eaton's and Simpson's – were thriving at the corner of Yonge and Queen Streets, and canny real estate entrepreneurs were purchasing and demolishing small shops, with housing above or behind them, to make way for prestigious commercial expansion along Queen.

After work, Frank might have missed the 5:20 p.m. return train and instead boarded the King streetcar, a slower and more crowded but less expensive journey. He ate dinner with his family, served by live-in maid Bessie Stephen. His mother, Clara Westwood, discussed plans for her forty-fourth birthday in the coming week. After dinner, twelve-year-old Emily played on her new piano, which had been delivered that afternoon. The family sang along.

At around 7:30 p.m., Frank again donned his overcoat and met up with his two closest friends. Ed Lennox was the son of Isaac Lennox, a local alderman and a manufacturer of excelsior, those wooden shavings so essential to packaging and insulation in the nineteenth century. Like Benjamin Westwood, Lennox was prominent in both the Parkdale Methodist Church and the Liberal Party. Temple Cooper was the son of the late Charles Cooper, a wholesale shoe and boot distributor, and lived next door to Frank's brother on Maynard Avenue.

The three young men wandered along Queen's retail strip. They visited Dr. Griffin, whose medical practice below his home on Macdonell just north of Queen was open on Saturday nights. There, Frank procured a prescription for liver pills, which he filled at Gray's drug store around the corner. Liver pills, according to advertisements of the day, relieved fatigue and flatulence and induced cheerfulness.

At some point in the next ninety minutes, the young men dropped by Mrs. Mitchell's, a grocery store a mile to the east on King Street West and Niagara, and ordered a pipe. Frank's father, aside from being an avid prohibitionist, didn't approve of Frank's penchant for tobacco, so the purchase needed to be made furtively and at a distance. When Frank and his friends returned to Parkdale, two more young men joined the group: Isaac Anderson, the son of a local lawyer, and William Andrew, another clerk at a downtown jewellery store. The five men perhaps retired to one of the four taverns in the area, but if they did, the secret was never betrayed by Frank's friends.

Just before 10:00 p.m., they were spotted sitting on a fence near Queen Street by Constable George Baird, who told them to go home. They walked to Cowan Avenue, where Temple lived. Frank parted with the other three at the corner of King and Jameson Avenues and then continued south.

When he got home, the light was still on in the front parlour. His father and the younger children were in bed, as was the maid, but his mother had stayed up, waiting for him, her favourite child, to return. They chatted for about twenty minutes, then they turned off the gas lamps and went upstairs. Frank kissed his mother goodnight and headed for the south bedroom, which he shared with his brother Willie. By the chiming of the hallway clock, it was 10:45 p.m.

A few minutes later, Clara heard her son go downstairs again. She wondered whether Frank was getting a snack from the icebox. She didn't hear the doorbell ring, but that wasn't unusual; she was slightly deaf, and the bedroom she shared with her husband was at the back of the second floor.

Frank lit the gas lamp in the hallway and unhooked the door latch. He held the door partway closed with his foot as he greeted the late-night visitor. His mother heard a sound like glass breaking, then the terrifying thump of a body falling. She rushed to the landing and looked down. The front door was closed, and Frank was propped against the wall clutching his stomach. Blood seeped between his fingers. "Mother, I've been shot," he cried.

"Ben! Bring your revolver, there are burglars in the house!" Clara screamed as she ran downstairs.

Benjamin, woken by the shot, joined her, still wearing his pyjamas. They could smell the residue of a gunshot. The door was closed but not latched. Frank must have slammed it shut after being shot. Benjamin tried to open the door, but Clara told him to stop, that the burglars might still be outside. He ran upstairs and threw on trousers and an overcoat. He grabbed the revolver he kept in his locked secretary desk and headed back downstairs, where Clara was telephoning their family doctor and friend, Adam Lynd. Benjamin opened the door and shot his revolver into the air, partly to scare off burglars but mostly in the hope that a police patrolman might hear.

Meanwhile, Frank staggered upstairs. Willie, still half asleep, asked whether it was morning and what the fuss was about. Frank said that he'd been shot and threw off his bloodstained jacket and vest. As Willie leaped from the bed, Frank collapsed on the floor. Willie grabbed a pillow to put under his head. When their mother joined them, Willie began to cry.

Downstairs, Benjamin phoned the police and two more doctors. He glanced at the clock in the hallway – it was just before 11:00 p.m. He wondered whether the burglars would catch the 11:10 p.m. train out of Toronto.

Within fifteen minutes, three doctors, one police detective, and two more police officers arrived on the scene. Frank was still conscious, but all the doctors in Parkdale could not cure an internal wound of that nature. Even if they'd removed the bullet from where it lodged near Frank's spine after piercing his liver, peritonitis (blood poisoning) had already begun to spread through his body, and penicillin had yet to be invented. When the initial shock of the injury gave way to agonizing pain, they gave him opioids. Remarkably, Frank was still semi-conscious. Detective Charley Slemin asked him, for the first of what would be many times, to describe his attacker. All Frank could or would say (or at least what was reported to the newspapers at the time) was that his assailant had been a medium-sized, relatively heavy-set middle-aged man in a dark overcoat and fedora. He had a thin moustache. Frank didn't recognize him, and no words were exchanged.

Clara and Willie sat with Frank, who slept fitfully, while Benjamin tried to console Emily. Outside, reporters gathered on the grounds as dawn broke. It was Sunday, October 7. Day 1 of the Parkdale mystery.

TWO

THERE'S

A GIRL IN IT

WHO SHOT WESTWOOD?

A Young Man, Eighteen Years of Age, Shot Down at His Father's Door.

PARKDALE IS AGITATED BY A SENSATIONAL MYSTERY.

Frank B. Westwood Lying Unconscious and at the Point of Death With a Bullet in His Body.

Headline, *Toronto News*, October 8, 1894

Bert Westwood, Frank's older brother, heard the news at 8:00 a.m. on Sunday, when Willie and Emily burst into his home while he was breakfasting with his father-in-law, wife, and baby.

Reverend Edward Scott of the Parkdale Methodist Church returned from visiting Frank's bedside just after dawn, and hastily re-wrote his sermon.

Emma Card, a widow with two children who had recently moved across the street from the Westwoods, heard the news when her eight-year-old son Austin returned from Sunday school.

In all of Parkdale's six churches – two of which were Anglican (High and Low), along with Presbyterian, Methodist, Baptist, and Congregational, but not Catholic – there was "no other subject of conversation" at the Sunday morning services aside from the shooting.

Hector Charlesworth, a twenty-two-year-old journalist with *The World,* didn't have time to attend church that day. He was too busy praying for a scoop.

Charlesworth was typical of a new breed of reporter: entrepreneurial, ambitious, and entirely without ethics. Born in 1872, Charlesworth was shaped by the attitudes of his father, who was active in Conservative politics during the 1860s, when Canada was officially neutral in the Civil War but unofficially supported Confederate slaveholders. According to his 1925 memoir, *Candid Chronicles,* the Yankees threatened Canadian invasion, while the southern states made every effort to cultivate goodwill: "Under the circumstances then the attitude of the Canadian people during the Civil War, so frequently censured by historians, was only human." Charlesworth grew up "terrified of Negroes" and anxious to avoid the kind of economic downturn that led his father to move from the border town of Windsor when his business failed in the mid-1870s. In the Toronto suburb of Yorkville, Charlesworth was a neighbour to the Westwood family and a contemporary of their oldest son, Bert.

In 1891, at the age of eighteen, Charlesworth was expected to make his own living. He joined *The World,* where his freewheeling attitude to accuracy was encouraged. As he freely admitted, sometimes the newspaper would "run fakes, but sometimes they were charged with fakes and it was true."

In 1894, there were seven daily newspapers in Toronto, and a good crime was their bread and butter. Tipped off by the police, journalists, including Charlesworth, gathered throughout the night outside of Lakeside Hall. They buttonholed members of the Westwood family, their friends, and curious Parkdale residents on their way to church, and they began to construct widely divergent narratives of the shooting.

Newspapers – both "quality" morning papers and their more working-class evening counterparts – were heavily subsidized by political parties and were often started as a launching pad to a political career. Founded in 1844, George Brown's party organ for reformers, *The Globe,* was Canada's first mass-market newspaper. Brown, who led the forerunner of the Liberal Party throughout the 1850s and 1860s, saw his party as representing the interests of up-and-coming businessmen against Conservatives (or Tories, as they were known). The latter were called the Family Compact, descended from Loyalists who fled America following the Revolutionary War to take up large land grants from the British Crown. They inherited both wealth and leadership positions such as judgeships, and they tended to intermarry. Brown's newspaper also held a brief against organized labour, viewed as the enemy of unfettered business.

Benjamin Westwood was an exemplar of *The Globe*'s desired readership. In October 1893, he'd been one of a thousand delegates at a massive national gathering in Toronto to push for a plebiscite on temperance, and he'd been elected to the organizing committee. In May 1894, he was one of three hundred Liberal Party delegates attending the candidate selection meeting for the provincial seat of West Toronto. In fact, he'd been a nominee, before he declined in favour of George Lindsey, a grandson of "W.L. Mackenzie, first Mayor of Toronto, and great opponent of the Family Compact." Westwood's good friends included Isaac Lennox, the local alderman, as well as Adam Lynd, who'd been mayor of the town of Parkdale before amalgamation. West Toronto was the backbone behind an unbroken line of reformer (Liberal) Ontario premiers from Canadian Confederation in 1867 until 1905.

In relation to the Westwood murder, *The Globe* was generally the newspaper least likely to print unsubstantiated rumour, in part because of its political affiliation with Westwood's Liberals and the business class more generally but also because it saw itself as the political establishment "newspaper of record."

While the Liberals were the natural governing party in Ontario, the nation as a whole voted Conservative in the late nineteenth century. John A. Macdonald had cobbled together a successful unity platform between farmers (the majority of Canadians) and Montreal-based businessmen who were alarmed by the Liberal Party's association with anti-French and anti-Catholic sentiments. Macdonald, a consummate politician, was prime minister for all but five years between Confederation and his death in 1891. But his skills in manipulating publishers were limited.

In 1866, Macdonald provided party funding to John Ross Robertson to start up *The Telegraph*. But Robertson, an independently minded and cantankerous politician, fell out with the

Conservatives, leading to the paper's collapse in 1872. Four years later, Robertson started up *The Telegram* under a different business model. Unlike the morning *Globe,* whose readers generally paid a five-dollar annual subscription, the *Tely* was an evening "family paper for those [waged labourers] liberated by the 6 o'clock bell." It sold for a penny, primarily on street corners. Rather than running stories on international news and the minutiae of national politics, it focused on local matters, sports, and crime. *The Telegram* would eventually take up Clara Ford's cause to such a degree that three of its staff became witnesses for her defence.

After being burned by Robertson, Macdonald tried again with *The Mail,* another failure. While *The Mail* flew the Conservative flag and was happy to take federal government money, it was associated with Canada First. The Canada First movement had been founded in 1868 by fervent white Anglophile nationalists, including Police Magistrate George Denison, who brandished a rhetorical sword against the twin evils of Yankees and republicanism. Alarmed by equal rights being given to the French language and the Catholic religion in the new Canadian Confederation, they strove to promote Anglo-Protestant values. Canada Firsters came from both parties, although most members were Ontario Liberals. Their great *bête noire* was Louis Riel, the Métis leader in western Canada (the Métis are an Indigenous people of mixed European – usually French – and First Nations heritage). By the time of the Northwest Resistance against the theft of Indigenous land in 1885, *The Mail* was sufficiently critical of the federal government's supposed inaction that Macdonald funded yet another start-up. *The Empire* was never the popular success of *The Mail* or *The Telegram* (it would merge with *The Mail* in February 1895). In the case of Frank Westwood's murder, both *Mail* and *Empire* printed a range of scurrilous rumours that libelled the Westwood family and, eventually, the accused murderer. It was *Mail* reporter John Miller whose drinking buddy Gus Clark provided the story that led to Clara Ford's arrest.

The *Toronto News* started as an evening edition of *The Mail* and aimed to attract streetcar commuters with its distinctive pink newsprint. But it took its own direction under American editor Edmund Sheppard. Sheppard took his lead from US newspapers, favouring short paragraphs, copious illustrations, and idiosyn-cratic capitalization and punctuation (exclamation points abounded in coverage of Frank's murder). The newspaper es-poused pro-union politics, including a regular column from the Knights of Labour.

The *Toronto News* continued to seesaw between Conservatism and radicalism, as did *The World,* a morning paper whose anti-monopolist and self-styled manly common-sense tone adapted better to Conservative Party backing than support from big-business Liberals. In 1894, *The World* was the only newspaper pub-lishing a Sunday edition; it appeared on the streets late Saturday night to avoid being sued under Sabbatarian laws. *The World,* and to a lesser extent the *Toronto News,* was the main persecutor of Clara Ford, and Hector Charlesworth would eventually be threatened with contempt of court for his articles published during the trial.

The last entrant in this overcrowded field was *The Star,* which became the third evening newspaper for the working man in 1893. The *Star* backed radical politics in a more straightforward manner than *The Telegram, World,* or *News,* all of which were happy to take Conservative Party money. But it would be a mistake to con-fuse the twenty-first-century progressive politics of the *Toronto Star* with the nascent newspaper of the 1890s: the *Star,* like the other six newspapers, didn't hesitate to apply racist rhetoric or manufacture fake news to win the newspaper circulation wars.

Reporters such as Charlesworth rang the doorbell and telephoned so often the Westwoods took to posting written bulletins on Frank's condition on their front gate.

On Sunday afternoon, Toronto Crown attorney James Curry ar-rived to take a statement from Frank. He was accompanied by the second in command of the Toronto Police detectives, Sergeant Henry Reburn. But Benjamin Westwood sent them away. Frank, he said, had already told Detective Slemin all he knew. On Monday, doctors operated on Frank to try to remove the bullet, or at least relieve his internal bleeding. He was too weak to speak to anyone, although Curry visited again. On Tuesday, the 8:00 a.m. and noon bulletins posted on the fence said, "There is no improvement in Frank's condition." The 5:00 p.m. bulletin read, "Frank is rapidly sinking." Frank had made a formal antemortem statement to Curry and Slemin that afternoon, and then he said his goodbyes. He told Ed Lennox to take his canoe, and he left Temple Cooper his part-share in the sailboat. He gave a ring from his mother to Bert, and he bequeathed his boating tools to Willie. Although calm, he broke down on Tuesday evening when Dr. Lynd was about to return home. He asked whether Lynd could stay for what he realized would be his last night on earth. Throughout the night, Frank became less coherent until he slipped into a coma. He died just before dawn on Wednesday, October 10.

The newspapers, along with the police and the public, spent those first few days searching for evidence and propounding theories. As is the case in any good murder mystery, their inquiries focused on three elements: means, opportunity, and motive.

The means were straightforward. Frank had been shot. His doctors confirmed, after their surgery on Monday, that the bullet had entered an inch below his right ribs, with the trajectory slightly downward. This suggested that an assailant roughly of similar height to Frank had fired from the top of the porch stairs toward Frank, who stood at the front door, a distance of about three feet (there were no powder burns on the clothes, so the victim and assailant were not next to each other). The type of gun was ascertained during the postmortem, performed on Frank's bed a scant two hours after his death on Wednesday morning. A .38 calibre bullet had pierced his liver and lodged near his spine. Benjamin's revolver was .44 calibre, and he'd given his son

Bert, on the occasion of Bert moving into his new home, a .22 calibre gun to guard against burglars. The Westwood family wasn't above suspicion, but if the father or older brother had shot Frank, they didn't use their own weapons.

The question of opportunity was more complex. Lakeside Hall was only two blocks from South Parkdale Station, a quarter mile from King Street, and a half mile from Queen Street. Both King and Queen Streets were served by streetcars that terminated in Parkdale. An attacker could have taken the last streetcar eastward at 11:15 p.m., and there was an 11:10 p.m. train that left South Parkdale Station for western Ontario. All these routes would have required someone to walk down Jameson Avenue, lit by new electric streetlamps. The grounds of Lakeside Hall were enclosed by a wooden fence, and anyone entering from Jameson Avenue would have had to use the gate. It would be difficult for an outsider not to be noticed.

Another form of access that received newspaper scrutiny was Lake Ontario. Numerous witnesses said that gunshots in Parkdale were not unusual because people hunted ducks on the lake in the autumn. There were four points of access from the lake. Two were private boathouses, one belonging to Westwood and another to his wealthy barrister neighbour William Clement. The third was Dean's public boathouse at Sunnyside Beach, about a quarter mile northwest of the Westwoods. And the fourth was a dock at the foot of Dufferin Street, a quarter mile to the southeast, used extensively during the Industrial Exhibition each September. Some newspapers hypothesized that a boat rented on Saturday afternoon from Dean's Boathouse hadn't yet been returned and could have been used for a stealthy night attack.

A third means of approaching the Westwood house gained surprisingly little attention. A pedestrian could have approached south of the rail tracks, either from the northwest or more likely from the southeast, using streets cleared and graded but not yet developed. Alternatively, they could have used the boardwalk along the lake. From there, they could have found a hole in the fence or entered via the Jameson Avenue gate. In either case, it was the least conspicuous approach, but it required an assailant who knew Parkdale's back streets, and, as we will see, police and journalists emphasized working-class outsiders.

The question of motive was the most mysterious and titillating element of the case. Benjamin Westwood contended that any member of his family could have answered the door and been shot. But the relatively sober *Globe* assumed from its first report that it had been a deliberate attack against Frank and that "there must have been some deep-seated feeling of hatred or resentment behind the attack."

Benjamin Westwood himself wasn't immune from suspicion. *The Empire* falsely stated in its initial coverage that Frank had been hit by "a .44 calibre bullet, the same calibre as Mr. Westwood's gun." Three days later, the same Tory newspaper reported rumours that "Frank Westwood and his father had not been on good terms for some time past, and that Frank had carried a large life insurance." *The Empire* hastily added that, of course, these rumours were untrue, that the insurance agent who'd sold Westwood his policy had been unsuccessful in selling him insurance for his second son. But it could not resist adding that Bert "had a small policy, but could not keep up the payments and his father refused to assist him." Charlesworth of *The World*, the most brazen reporter from the start, on Monday morning sought a denial from Benjamin Westwood that the shooting wasn't "a family affair."

The most popular theory was that the murderer had been a male relative of a girl wronged by Frank and that the Westwoods knew more than they were telling the police. The police thought so as well. *The Star* quoted Inspector William Stark, the senior detective on the police force, "My own opinion is that there is a woman somewhere in this case." Local detective Charley Slemin concurred with his superior officer, confidently asserting, "There's a girl in it."

Slemin, the first police officer on the scene, had asked Frank about lady friends and got the defensive response, "You can't pump me." Frank told the detective not to search his clothes, which Slemin immediately proceeded to do. However, the detective said he found nothing in the way of a suspicious note or other evidence. *The Empire,* eager to publish the most scurrilous rumours, told the story of Henry Hornsby, a travelling salesman living in North Parkdale. Hornsby was scouring the Westwood's fenced-in lawn on Monday morning after the shooting and was just about to pick up some paper scraps from the ground when Bert came out of the house and shouted at the trespasser. Hornsby "withdrew, not wishing to be observed or suspected of anything, but upon his return found all of the remaining bits had been picked up."

As he lay dying, rumours spread about Frank, often under the guise of one newspaper correcting false accusations from another. On Monday morning, when the first reports of Frank's shooting hit the streets, *The Empire's* subheadline cut to the chase: "Are the Relatives Keeping Something Back? Is there a Woman in the Case? It is Freely Hinted That There Is." In the second paragraph, it suggested that "young Westwood and another man were rivals in love, and that the shooting was done by a jealous lover." However, the Reverend Edward Scott of Parkdale Methodist Church, interviewed between Sunday services, insisted that Frank "did not pay any particular attention to anyone of the opposite sex" and that he would have been "pretty well cognizant of any such attachment if any existed." *The World* also reported rumours that "there might be a woman in the case. This probably arose from the fact that [Frank] was always well dressed and a general favourite with the fair sex. But his parents and friends who know the young man best scoff at this theory as absurd." By Monday afternoon, the *Toronto News* didn't even bother providing a rebuttal for its assertion that "the father of a young lady who lives not far from the Sunnyside Club" was a suspect. The next day, *The Star* could cite "another groundless story ... that there was a young lady in Victoria Crescent whose father resembled the assailant."

In the same *Star* story, "a boy who knew Willie said that Willie said that Frank knew who shot him but would never say because it would bring disgrace to the family." When the reporter showed up at the Westwood's home to confirm this rumour, Willie was brought to the drawing-room and strenuously denied the story. The *Toronto News* published a supposed interview with Frank's nurse, Miss Eastwood, who'd overheard Ed Lennox telling Frank: "Edith told me to be sure and tell you how much she loved you," to which "with tears in his dim eyes the dying young man replied, 'Ed, thank her for me and return my love.'" The following day, *The Mail* asked Lennox to clear up a rumour in an unnamed "evening paper" that Frank had discussed an "affectionate message from a young lady named 'Edith'" with him. Frank's best friend said the rumour was "utterly false," which allowed the fake to be duly printed in *The Mail*.

Frank's position as secretary-treasurer of the Maroons Canoe Club was treated as particularly suspect by the gentlemen of the press. *The Mail* reported that Frank had "been accompanied by young ladies on his boat," a claim that was strenuously denied by Walter Dean, the owner of the boathouse where the club was quartered. Boathouses were considered prime sites for sinful activity. C.S. Clark, the reporter who in 1898 published the salacious and sarcastically titled "tell-all" *Of Toronto the Good,* alleged that "a man who owns or rents his boathouse might furnish it with some household possessions such as a sofa or camp bed" to turn it into a site for sexual assignations. He gave an example of two boathouses near York Street, "rented by well-paid clerks in the summer, [who] lure innocent girls into boats and thence boathouses." One of them was a sixteen-year-old girl named Sadie Lavelle, who in summer 1891 went on a boating trip to Toronto Island with her friend Ida Simmons and two brothers and subsequently died from an abortion on Terauley Street. The two girls' names and addresses were published in *The Globe* in the initial report on the death. Ida Simmons was immediately brought before Police Magistrate Denison on a charge of "attending a house of ill fame" and sentenced to six months at "the Haven," the reformatory run by the YWCA for "fallen women" at the gate of the Central Prison. The two men remained unnamed and uncharged; one claimed that "he and his brother ... were not the only ones who enticed young girls into their boathouses, and if the truth were known it would be found that many prominent young men were deep in the mire."

There were even allegations that eighteen-year-old Frank had seduced his twenty-one-year-old sister-in-law, Maggie. The *Toronto News* lost no time in publishing, less than thirty-six hours after the shooting, that "the son [Bert] who was married about five years ago [actually, ten months previously] had to hurry along the date in order to avoid a scandal, and Frank, while to all appearances a model young man, had his own difficulties and secret vices." Indeed, Bert and Maggie had been married on December 12, 1893, by Reverend Scott, in Maggie's home rather than the Parkdale Methodist Church. Their healthy and hardly premature child Harry was born six months later, on June 3, 1894.

Charlesworth confronted his old primary school chum on Tuesday, October 9, after the police came to Bert's home to obtain his revolver: "In the event of the Crown's endeavouring to show that your brother came to his death through you by either accident or intention, would you be prepared to meet them?" Fortunately, Bert had a good alibi. His friend Harvey German, son of a Methodist minister in the North Toronto suburb of Davisville, had been over to dinner on Saturday night and stayed until the last eastbound streetcar left at 11:15 p.m. They discussed a topic near to the hearts of so many nineteenth-century middle-class households: the difficulty in finding a good servant.

The miasma of rumours that surrounded the Westwoods as Frank lay dying reflected deep-seated hypocrisy about consensual heterosexual relations and sexual assault. Sex outside of marriage was common, but it was considered shameful. While women and men – and women and women, and men and men – must have had pleasurable carnal encounters, this reality was denied by religious and social leaders. Few births in Canada occurred out of wedlock – only about 5 percent. But it was common for marriage to occur after a baby had been conceived, as was the case for Bert and Maggie Westwood.

In the case of a child being born out of wedlock – or indeed, any other evidence that a woman had engaged in sex with someone who wasn't her husband – the assumption was that the woman had either been tricked by a promise of marriage or had exhibited "personal depravity." Women, whether married or unmarried, who were portrayed as sexually promiscuous were assumed to be doomed to fall into further vices such as prostitution, followed by disease and death.

The notion of consent was rudimentary, at best. If a woman had been sexually assaulted by a man, she needed to produce physical signs of having struggled. If she'd engaged in sexual intercourse, companionship with a man other than her husband, or even friendship with an unmarried woman who was reputed to have engaged in sexual relations, she forfeited any claim to protection from the law. Ida Simmons's reputation as a "fallen woman" was given as the reason why the boathouse brothers felt comfortable "seducing" Sadie Lavelle.

The Globe had supported the 1880s campaign led by Liberal MP John Charlton to criminalize "seduction," a term that would translate to "statutory rape" today but that legally meant taking the virginity of a girl under false pretences. The 1886 Seduction Act made it illegal for a man to have sex with a twelve to sixteen-year-old "of previously chaste character" who'd been seduced under "promise of marriage" (girls could marry at fourteen). Even before the passage of the act, male relatives could and did sue for damages to their reputation when their daughters or sisters became pregnant.

An 1862 article in the *Upper Canada Law Journal* summarized the attitudes of many judges, who believed that women manufactured false claims for mischief and profit: "Her real seducer it may be is a young man of buoyant expectations but no substance. Her speculation is much more likely to pay if she can only get a jury to believe that a man of property, who perhaps innocently was once or twice in her company about the time of her seduction, is her seducer. If a married man, so much the better – he is likely to pay handsomely in order to prevent the exposure of a trial, however innocent he may be of the charge."

The National Council of Women in Canada was appalled by these judicial attitudes. It pointed out, before and after the Seduction Act, that "false charges of this kind are of very rare occurrence." In fact, the obverse was true. It was almost impossible to get a woman to press charges of seduction or rape because her sexual background would then be put under scrutiny. Newspapers didn't hesitate to publish the names and addresses of those involved in police matters, destroying the reputation of women such as Ida Simmons. If an accused man got a friend to testify that a girl had been unchaste with a friend, charges would likely be dropped. If a child had been previously raped by someone other than the accused seducer, she (and the legislation was clear on the gender of victims) would not be able to file a complaint.

Given the difficulties in obtaining legal redress, the "unwritten law" – an outraged male relative or, sometimes, the victim herself had a right to kill the seducer or rapist – was a common enough reality in nineteenth-century Canada, as it was in the United States and other countries. In 1856, a man named Brigdin in Port Hope, a village east of Toronto, was acquitted of murdering his wife's lover on grounds of justifiable homicide. *The Globe* didn't approve of the verdict. Using the notion of woman as property, the reporter noted that it was one thing if the couple had been found *in flagrante delicto*; in that case, "the destruction of a seducer may be viewed as justifiable homicide, the same as the destruction of a burglar in your house would be, or one in the act of burning your house." But to murder someone in cold blood was barbarism; if everyone took revenge in such a manner, he concluded, Canadian society might revert to "savage Indian life."

Race played a role in the unequal justice system of the day. Black Canadians and Indigenous people, as offenders, received much harsher sentences than white men, and women of colour rarely won cases against white male assailants. Under these circumstances, "the unwritten law" may have seemed like the best alternative. In 1874, at a Dominion Day celebration in western Ontario's Kent County, a Black man named William Custard raped a Black woman named Mary Smith. James Smith, Mary's brother, later got a gun from the house and shot Custard dead. Numerous witnesses attested to Smith's good character and Custard's bad character. Smith was convicted, although his sentence was commuted from death by hanging to ten years in the penitentiary.

In 1897, Euphemia Rabbitt, a First Nations woman, shot a white neighbour the second time he tried to rape her. The trial, in the Okanagan Valley of British Columbia, ended in a verdict of justifiable homicide. As was the case with the Smiths, Euphemia and her husband had a "good reputation" within their community, and her attacker was known to be a "bad man" – though not bad enough, apparently, for him to have been charged after the first attempt. Solving repeated assaults with a gun appeared to be more effective than relying on the forces of the law.

The testimony of Frank's friends and family at the inquest did little to refute the suggestion that sex motivated the shooting. Cora Wesley, aged eighteen, was probably the young lady with the potentially angry father referred to the initial *Star* report, as she lived on Victoria Crescent. She testified that she knew Frank from Sunday school and had "walked out frequently" with him. Isaac

Anderson, who'd known Frank since high school and spent time with him on the night of the shooting, was asked whether he'd ever heard of Frank having "girl trouble." Yes, he said, but "not during the past year." Ed Lennox, Frank's best friend, stated that "during the present year he was certain that the deceased had led a proper life." Maggie Westwood testified that Frank had a "sweetheart" who lived in another town, presumably the attachment spoken about by his friends.

Immediately after Frank's shooting, *The Empire* quoted "a servant girl" who worked at William Clement's residence and evoked the unwritten law: "There was a girl in the case ... and if young Westwood had injured a girl he got his just desserts."

Benjamin Westwood's prominence in Toronto's political and business elite did little to shield his family from the storm of conjecture unleased by newspapers. Indeed, that he was a prominent Liberal in a city where five of seven newspapers received Conservative funding fed the media frenzy. On Friday, October 12, when Frank was interred at Mount Pleasant Cemetery, Reverend Scott preached from the Book of Job and spoke with "warm indignation of the many black and unmanly aspersions cast on many innocent and respectable people." *The Globe* reported that numerous friends, family, and residents of Parkdale attended the funeral and expressed disbelief at the "vague and malicious rumours." But they were vastly outnumbered by "people who gathered about the grounds of the residence and on the sidewalks leading up to King Street" seeking a glimpse of the family at the centre of the Parkdale mystery.

In the absence of a viable suspect, Torontonians needed an outlet for the consternation they felt at seeing justice delayed. Enter the police.

THREE

AMATEUR DETECTIVES

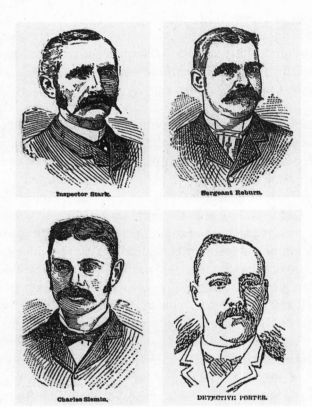

Inspector Stark, Sergeant Reburn, and
Detectives Slemin and Porter

The inquest into Frank Westwood's death opened on Friday, October 12, the evening of Frank's funeral. At 7:30 p.m., Parkdale's former town hall on Queen Street West was surrounded by a crowd of would-be spectators, and it took the best efforts of the two police constables to keep them from storming the entrance when the doors opened.

The jury, who'd been sworn in the night of Frank's death, were all Parkdale residents, and many – including foreman Isaac Lennox, father of Frank's best friend Ed (who testified at the inquest) – had been in the Westwood home for social reasons. Hartley Dewart, York County Crown attorney and Liberal Party stalwart, questioned witnesses alongside Toronto Crown attorney James Curry, who shared a law practice with Frank's chum Isaac Anderson's father. The York County coroner, R.B. Orr, a Liberal Party appointee, presided.

Charley Slemin, the local police detective, was joined by a trio from the downtown precinct: Inspector William Stark, head of the detective squad; Sergeant Henry Reburn, his second in command; and Detective George Porter, a relatively new recruit to the detective force.

Benjamin Westwood, the first witness, arrived late and "in deep distress," hardly surprising given that the funeral had ended only two hours earlier and it had been less than a week since Frank had been shot. Haunted not only by terrible memories but also by the relentless crowd of reporters and spectators trespassing on their grief, Benjamin, his wife, and their two younger children had decamped to Clara's brother's home in the northeastern suburb of Rosedale. By the time the inquest ended, Lakeside Hall would be for sale, and they'd moved to a rental home on Spencer Street in Parkdale, far from the public's gaze.

For the convenience of the white-collar residents who made up the jury, the inquest proceeded by stops and starts on weekday evenings. After hearing from seven witnesses on the first day, it met again five times over the next month, calling a total of sixty witnesses, of which five were recalled. By Monday, November 12, the Crown admitted defeat. The police said they'd followed up every inquiry, spoken to every neighbour who saw or heard anything, and eliminated all possible suspects. The jury returned a verdict of "murder by person or persons unknown."

The inquest process was "destructive rather than constructive," according to *The Globe,* as every clue, motive, and suspect presented at one session of the inquest had been refuted at the next week's session. The inquest appeared to be a stage-managed performance rather than a focused investigation. Newspaper rumours and public gossip were given an airing and then dismissed. Midway through the inquest, on October 26, the provincial government offered a five-hundred-dollar reward for information leading to an arrest.

According to the newspapers, there was no shortage of dubious characters who might have a grudge against Frank and who needed to be interviewed by the police. On the day after the shooting, Bert told *The Globe* that Willie and Willie's friend Frank Rice had been accosted the previous day between 5:00 p.m. and 6:00 p.m. near the train station by a suspicious man who asked where the Westwoods lived. The fellow was "rough looking" and wore dark shabby clothes and a fedora. Willie said the stranger "had murder in his eyes."

At the inquest, James Burns, one of the men who delivered Emily's new piano, testified that he had, indeed, asked some boys for directions to the Westwood home that afternoon.

Emma Card, a widow who lived across the street from the Westwoods, told *The Star* about a suspicious occurrence the night of the murder. She'd gone to see *The Black Crook,* a popular musical, at the Grand Opera House. When she alighted from the King streetcar at around 11:00 p.m., a man she didn't know also got out. At first, she mistook him for Frank, who she knew by sight, but he was taller and stouter and had dark hair and a sallow complexion. The Wesley sisters, Ellen and Cora, who'd been minding Emma's two children, waited for her with the children at the corner of Jameson and Victoria Crescent. They all saw the man cross the street and then linger. At one point, he gave a soft whistle that appeared to be some sort of signal. Emma's eight-year-old son, Austin, told his mother the next day that he'd heard a shot while she prepared them a midnight snack in the kitchen. At the inquest, the room convulsed with laughter when Austin told Crown Attorney Curry at his swearing-in that he had no idea where boys who told lies went after they died. Austin provided levity to a generally dull session. When asked whether he was on speaking terms with the deceased, he responded with an emphatic yes.

"You spoke to him often?" Dewart asked.

"I said hello once."

"And what did Frank say?"

"He said ... hello!"

At the next session, the stage manager of the Grand Opera House, O.B. Sheppard, testified that the Saturday performance of *The Black Crook* ended at 10:55 p.m., five minutes after Frank was shot. The streetcar conductor, Samuel Sheppard, also took the stand and explained that since it was the last westbound streetcar for the night, he waited until 11:06 p.m. to leave, to accommodate passengers emerging from nearby theatres. The trip to Parkdale took eighteen minutes. Dorr Keller, a lodger living on Victoria Crescent, explained that he'd been at the same show as Mrs. Card and had seen three young ladies and a boy greet the older woman at the corner of Jameson and Victoria Crescent. The door to his lodging house had been locked, and he'd whistled for the fellow who rented the front room upstairs to let him in. It was probably twenty-five minutes to midnight when he entered the house, well after the attack.

Cora and Ellen Wesley, both tearful when a *Star* reporter called on their Victoria Crescent home the day of Frank's death, said they'd heard two equally suspicious men whistling to each another on the train tracks just before Emma Card appeared. Three men emerged on Jameson Avenue, and one wore a dark overcoat. Dr. Lynd also saw two men loitering at the train station as he hurried to the Westwood house to attend to Frank just after 11:00 p.m.

Stephen Leslie, who also lived on Victoria Crescent and managed the Grand Trunk Railway office, testified that he'd had a drink on Queen Street with his neighbour William Clement that Saturday night. He was returning home, crossing the train tracks just before 11:00, when he heard a gunshot. He lingered there for six or seven minutes and heard another shot near the Salvation Army premises. He, too, saw two men emerge from the shadows by the train station. But these suspicious men were also accounted for. John, the son of Robert Carswell, the legal publisher, said he'd hopped off the 11:10 p.m. train before it stopped at the station and whistled to his friend to wait up for him.

So much for mysterious loiterers who might have had a shadowy motive to do Frank harm.

The police paraded two other sets of suspects before the inquest: stone hookers and duck hunters. The story of the stone hookers goes like this. Four weeks before the shooting, a scow used for hauling rocks was anchored near the Westwood boathouse. The annual Industrial Exhibition, held at the beginning of September, included several nights of fireworks, and boats commonly gathered on the lake during those last evenings of autumn to watch the show. There were concerns about the shoreline at Parkdale being undermined by men gathering rocks for use in construction. Angered by the presence of the stone hookers, Benjamin fired his revolver from the house, narrowly missing the scow. Perhaps the stone hookers had taken revenge.

The police found the father-and-son stone hookers, Albert and William Peer, in Port Credit west of the city. They said they had been watching the fireworks from their scow that night when someone rapped on the hull. Two men in a canoe told them that if they went ashore, they'd "get some lead in them." They took a nap and heard shots as they lifted anchor. They hadn't thought about that night until they were told by the police to testify at the inquest. Benjamin Westwood was recalled and said he'd fired the revolver to stop a burglary in progress at his boathouse.

The duck hunters were two Parkdale residents who'd rented a boat from Dean's Boathouse on the afternoon of Saturday, October 6. They said they only wanted the boat overnight, but never returned. A week later, they were found at Stoney Creek, another town on Lake Ontario, trying to sell the boat for ten dollars. They may have been thieves, but they didn't know the Westwoods and had no connection to the murder.

One final bit of theatre regarded Henry Hornsby, the Parkdale-based travelling salesman who, in his own words, "sometimes undertakes to find out criminals." He was the man who'd prowled the Westwoods' grounds on Sunday, October 7, and seen the suspicious pieces of torn paper. Based on a glance, he claimed "the handwriting was that of an experienced lady penman ... not a young girl" and included the words and phrases "Protect myself," "I will be at," "I have never," "ourselves," "If you don't," and "I will." The papers were torn because "the one to which it was sent did not intend any other person to see it." Hornsby told the *Toronto News* that, as a private detective, he would need to be paid before disclosing more information. However, he was happy to expound on his deductions at considerable length to a gormless reporter for *The Empire,* who effused that "Hornberry," a "pleasant featured man of middle height, wearing a dark moustache ... will probably be one of the most important witnesses at the inquest." Hornsby had deduced, based on his glimpse of the torn scraps of paper, that the "shooting was done by a woman in male attire ... She was not the party who sought revenge, but was the hired assassin of the vengeance seeker."

However, when called to the stand, the paper scrap "clues" he provided from a "fairly large radius" were contemptuously thrown away by Dewart, to the derisive laughter of the public. Ironically, Hornsby, who sounded delusional, may have stumbled on a clue. After all, Frank didn't want his clothes to be searched by the police, and an incriminating note could have been torn up by his father and scattered over the grounds.

Hector Charlesworth, perhaps inspired by Hornsby the amateur detective, pulled off a publicity stunt. In 1894, Arthur Conan Doyle and his creation, Sherlock Holmes, were at the height of their popularity. *A Study in Scarlet,* which introduced Holmes, had been published in 1887 and followed by another novel and short stories. When Conan Doyle arrived in North America for a three-month lecture tour in autumn 1894, it was as the English-speaking world's most famous author, the man who'd just killed off Sherlock Holmes at Reichenbach Falls.

Conan Doyle was scheduled to speak at Toronto's Massey Hall on November 26. On October 13, a week after Frank was shot, Charlesworth sent Conan Doyle a thick sheaf of clippings on the Parkdale mystery and asked for the writer's "expert opinion." Conan Doyle politely responded: "Dear sir, I shall read the case, but you can realise how impossible it is for an outsider who is ignorant of local conditions to offer an opinion." This noncommittal response was published on the front page of *The World* on October 29 under the headline "Even Sherlock Holmes Puzzled." Charlesworth followed up with an offer to personally brief Conan Doyle on the case when he arrived in Toronto. By the time Conan Doyle arrived, Clara Ford had been arrested, but a book published in 1991 still claimed personal intervention by the author helped solve the mystery.

Several times the jury heard testimony from witnesses such as Emma Card and Benjamin Westwood, only to have it refuted a week later. It was a public embarrassment for the police.

On the day Frank was buried, *The Mail*'s headline was "Still Unsolved," a headline mimicked by other newspapers that suggested the detectives were "entirely at sea" and "baffled," and that the mystery was "darker than ever," with "no light yet," "no clue," and "still no clue." Angered by Inspector Stark's contention that seduction was involved, Benjamin Westwood turned on the police. By Monday, in the first coverage of the case, he was quoted as saying that the police were trying to cover up their incompetence by making unsubstantiated allegations.

The Telegram, for the moment agreeing with Westwood that the shooting had been done by an outsider, argued in an October 9 editorial that "the southern part of the Flowery Suburb is a route used by tramps and requires special police surveillance." By October 11, the day after Frank died, it added that "the reticence of the police, and their failure to make any movement toward effecting the capture of the guilty man or woman, has given an impetus to the wild rumors that have been spreading so rapidly in the west end ... The detectives shake their heads and look confident when it is hinted that their reputation is at stake." Toward the end of the inquest, that newspaper was simply bemused by the lack of progress: "The police have a theory in the Westwood mystery. The public have a dozen theories, and are that much ahead of the police."

Any discussion of the Toronto police, then as now, brings up "questions of ideology, political partisanship and class" – along with racism. Certainly, the force was enmeshed in sectarian politics. After the founding of the town of York in 1793, public order was kept by military men under the direct command of the lieutenant-governor and the indirect control of the Family Compact. Toronto's first city council, led by reformers, hired a bailiff and five constables in 1835, four years before the first "Bobbies" hit the streets of London. From the first, the Toronto Police had an agenda focused on controlling a particular group of people: Irish Catholics. This stemmed from the fact that, without exception, the first Toronto police were Orangemen.

The Orange Order had been established in 1795 in Ireland as a semi-secret society sworn to uphold Protestant ascendancy in that country. By 1830, it had established a stronghold in Canada, and membership quickly grew among Scottish, English, and Irish Protestant settlers. There were no fewer than forty-five well-subscribed Orange Lodges in Toronto by the 1860s, when the city was widely described as the "Belfast of Canada."

The Globe, whose founding editor, George Brown, had been attacked during a mid-century sectarian riot, had an equivocal relationship with the police force. On the one hand, a flattering *Globe* article on police detectives in 1889 emphasized their "scheming brain and steady purpose" in protecting citizens from criminals. Inspector William Stark, the new head of detectives, the article related, had toured eight US police headquarters. He was described as a "lithe, spare man of 38 years, with iron grey hair and a heavy dark moustache," whose "keen perception" and "unparalleled memory for names and faces" had cracked many a case. His second in command, Sergeant Henry Reburn, was "a stout man with black hair and moustache, large steady gazing grey eyes that must make an evil-doer feel uneasy, and a slow, deliberate way of talking that gives one the impression that every word uttered is thought over first." "Charley" Slemin, who was head of detectives in the western district, including Parkdale, was Irish Protestant, like Reburn and five of seven other detectives on the force. The article described the thirty-year-old as "a favourite with reporters, with a trace of brogue in his speech." As these sketches attest, a handlebar moustache was a badge of office.

On the other hand, *The Globe* had also undertaken an investigation in 1887 that highlighted "the brutal treatment of prisoners by the police of the city." *The Globe* hired a journalist to get arrested on a charge of drunkenness. He then reported on his arrest, the holding cell, Magistrates' Court, and a month-long prison stay. The seven-part series reported he'd been "shaken, shoved, pulled, jostled, told imperiously to stop, to move on, to be quick, to go slow, and all apparently because the dull-witted dogbodies who are supposed to be guardians of the peace have not the slightest knowledge of what they wanted to be done."

C.S. Clark differentiated between working-class constables and slightly higher-status detectives. The latter, "under the supervision of Inspector Stark ... are men of experience, intelligence and industry ... distinct from the Police force." Clark had nothing but contempt for police on the beat. He approvingly quoted a heckler who responded to Mayor Fleming's contention on the hustings that "there is not another force on this continent who will compare with ours" by shouting, "At drinking lager." Clark accused the police of petty corruption; saloon keepers presented police with bottles "that undoubtedly contain water." He also argued that they were bullies. Like *The Globe* journalist, he concluded: "I can only ascribe the tyranny of the police force to one cause. An overwhelming majority of them, knowing themselves to be the scum that they are, are aware that the only chance they have of speaking to a gentleman is to tell him to 'move on.'"

These exposés focused on the experiences of white, middle-class, Protestant men. Police brutality against working-class Catholics or Black people received considerably less coverage.

Police officers were under the authority of Magistrate George Denison, and he liked quick results. Denison was the best-known public figure in nineteenth-century Toronto and the most terrifying to the working-class Black, Irish Catholic, and union members who crossed his path. During the forty-four years he was magistrate, from 1877 to 1921, there were sixteen Toronto mayors but little doubt about who really ran the town.

Born into one of the more prominent Tory Family Compact clans in 1839, he inherited two "park lots" of prime West Toronto real estate, as well as "a legacy of antipathy to the United States, loyalty to the crown, conservative political values, and military service." Trained as a lawyer, he saw himself primarily as a military leader. In the early 1860s, when he was the young commander of Toronto's volunteer militia, his home became a centre for US Confederate agents and their smuggled documents. This scheming ended his military career but not his political one. After all, John A. Macdonald, Denison's idol, was also a strong supporter of southern slaveholders.

Denison argued that a war against the United States, weakened by the Civil War and the assassination of President Lincoln, would unify the Canadian colonies in much the same way that the American Revolution eighty years earlier had galvanized thirteen disparate colonies into a strong nation. Denison's colleagues were less overtly war-mongering but equally bloody-minded. Canada First gained its first martyr when Thomas Scott, an Orangeman and Canada Firster, was executed in Winnipeg in 1869 after trying to overthrow the elected government of Louis Riel. To the utter fury of the Canada Firsters, the Conservative government's military response to this failed white supremacist coup combined persecution of Riel (who'd led a legal government but committed the unpardonable sin of executing a white man) with acknowledgment of some Métis rights. Manitoba became a province where the French language and Catholic education were protected.

The Canada First movement soon collapsed, as it became clear that Ontario's obsession with Anglo-Protestant racial purity didn't translate well in other provinces. The movement folded into the Ontario Liberal Party. To everyone's surprise, perhaps

Denison's most of all, he ran unsuccessfully as a Liberal candidate in the 1872 federal election and was rewarded with an appointment as Toronto's police magistrate in 1877.

Although Denison was bored by the finer points of the legal process, he was a showman. The Magistrates' Court became a model of military efficiency. Daily reports quoting Denison's *bon mots* ran in all seven dailies. Denison tried all crimes except capital offences such as murder, and even those crimes received a preliminary hearing at his court. It's estimated that Denison judged 650,000 cases over his career. In his memoirs, he bragged about his faultless instinct for the truth of the matter, which really meant he could rapidly dismiss the facts before reaching a verdict.

The truth, to Denison, was that crime was innate to certain "races," particularly Irish Catholics (often referred to as a "race" in the nineteenth century) and Black people. He saw his magisterial mission as instilling terror in potential miscreants rather than upholding some abstract ideal such as justice or the right to a fair trial. Denison's speed adjudication record was 250 cases in 180 minutes. In the admiring words of a *Telegram* reporter, he "scatters legal intricacies to the wind ... cleans off the 'slate' before the bewildered stranger has finished gaping, shuts the book with a bang ... [then] strolls off to lunch at the National Club." The magistrate, who was also chairman of the Police Board, ensured that Toronto had an unjust justice system.

From the first coverage of Frank's murder, several newspapers noted that it had been seven years since Parkdale's last shooting mystery, back in the days of gas street lighting and an independent town. The Priestman case was used as a cautionary tale of police incompetence. At around 9:00 p.m. on the evening of August 25, 1887, Joseph Priestman, an insurance agent living in South Parkdale, told his wife that he was meeting someone at the King Street underpass and would be home in an hour. At dawn the next day, York County constable Alexander Smith started on his rounds, which included extinguishing the street lamps. He saw a man lying south of the train tracks and assumed he'd stumbled across a drunk. He turned the body over, only to find that the man's head had been shattered by a bullet. Smith ran to the home of the mayor and York County coroner Dr. Lynd, the same physician who would attend to Frank Westwood.

A gun was found lying next to the body, and scorch marks indicated it had been adjacent to Priestman's temple when fired. The dead man was in severe financial straits and had recently taken out a $20,000 life insurance policy. Although the facts strongly indicated suicide, the inquest jury – led by John Clark, the Westwoods' next-door neighbour – returned a verdict of "murder by person or persons unknown." This verdict allowed payment of the insurance policy to Joseph's wife, who would otherwise be penniless. The distraught wife hired a private detective to find her husband's "murderer."

Almost a year later, in June 1888, Constable Smith answered the door to his home on Cowan Avenue, Parkdale. A Toronto detective, probably Charley Slemin, said he'd received a lead on a horse thief and asked Smith to accompany him in a cab. When Smith entered the cab, he was put in handcuffs and arrested for Priestman's murder. His wife, Rachael, was also arrested, and his fifteen-year-old daughter Sarah was taken into custody as a material witness, leaving the younger children without an adult in the home. Disturbingly, reporters were alerted to chronicle the arrest and the search of the residence. *The Globe* offered a harrowing tale of the Smiths' living conditions: "The house was small, wretchedly furnished and covered in filth. The [eight children, age three to fifteen,] are miserable and hungry ... [Smith] is a heavily built man of 38. His wife is 37, but looks older than her years."

When the couple and their daughter were brought before Magistrate Denison the next morning, the charge of murder brought against them was based on the fact that Priestman's silver watch had never been retrieved, nor had a roll of bills, valued at between one hundred and two hundred dollars, allegedly in his pocket at the time of his death.

Coincidentally, the witness who testified to Smith discovering the body just after 5:00 a.m. was David Low, the father of a future suspect in Frank's death.

In any case, no money or watch was found in the Smiths' home, and there was no evidence that Smith had acted suspiciously or improperly before reporting the crime to Lynd. The arrest was related to a rumour that Smith had Priestman's revolver in his possession. Although another revolver disappeared from the station and was sold to a "Parkdale resident," there was no proof that Smith had been involved in this sale of a gun submitted into evidence. *The Globe*'s summary – "the case is a weak one" – was an understatement.

Still, Denison liked having an arrest in the case. All three Smiths were held for a second night until the murder charges were dismissed by E.F.B. Johnston, deputy attorney general of Ontario (and later Clara Ford's lawyer). A month later, Rachael Smith, the constable's wife, was reported to be seriously ill from the trauma of the arrest. The family moved north of the city to get away from the scandal. By 1894, when the Priestman case was being bought up again, Alex Smith was employed by the Toronto fire brigade, and Rachael Smith was dead.

The Globe opined that the arrests were based on "a peculiar chain of suspicions that could have been easily broken by more thorough detective work." Specifically, the reliance on the work of a private detective, whose "bread and butter depends on the number of people he sends to prison," should have been treated with more caution by Toronto police, who seemed "more anxious to convict than to clear the suspected" and could have "saved an innocent couple much pain and suffering."

The arrest of Constable Smith led to a side debate in *The Globe* about the low rate of pay for police constables. It was reported that Smith had earned $6.50 a week working for York County, and yet his family was impoverished. One "ex-policeman" wrote, with justice, that the $1.21 a day pay for a rookie Toronto police-man was considerably less than the amount paid to a semi-skilled labourer. Even after five years on the force, a daily wage of $1.95 (with 3 percent deducted for the police benefit fund, which cov-ered insurance for injury and illness) would not be enough to comfortably provide for a family. Another correspondent, who signed himself "Justice," argued the opposite – that Toronto policemen were overpaid and incompetent: "If a London police-man, at $7 a week, can stand threats and chaff and still control himself, why can't a Toronto policeman at $10 or $12? ... Canadian officials generally, from janitors and policemen on up till you get to the top, seem to consider themselves the master of the people and not their servants."

The Globe, as revealed in its exposé, agreed that Toronto police abused their authority, or at least didn't restrict their violence to the underclasses they were supposed to control. It ran the follow-ing "observed" dialogue in June 1888 to suggest police were un-chivalrous to the "weaker sex":

Timid young mother: Please, good kind mister policeman, may I wait on this corner for the streetcar?
Policeman: Naw, you just get on or I'll attend to you, my lady. It's my instructions to treat you as an ordinary tough.
Timid young mother: But my baby is heavy, sir, and I am very tired.
Policeman: Move on and be quick or I'll have you up before the Colonel [Denison] and you'll get a dollar and costs or ten days.

The Priestman case revealed detectives following up on vague ru-mours, arresting innocent people on flimsy evidence, and bully-ing women. The force was portrayed, generally in the media and specifically in the Westwood case, as incompetent boobs. Toronto

Police needed an arrest in the latest Parkdale mystery. They also knew who they needed to lean on: the most likely suspect, the son of the jury foreman in the Priestman case, Gus Clark, who, along with his friend David Low, had been shot at by Benjamin Westwood four weeks before Frank's murder while attempting to rob his boathouse.

There was only one problem. Detective Slemin was out to protect him.

FOUR

THE
BAD HAT

"How the Shooting Occurred," according to the
Toronto News, October 8, 1894. Frank was actually shot
from the top of the stairs.

On the night of the shooting, Frank Westwood revealed himself to be desperately afraid of his former next-door neighbour, Gus Clark.

After he made his initial statement to Detective Slemin, he was left alone with police constable Charles Coombes for a few minutes while Dr. Lynd briefed Slemin and his father on his medical status. Coombes, a North Parkdale resident, had a nodding acquaintance with him. Frank opened his eyes and said, "I think I saw you on Queen Street tonight, Sergeant." (It was actually the other constable, George Baird, who moved the young men along.) A few minutes later, Frank opened his eyes again: "Gus Clark is in the cooler, isn't he?"

Coombes, who knew of Gus Clark's career as a petty criminal, answered. "Not that I know of."

"That settles it."

"Do you think Gus Clark shot you?"

"No ... I don't know ... Mum's the word."

If there is a clear-cut villain in this melodrama, it's Gus Clark, the very definition of a "bad hat" – the nineteenth-century term for a dissolute wastrel. Clark, like Frank, had a middle-class father. John Clark worked for thirty years as an inspector for the Customs House, the federal government office in the Port of Toronto that registered all incoming and outgoing boats and their contents and collected taxes on imported goods. Clark benefitted from Toronto's patronage system, in which a wide variety of jobs, from the federal post and customs offices to municipal policing and firefighting, were controlled through the Orange Order.

Like Benjamin Westwood, Clark was prominent in local Liberal politics and the Methodist Church. As one of Parkdale's town fathers, Clark had donated money to establish the first primary school, and he'd been the chairman of the committee to incorporate Parkdale as an independent municipality in the late 1870s. From 1889 to 1893, the Clarks and the Westwoods were next-door neighbours.

This is where the resemblances between the two families end, at least on the surface.

Clark was one of the earliest settlers in Parkdale and lived in a large new house, even grander than Lakeside Hall, constructed in 1875. In 1877, he claimed he was "aroused and indignant" (ironic, in light of subsequent events) in a letter to *The Globe*. Parkdale, he argued, should become a politically independent suburb because Toronto had "six or seven burglaries each night" and the "expensive" police force could not "detain or bring to justice the perpetrators." In 1885, at a Village of Parkdale public meeting described as "a circus" by *The Globe*, Clark, a Liberal candidate for deputy reeve and an ally of Adam Lynd, denied "infamous" rumours that the prodevelopment Grits were about to flood the village with whiskey shops. Then he took the offensive and accused Reeve McMath, a Tory, of lending the council money at exorbitant rates. When Reeve McMath attempted to answer these allegations, Clark threw off his coat, stood "arms akimbo" in a fighting posture, and shouted that he had the floor. Clark, like his son Gus, probably had a drinking problem, and he definitely had an anger-management problem.

Clark, like so many colonizers before and after him, hoped to make it rich through land speculation. Unfortunately for his family, he was terrible at it. He was the first of several developers to lose money on the eventual site of Lakeside Hall, having tried and failed to sell the lakeside lot for over a decade.

He then tried an even more ambitious path to real estate riches. Alarmed by Métis and Indigenous self-government in the West, the federal government was trying to encourage white settlement by selling land stolen from Métis, Dakota, Cree, and other nations for one dollar an acre. The Temperance Colonization Society, one of many speculative firms that responded to this call, promised a haven from "intoxicating liquors" in what is now Saskatoon. While negotiating the purchase of one hundred thousand acres from the federal government, the society offered "subscriptions" for its new settlement at two dollars an acre. By January 1882, over three thousand subscribers had purchased 2.5 million lots. Clark was one of them. He purchased over three hundred dollars' worth of property. In March 1882, he went west to take possession of the land, an arduous journey of several weeks. He had to camp out until July, when the directors of the society arrived from Toronto and told him that their negotiations with the government had been unsuccessful and his scrip would not be honoured. Clark returned to Toronto, where he hired Canada's most famous attorney at law, B.B. Osler. He sued for breach of contract and was awarded $3,500 in 1884. However, the society, a Ponzi scheme, was in default by then, and Clark didn't collect any money. By 1884, Clark was severely ill with Bright's Disease, the nineteenth-century term for a range of kidney-related ailments, and was forced to retire from his job at the age of fifty.

While the Clarks were wealthy enough to have a horse and a servant who lived in separate "stables" in 1881, when John Clark died in May 1889, his wife, Catherine, inherited the property but no money and had nine children between the ages of one and nineteen to feed. She had a hard time selling the Clark house during the recession of the early 1890s. It was heaven-sent when the Salvation Army, established less than a decade earlier in Canada, purchased the house in 1893 to become "a refuge and home for young girls who have fallen into evil and have been persuaded to place themselves under the care of the Army." While the sale went through, Clark rented a smaller house a few blocks away on Cowan Avenue for a year. Then she used the proceeds to buy the CPR Hotel, a tavern at Yonge and Price Streets, in late 1894, just after Frank was shot. Her younger children moved to North Toronto with her. "Guster," as his family called him, had already moved out following a dispute with his mother.

Gus Clark's run-ins with the law had gained him local notoriety. In April 1888, the sixteen-year-old, along with two other teenaged chums, appeared in Magistrates' Court. They were committed to trial for breaking into broker Frederick Clarry's Jameson Avenue house and stealing five dollars, a sealskin coat, and other goods.

On January 1, 1892, he was convicted for being on a train without a ticket, in Hamilton, the next major city west of Toronto. He gave his name as George Anderson then "admitted his name was Gus Clark and he changed his name because he didn't want to disgrace his mother. He was fined the usual $10 or ten days."

At the time of the shooting, Clark was twenty-three, the same age as Hector Charlesworth and Frank's older brother, Bert. He was a clerk at Dorenwend's Electric Belt and Truss Company, owned by his sister Carrie's husband, Christian Dorenwend. Dorenwend was a household name in Toronto. His father, "Professor" Hildebert Dorenwend, owned the "Paris Hair Works" emporium on Yonge Street, which provided "waves [hair extensions], wigs, toupees, perfumes, hair-washes, haircuts and removal of superfluous hair from ladies' faces."

Clark was connected to one of the more outrageous examples of nineteenth-century medical quackery. Tens of thousands of electric belts were sold between the 1890s and 1920s. While trusses were and are used to ease hernias and aching backs, the addition of copper coils and wires that delivered small-dosage electric jolts promised to cure "seminal weakness" and "impotency or lost manhood" in men and "nervous exhaustion" and "sleeplessness" in women. Advertisements were particularly directed at women, and their belts were more expensive than those marketed to men. The Toronto Electric Light Company, seeking to diversify its business, advertised its household product: "The Electric Vibrator is a very essential article in my lady's boudoir. By its use, vibratory treatment may be applied at one's own convenience." The drawing in the ad shows "my lady" applying the hand-held device to her face, which wears a satisfied expression. Despite a successful lawsuit for fraud – brought in 1892 against the first mass manufacturer of electric belts by a man with the excellent name of Cornelius Harness – heavy advertising for "medical" vibrators ensured that Christian Dorenwend's establishment, in the industrial heartland of Queen and Shaw, east of Parkdale, was thriving.

Vibrator salesman by day, Clark continued to lead a gang of "boy burglars" that terrorized Parkdale at night. In February 1895, Clark was found drunkenly insensate and half-frozen in a High Park snowbank. He was arrested and sentenced to six months in Central Prison for stealing thirty dollars from his mother's hotel on Yonge Street. While in prison, two teenaged accomplices testified against him, and he received an even more severe custodial sentence for having broken into the Parkdale Methodist Church and at least two residences in late 1894. He wasn't released until July 1895.

Although his name wasn't mentioned until midway through the inquest, Clark became a suspect within hours of the shooting. Constable Coombes reported his conversation with Frank to Detective Slemin, who asked Frank about Clark the next time he opened his eyes.

But Slemin wasn't an objective actor. Slemin's father, also named Charles, had been a police constable, one of the original Orange Order hires. By 1870, he'd moved on to being a messenger and caretaker at the Customs House, where he worked for Gus Clark's father, John. As would become clear, Slemin had no problem falsifying evidence. It is impossible to say what Slemin and

Frank discussed, but there are good reasons to distrust Slemin's version of events.

According to Coombes, Frank seemed frightened about implicating Clark but eventually said: "I had some trouble with Gus Clark. The man who shot me, I think, looked like a man who chummed with him. Possibly it might have been him. Low, I think, is his name. He is at the rail works." Frank also mumbled, at one point in the next few days, "we were only fooling in the hall," which might have been a reference to the Parkdale Methodist Church break-in in September 1894, for which Clark was convicted in 1895.

David Low was nineteen years old. He worked in the Canadian Pacific rail yards at Queen and Dufferin Streets and lived nearby, on Jefferson Avenue. He had undergone a severely traumatic experience in July, when he'd seen his father of the same name, the man who testified in the Priestman inquest, dismembered and killed by a runaway engine in the yards. He would continue to work in rail yards until he, too, died in an industrial accident in Orangeville, ten years after his father.

The first reports of the shooting quoted police sources as saying that Frank "may have become involved in some affair in which he has roused the anger of a desperate and unscrupulous man." The following day, Tuesday, October 9, *The Empire* was even more explicit: Frank had "incurred the enmity of a man of the neighbourhood by informing Barrister William HP Clement ... that the man had been prowling about his boathouse with the evident intention of doing mischief." However, Benjamin Westwood "would not acknowledge that he suspected this man. [Clark] had lived in close proximity to the Westwood home for years, but had recently moved to another part of the city. Although he bore a bad reputation, and had for years been the terror of the locality, there seemed to be no sufficient motive for him to commit the crime."

The story that emerged was that Frank and his chum Ed Lennox had seen Clark and a man who was either David Low or David Boyd (another member of Clark's gang) in a canoe on the third night of the Exhibition fireworks (Saturday, September 8) attempting to break into the Clement and Westwood boathouses. Clark and Boyd were the men who threatened to shoot the stone hookers if they ventured any closer to the shore. Frank alerted Clement and his father. Benjamin Westwood fetched his gun from the secretary desk and fired it from the bedroom window in the general direction of the canoe. The stone hookers heard the shots. Although no charges were laid, Frank allegedly told his friends that Clark had threatened to "get even" with him.

This appears to be the reason the police believed an arrest was imminent on the Monday after Frank's shooting. The *Star* reported that police had detained "a young man who was one of two who were said to have robbed the Clement and Westwood boat-houses. But he gave a satisfactory account of his movements on Saturday night and was released." The "satisfactory account" given at the inquest was that Clark had been repairing a house on Melbourne Avenue in Parkdale, before retiring to bed at 10:30 p.m. David Low said he'd been to a performance of a play on Saturday night, *Rob Roy* at the Academy of Music, and returned on what must have been a packed streetcar with the other theatre-goers. David Boyd said he'd been on a train to Chicago.

Clark's alibi made no sense. Although he didn't mention it at the inquest, his youngest brother, Percy, aged seven, had died of croup in the Clarks' Cowan Avenue rented home two days before Frank was shot. His funeral took place that Saturday, October 6. It beggars belief that Clark wasn't with his mother and siblings, who were literally around the corner from where he said he was work-ing, on that tragic occasion.

There are other highly suspicious circumstances. To get him to testify at the final session of the inquest, police first had to locate him, and he was found in Parry Sound, 150 miles north of Toronto, where he'd taken a job working on the Algoma Railway midway through the inquest. (His travel was possibly funded by the thirty dollars he'd stolen from his mother, for which he was arrested in February 1895.) At the last session of the inquest, Clark testified that he hadn't seen Frank face to face since June and that "they were the best of friends and never had any trouble." He also said that he and David Boyd "took a boat that was lying" near the lake the night of the fireworks, but they hadn't heard any gun shots. Clark's testimony contradicted the dead man's story, not to mention the testimony of the two stone hookers, but there were no follow-up questions before the jury returned a verdict of murder by person or persons unknown. The police never mentioned checking the calibre of Clark's gun (as a petty criminal who'd threatened to shoot people, he would almost certainly have had a gun). There was no further discussion of his alibi.

Benjamin Westwood seemed reluctant to implicate Clark. In his original testimony, he said he'd been shooting at the stone hookers, who were "not welcome in Parkdale." Then when he was recalled after William Clement's testimony in relation to the attempted burglary in the boathouses, he changed his story, saying he fired warning shots to scare Clark away.

To recap: Clark and another man threatened to fill two men with lead in September 1894. They were then shot at by Frank's father during an attempted burglary at the Westwood boathouse, which Frank foiled. After this incident, four weeks before Frank's shooting, Clark threatened to "get even" with Frank. Clark had a criminal record for burglary and was well known to local police. He had lived next door to the Westwoods for four years and presumably knew Lakeside Hall well enough to sneak in and out of the grounds without being seen. The night he was shot, Frank muttered "mum's the word" as he dropped Clark's name. Clark's alibi was that he was in bed on Melbourne Avenue, one block away from his mourning family and less than a quarter mile from Frank's house.

Why was Gus Clark not under arrest?

It appears that Gus Clark, even after two stints in jail, got extra careful handling as a fallen member of Parkdale's elite. Slemin's father had worked for Clark's father, and they were both members of the Orange Lodge and the Liberal Party. In the small world of Parkdale, insiders looked after their own. It is also possible that the police wanted to be sure they had the right man before arresting him. But at this point, Clark felt his arrest was imminent – unless another suspect was found. The police told Clark he wasn't to leave Toronto, and he was "questioned minutely" outside the public forum of the inquest.

According to his friend, journalist John Miller of *The Mail,* Clark had been provided with twenty dollars from Crown Attorney Dewart "to cover expenses to and from where he had been working [in Parry Sound]. Instead of returning, he remained in the city and had a 'good time' with the cash. As a result of that 'time,' he became communicative." In case it's not yet obvious, Clark was an alcoholic. The night after the inquest verdict, Clark was in a tavern with Miller, with whom he was staying (again suggesting a serious break with his bereaved family). Clark talked about a woman who'd lived behind the Clark house, next to the Westwoods, several years previously. The woman, Clara Ford, was Black, although that was probably not the term Clark used.

Clark told Miller that Clara possessed two revolvers and frequently dressed in men's clothes. She'd lived with "an old invalid lady" and two young girls in the old servants' quarters in the stables. Clark's mother, Catherine, invited Clara to stay in the house "for protection" while he was "away" (in jail) and his father was dying in 1889. Clark's sisters got in a nasty fight with Clara and notified the police about her strange ways. According to Clark, Clara had a violent temper and had publicly quarrelled with Frank, who was then thirteen, in an incident that led to her being ejected from the Clark house. Clark also intimated that Frank had been the source for an article run in *The Telegram* in late

August 1894 calling attention to a girl who masqueraded as a man and demanding that police arrest her. He said that Clara had vowed revenge against Frank.

Miller went to the police with this information and was asked not to publish anything for a week while the police followed up. Called in by the detectives on Thursday, November 15, Clark repeated the story he'd told Miller. Christian Dorenwend – who came to the station with Clark, his brother-in-law – provided the police with two anonymous letters, allegedly written by Clara, which told lies about Clark's younger sister, Carrie (Dorenwend's wife), and older sister, Eva, mentioning Frank as a source of information. Neither Clark nor Dorenweld knew where Clara lived. The following Tuesday, the police found her on York Street, the commercial hub of the small Black community, living above a restaurant owned by the Dorseys, a prominent Black family, and working for a Jewish tailor who lived next door.

At about 3:30 p.m. on Tuesday, November 20, one week after the inquest ended, Detectives Slemin and Porter entered Samuel Barnett's tailoring establishment on York Street. Barnett pointed out a tall, muscular Black woman working a large steam-powered iron. As Porter approached Clara Ford, she lowered the clothespress, faced the officers with a steady gaze, and entered history.

CLARA'S TURN

Clara portrayed in men's clothes

FIVE

FROM
WHENCE SHE
CAME

The Ward in 1910, with 1850s houses in the foreground

Clara grew up surrounded by lies. In the days following her arrest, newspapers told wild stories about her birth. Her father was a prominent white merchant and the son of a retired British officer, her mother a nameless "mulatto maid." She'd been abandoned, a "plump infant so dark it evidently had African blood," on the merchant's doorstep, only to be adopted by their old spinster housekeeper, Jessie McKay, who loved children but was unable to have any of her own. In fact, according to *The Star*, that servant had eventually adopted four mixed-race children: Clara, a boy who died young, a girl named Florence many years later, and another unnamed child.

The Mail said Jessie's motives were less altruistic: a childless widow, she was paid as a "baby farmer" to tend Clara, while the Orphan's Home was shut down due to infectious disease. After Clara was returned to the Orphan's Home, Jessie continued to visit the baby and decided to keep her, even as payments from the white father's family were cut off. The origin of Clara's name lay with the matron of the Protestant Orphan's Home, who named the child after herself.

Clara, when pressed by the police the day she was arrested, said she was "half Spaniard." Her father, a lawyer from Spain, died before she was born; her mother, who was white, died just after her birth. In Toronto's newspapers, Clara's titillating origin story held the same interest as the question of her innocence.

The only words we have directly from Clara's family came during Flora's testimony at her mother's preliminary hearing. When asked about her time in Parkdale, she said their household consisted of "Grandmother, my sister Annie, Clara and me."

Jessie, whether Clara's biological or adoptive mother, remains a shadowy character. Unlike Clara, she never seems to have fallen afoul of the law, and so the only information we have relates to her daughter. She was considered a "good-natured, hardworking woman." She was poor, illiterate, and of little interest to those gathering information for street directories, censuses, or assessment records.

In 1862, just after Clara was born, *The Upper Canada Law Journal* explained that unmarried mothers frequently committed infanticide out of a "sense of shame" to prevent "loss of reputation ... The loss of character is the loss of earthly prospects. The consequence at times is a life of prostitution, loathsome disease – in a word, a living death." The stakes in being identified as an unmarried mother were high, and it was far more dangerous to be the unmarried mother of a mixed-race child.

All accounts agreed that Clara was the product of a mixed-race relationship, and they typically used the term "mulatto" to describe her. Two decades after Clara's birth, in 1884, Frederick Douglass, America's most respected and renowned Black leader, married Helen Pitts, a white suffragist from a prominent family. This event occasioned a particularly poisonous screed printed in the *Chicago Tribune* and carried in *The Globe,* which portrayed itself as an ally of Black Canadians. In it, the "evil effects" of miscegenation were "set forth in vivid colours by a Chicago physician." According to the article, although "Mr. D. is but half African, and therefore, as he himself says, not a Negro [that is, he was being classified as 'mulatto']," Douglass's claim that there is "but one race of mankind" was false. Nature herself had "placed a limit to such admixture." Mortuary statistics showed that the "average life of a half breed is but one quarter that of their parents." (Douglass was, at the time, well into his sixties, so his parents must have been Methuselan.) The "average life of quadroons [is] ... about one third of their parentage," and "a male and female octoroon cannot have children together."

Although no law prevented Black men and white women from marrying in Canada, "Blacks in Canada lived in a state of paradox, caught between formal legal equality and deeply entrenched societal and economic inequality." Marriages between Black men and white women were rare in nineteenth-century Canada (with marriages between Black women and white men only slightly more common), and mixed-race children were characterized as genetic mistakes. In such circumstances, it's hardly surprising that Clara was differentiated, by surname and legend, from her white "foster" mother.

It is true that in 1861, the matron at the Protestant Girls' Home, an orphanage and day nursery, was named Martha Ford, and she had two children, one of whom was a nine-year-old named Clara. When the census official visited, none of the other thirty-two children who lived there full time were named Ford, and it seems highly unlikely that a mixed-race orphan would have been given the same name as the matron's own daughter.

Chloe Dorsey was personally acquainted with Clara Ford's white mother and knew her father, "who had a considerable infusion of colour," by sight. According to Dorsey, who lived on York Street from 1832 to 1896, Clara resided with her parents in a roughcast house on the north side of Queen Street, west of James Street. After her husband died, the mother supported herself by taking in washing. The mother died when Clara was six, at which point she was adopted by Jessie. It is unlikely that Jessie adopted a child who lived at the same address (Jessie lived at the northwest corner of Queen Street West and James Streets in 1867) and whose mother had the same employment as her. Chloe was describing Jessie herself.

According to Jessie McKay's death certificate, she was born in Scotland in 1826 and was a member of the Church of England. Her family was from the Scottish Highlands, and she grew up on Cape Breton Island, Nova Scotia, within a majority Scottish culture. Her first language might have been Gaelic. By the mid-nineteenth century, half of the wealthiest businessmen in Canada were Scots in origin. So were many of the most prominent politicians, including William Lyon Mackenzie and John A. Macdonald. However, most Scots immigrants were not businessmen or politicians but impoverished farmers.

At an early age, Jessie became a servant. She worked as a nursemaid with a family in Sydney, Nova Scotia, then followed them to Toronto in the 1850s. In March 1861, before Clara was born, Jessie McKay was unmarried and working as a nursemaid to the three children of Frederick and Catherine Stow. Frederick Stow was a wholesale broker who lived above his business on the corner of Yonge and Gould Streets. Yonge Street was the main north-south thoroughfare of Toronto. It led north to the farms, forests, and mines of northern Ontario. Like Queen Street, the main east-west road, it was lined with shops, taverns, stables, and hotels that catered to travellers and residents.

Just behind these brick-fronted shops, with living quarters above them, lay wooden shacks interspersed with empty lots, evidence of a fast-growing, unregulated city of forty-five thousand people. The corner of what would become Bay and Dundas but was then Terauley and Agnes Streets was three blocks away. There, a twenty-seven-year-old single man named Tory Ford, a labourer born in the United States, lived as a lodger with a married white woman named Sarah Shields and her sister-in-law, Cath. Sarah's three young children (including a seven-year-old named Clara) were listed as "Negro" in the 1861 census, as was Tory. He was the only Ford in Toronto listed as "Negro." His religion was Episcopalian, the American term for Anglican.

At that time, the closest Anglican Church to both Jessie McKay and Tory Ford was Little Trinity. Most churches charged for the use of their pews, but thanks to charitable bequests, Little Trinity was open to all. The church had many Black congregants, including businessman William Hickman, whose daughter Chloe Dorsey would play an important role in Clara's life. Perhaps Jessie and Tory met at church. This is the most plausible origin story for Clara, one that might explain her surname.

Whether Jessie gave birth to Clara or adopted her, by 1862 she was no longer a live-in servant. She'd moved to a tiny shack on McGill Street at the southeast corner of Church Street, two blocks northeast of where she'd lived with the Stows. The most likely date of Clara's birth is sometime between mid-May and early November 1861.

Clara possibly spent some part of her first years in the Protestant Girls' Home and Nursery, which took in both orphans and children whose parents could not provide for them. Jessie is not listed in a street directory between 1862 and 1867, and she may have been homeless for part of that period. The nursery department was "designed to enable the poor parents of small children, by the payment of a small fee per month, to obtain leisure for earning their living." By January 1864, when Clara was two, there were a total of eighty-eight children in the nursery, either during the day or full-time. No more than eighty children were allowed at any time in the converted single-family house, so the charity turned away children often.

Clara moved a lot during her childhood, as Jessie rented a succession of run-down wooden shacks one step away from collapse or demolition. Their home on McGill Street was torn down in 1863. By 1867, Jessie and Clara had moved to the rear of 34 Queen Street West, at the corner of James Street, where Old City Hall now stands. They paid four dollars a month for a single room, and there was another tenant upstairs. The main building was shared by Alexander Julius and Abraham McCauley, Jewish tailors with a second-hand clothing shop. In adulthood, Clara would work for several Jewish tailors, and her skills as a seamstress likely began in this period.

One of the anonymous middle-class sources said Jessie made "a comfortable living" in Clara's early childhood by taking in sewing, perhaps the most unlikely newspaper rumour related thus far. A *Globe* correspondent who used the pseudonym "Bertha Brusk" laid out working conditions for women in 1868. The most common legal profession for women, after domestic service, was seamstress. Their wages ranged from $1.50 to $6.00 per week, which was barely enough to pay rent, let alone for food, fuel, or clothing. If forced to take in piecework at home, a process known as "sweating," sewing a buffalo robe would only provide a seamstress with fifty cents for two days' work. The same price would be paid for "twisting" one thousand cigars, at a time when three hundred a day was considered the maximum number a person could manufacture in their home. In other words, it was possible to earn as little as $1.50 a week working ten hours a day, six days a week, an insufficient amount for even the cheapest accommodation plus food. Under those conditions, it was hardly surprising that children were kept home from school to help their mothers with piecework or washing.

John Hoskin, a founding partner of the law firm Osler Hoskin Harcourt, still one of the most prestigious in Toronto, recalled a "little dark-skinned girl ... in the habit of accompanying" his washerwoman, Jessie McKay, to his home in Rosedale, north of the city. The girl would get "ugly if spoken to about her color, and she was simply tolerated around the house on account of Miss Mackay."

Rebecca Alexander, the Jewish owner of a second-hand clothing shop next to the Dorseys, remembered Clara playing on York Street along with the other children who went to Louisa Street School in Macaulaytown.

St. John's Ward, dominated by Macaulaytown, was the poorest part of the city. In the late 1850s, assessment rates based on the value of property were $25 per head. In contrast, in St. George, the ward to the west dominated by land developed by the Denison family, rates were $110 per head. With rates of only $30 per head, St. David's Ward, to the east of Yonge, was also poor. The west and east slums differed in terms of religion and ethnicity: Macaulaytown was only 19 percent Catholic, at a time when one in four Torontonians was Catholic. In the eastern neighbourhoods, "Corktown" south of Queen Street and "Cabbagetown" to the north, the proportion of Catholics was 35 percent, mostly because of an influx of Irish Catholics after the 1847–48 famine. They lived close to the cathedral on cheap, swampy land near the Don River.

Macaulaytown had a distinct Black community. As with the Scots, there had been Black people in Canada since the early seventeenth century. Unlike the Scots, there was nothing voluntary about their migration. For two centuries, in both the British and French colonies, Black people were slaves, "bought, sold and compelled to submit to a lifetime of forced labour." In 1790, white American Loyalists were lured to Upper Canada with the promise of free importation of "Negroes, household furniture, utensils of husbandry or clothing." The first census of Upper Canada listed 384 slaves in 1794, out of a total population of ten thousand non-Indigenous people.

The lieutenant-governor, John Graves Simcoe, had been an ardent abolitionist in England's Parliament and brought this conviction to Upper Canada. At the inaugural meeting of the Executive Council in March 1793, Peter Martin, a Black man who'd been freed after fighting for the Loyalists in the Revolutionary War, brought a petition to the council. He spoke of the recent case of Chloe Cooley, a young woman who'd been publicly beaten by her slaveholder before being forced on a boat to be sold in the United States. One of the three Executive Committee members listening to Martin, William Jarvis, was a slaveholder and vociferous advocate for slavery in the new colony. Simcoe forged a "compromise" to phase out slavery over the next fifty years while respecting the "property rights" of the new Ontario aristocracy. No new slaves were to be imported to Upper Canada. Children of slaves born after 1793 would be freed at twenty-five, and any children born to these slaves before they were twenty-five would be free at birth. This hardly generous virtue-signalling arrangement was superseded by the abolition of slavery across the British Empire in 1834. By that time, the sight of "black men in red coats" (African Americans lured to the Canadian militia with the promise of freedom and land) burning down Washington in the War of 1812 had spread news of a Land of Canaan up north where Black people could be free and equal.

For the first five decades of Toronto's history, a relatively small and steady flow of Black migrants, both enslaved and freeborn refugees from the United States, settled in the city. Whether constrained by racist landlords or preferring proximity to others with the same religious beliefs (in addition to Anglican Little Trinity, there were African Methodist Episcopal and African Baptist churches in Macaulaytown by the 1840s), a small Black community began to develop.

In 1834, the newly named City of Toronto had nine thousand residents. One of the city's four hundred or so Black residents was grocer William Hickman. Ironically, he'd been freed from slavery after fighting for the Americans in both the Revolutionary War and the War of 1812. But when his shop in Richmond, Virginia, was threatened with arson by an angry white mob, he and his family fled north to Canada. His next-door neighbour on York Street (the main commercial thoroughfare of Macaulaytown) was also from Richmond. John Gallego was a young Black theology student. In 1840, he was hired by Bishop Strachan, the head of the Anglican Church in Upper Canada and a key member of the Family Compact, to carry out a census of Black residents across Upper Canada. Strachan's support of Gallego was part of a Tory political project to differentiate superior British values from those of the Americans, and, indeed, many of the early Black settlers in Toronto were Tory converts to Anglicanism who had been the first to sign up for militia duty during the 1837 Rebellion. Gallego noted the presence of general labourers and merchants, skilled tradespeople, and landowners among them. After US migrants were granted citizenship in the 1830s, Black men could, and did, vote. In 1827, future mayor William Lyon Mackenzie boasted of Toronto's racial equality, asserting that "a black family [could] ... keep white men and women servants from Europe to wait on them and their black children." Given that slavery had yet to be abolished in Canada, this was quite the ambit claim. But it's true that John Butler, a successful barber, employed white people in his shop and home during the late 1820s.

In 1850, the US Fugitive Slave Act changed the political landscape. While escaped slaves from the southern United States had previously found safe havens in northern states, the act penalized anyone who harboured a fugitive and allowed free Black people in the northern United States to be arrested on suspicion of their being slaves. Canada already had a history of opposing the extradition of fugitive slaves. In 1831, Lucie and Thornton Blackburn fled slavery in Kentucky for Detroit. After two years in that city, they were arrested. A riot by Black residents allowed them to escape to Toronto, where both the Blackburns' slaveholders and the State of Michigan sued to have them extradited and charged with attempted murder in relation to the uprising (they were, of course, in jail at the time). The decision against deportation was well publicized across North America.

A trickle of Black people escaping north to Canada through a series of safe houses in the 1830s and 1840s became the more established Underground Railroad by the 1850s, and Toronto was the terminus. Black men such as Tory Ford – who was born in Illinois but whose mother, Bettie, had been enslaved in Virginia – feared being kidnapped and forced into slavery. However, claims that between forty thousand and sixty thousand African Americans moved to Canada during the 1850s were exaggerated by both abolitionists and racists concerned about Canada being overrun by Black refugees. In 1854, another independent census of Black people in Ontario listed just under one thousand in Toronto, about half in Macaulaytown. Another thousand Black people lived on the outskirts of Toronto, most prominently in Seaton Village north of Bloor at Bathurst. This was a drop in the foul bucket of slavery in the United States: over 4 million Black people were freed after the Civil War.

During and after the Civil War, there was a slow exodus of Black Americans back to the United States. Attitudes hardened toward Black Torontonians, as their utility in the game of Canadian moral righteousness relative to the United States waned. Sometime in the mid-1860s, Tory Ford moved back to Peoria, south of Chicago. He lived the rest of his life in Chicago, where he was a baker and cook until at least 1910. Whether Tory Ford was Clara's father is unknown. If he was, whether Clara had contact with Black family members is also unknown.

Unlike many Black children growing up in western Ontario who were excluded from white-dominated public schools, Clara was integrated into one of the three large "common schools" in central Toronto.

The Globe went on a tour of Toronto public schools in 1853 and approvingly noted that Louisa Street School put girls and boys into separate classrooms, unlike some smaller schools. The school provided a space of racial equality and moral rectitude where "the innocent [are] preserved, the vicious reclaimed": "There are 283 girls on the ground floor [and 274 boys on the second floor], with Mrs. Corbett, Miss Keown and Miss Robinson. [There are] several coloured children, seated alongside others, without any semblance of dislike or prejudice on behalf of teacher or scholar; and we believe, in many instances, that the coloured students are

great favourites in the school and evince the best moral and in-
tellectual habits."

Six years later, a report on the first decade of the public school
system in Toronto provided a sense of the curriculum. The hours
were 9:00 a.m. to 12:00 p.m. and 1:00 p.m. to 4:00 p.m. Students
had fifteen minutes for exercise at 10:30 a.m. and again at 2:30
p.m. After an attempt at a six-day school week failed, there was no
school on Saturdays. Rather than grades, the schools were divided
into three "divisions," and graduation to the next division was decided by examination.

Girls and boys had different curriculums. In the first division,
all learned letters, reading, writing, and use of pen and ink; the
boys learned basic mathematics, and the girls learned needlework. By the third division, the boys had advanced to book-
keeping and Euclid while girls engaged in more complex forms of
needlework such as crochet and embroidery. A typical schedule
for girls in the third division might be reading, history, and handwriting before morning recess then arithmetic before lunch. In
the afternoon, there might be grammar, history, and geography
before afternoon recess then sewing, singing, and "natural philosophy" (science).

The main problem was low attendance by impoverished students. According to the 1859 report, frequent absences could
cause suspension and then dismissal from school.

By 1870, the building on Queen Street West that had been Jessie
and Clara's home had been demolished. The following year, they
moved to 17 James Street, around the corner from Louisa Street
School. It was a single-storey frame house with two rooms, only
thirty by eighteen feet, and in "third-class" condition (that is,
barely habitable). The household had three Scots-origin labourers
as boarders. Conditions must have been unpleasantly crowded.
At a time when pay for labourers and washerwomen was so low,
sharing a house with others would have been a necessity: those

who rented a room or bed as a lodger or boarder got "inexpensive housing while hosts supplemented their often-meagre incomes."

When the home on James Street was torn down in 1873, Jessie and Clara had to find new accommodations. There was the House of Industry for the truly desperate. As *The Globe* helpfully clarified, "It is not truly a House of Industry, since ... inmates do little work except for some washing and scrubbing." However, the newspaper recognized that the house was so overcrowded that indigent women were forced to sleep on the floor where "day relief" such as food and fuel was distributed. In December 1874, when Clara was thirteen, the building sheltered four men, twenty women, and five children. The day-relief aspect scaled up as Toronto faced the beginning of the Long Depression from 1873 onward. From December 15, 1876, to February 24, 1877, the House of Industry provided 400 tonnes of coal, 12,894 loaves of bread, and 170 gallons of soup and accommodated up to fifty casual lodgers a night.

Although Jessie and Clara eventually found a new home in Cabbagetown, Clara's school days were over. A "most reliable gentleman" who knew Clara as a child (probably John Hoskin) said that although she "got along well with her studies," she "quit school at an early age." By the age of twelve, Clara was out of school – and in trouble with the law.

SIX

GO WEST,
YOUNG MAN

Unknown Torontonian, 1870s

Clara's arrest for Frank's murder in November 1894 wasn't her first run-in with police. During the trial, she said she had to earn her own living from the age of twelve. Her first job was as a barmaid at Roach's Tavern on Parliament Street in Cabbagetown. The landlord was frequently arrested by the police for "disorderly conduct," which may have brought her into conflict with the law. On August 11, 1874, when Clara was twelve or thirteen, she appeared before Magistrates' Court on a charge of vagrancy. The charge was dismissed, but eight days later, she was charged again. This time, she was convicted by Alexander McNab, George Denison's predecessor as magistrate, and was fined "$1 and costs or 6 months [imprisonment]."

Vagrancy was a catch-all status offence. According to the 1845 legislation that established the offence, the onus was on the "persons found wandering around the street with no visible means of livelihood" to provide a "satisfactory account of themselves." Vagrancy could be charged if people were sleeping rough, suspected of street prostitution, or simply in the way of a disapproving police officer. Clara may have been selling newspapers or other goods on the street to supplement the family income. She and her mother may have been temporarily homeless. She may have been selling her body. She may simply have been Black and therefore at risk of police harassment in public space. The Police Court often tried the cases of "children whose heads barely reach above the dock, awaiting their turn, with drunkards, prostitutes and burglars. On conviction of some petty offence, the Police

Magistrate has no option but fine, or imprisonment; and so young boys [or girls], in default of payment of a fine entirely beyond their means, are committed to gaol."

Clara received an unusually long custodial sentence. Most vagrancy offences were punished with a standard "$1 and costs" (costs of the court were about fifteen dollars, the equivalent of three weeks' wages) or ten days' imprisonment. Children were often removed from parents "for their own good," and young girls were imprisoned in institutions at the slightest hint of loss of respectability. Clara's sentence suggests she was being removed from her mother because the court had decided she wasn't in a suitable home environment. In 1866, *The Globe* fulminated against children who were not in school, using the racist term "Arabs of the street" to describe them: "It is first necessary to take control over them ... Children found begging, not attending school, and whose parents, evidently, were unable to provide for them properly, should, on proper proof of the facts, be sent by the Police Magistrate to an institution where they would be clothed and educated for a time, after which they should be sent to the country [to work on farms] ... The unruly subjects of which we speak must be controlled by the authorities, and an institution under the control of officers of the law seems to be absolutely essential." In 1882, William Howland, city alderman and future mayor, wrote in the annual report on prisons and charities about the need for longer sentences to get girls off the streets: "Once again we would desire to call attention to the fact that a short term does not give the time necessary for the building-up of character and of moral strength. The experience of this year, as of the last, is that the best results have, in nearly every case, been obtained from among those sentenced for the longer terms."

If Jessie was unable to pay the fine (a virtual certainty), there were three possibilities. Clara may have been sent to Central Prison in West Toronto for half a year. In 1874, 2,065 men and 558 women passed through its walls, including 16 girls under the age of sixteen. Sixty-one of the women were in prison for vagrancy. In 1878, the Mercer Reformatory for Women was constructed adjacent to the Central Prison to accommodate the growing number of women serving time for morality-related offences.

The second possibility was the Girls' Home. If Clara's age and lack of previous convictions were taken into account, she might have ended up there. By 1874, the Girls' Home had moved to a larger building in the northern part of the city. There were ninety-five inmates that year; most were under seven years of age, but the oldest was sixteen. In 1882, a *Globe* reporter (possibly the social reformer J.J. Kelso, who later set up the first Children's Aid Society) spoke of ninety girls over the age of two being in the Girls' Home "under the management of Auntie Jane, a mulatto girl of 15." However, that institution was, in 1873, "bordering on the verge of bankruptcy due to lack of subscriptions."

The third possibility, and the most likely one, is that Clara was sent to the Protestant Magdalen Asylum, a home for "wayward" girls and women who were pregnant or arrested for prostitution-related offences. In 1874, the Protestant institution had just been deeded a home on Yonge Street near Belmont, in North Toronto. It might have been the best of a bad lot of alternatives. According to *The Globe,* it only had "34 inmates ... engaged in useful activities such as sewing, knitting, washing etc." Clara would have done work she was trained in, and the institution boasted "a library, with writing slate and all of the accessories of a school." Inmates received instruction each day. The Magdalen Asylum claimed to morally reshape its inmates: "During the past year, a good many of these unfortunate girls have been apparently completely reformed under the gentle discipline they undergo, and gone out into respectable service."

It is doubtful that Clara wanted – or received – "reformation," and it's also unlikely that her life goal was to become a servant.

There are numerous stories about Clara's travels in the two decades between her first arrest at age twelve or thirteen and her most famous arrest at age thirty-three. At the preliminary hearing, Clara said she "was born in Toronto and has lived here, off and on, her whole life, though at intervals she has spent time in the States." Clara was generally reticent about her life. Acquaintances remarked after her arrest: "She never talked of her affairs and encouraged no one who enquired of them." Occasionally, with close friends, she would tell stories of her travels abroad, but they tended to be polished for entertainment value. Mary Crosier, probably her closest friend, said, "In speaking of the many amusing adventures and ... escapades, she did so with evident amusement but without bravado."

With no other evidence, we are left with her words, and the words of her confidantes, many of whom testified at her preliminary hearing and trial. One such confidante was the Reverend Charles Ingles, the Anglican priest for St. Mark's Church, Parkdale, from its opening in 1881 to his death in 1930. Ingles had known Clara for fifteen years, including the period just before the birth of her daughter Flora. In 1879, when he first met Clara, Ingles was twenty-three years old, had just received a bachelor of arts in theology from the University of Toronto, and was in training at Clara's church, St. Luke's. Ingles was a middle-class establishment figure who lived an unexciting life catering to his congregants and occasionally speaking at Anglican Synods. He was a strong supporter of Clara and visited her regularly during her time in jail awaiting trial. He served as a character witness at her trial.

Despite Gus Clark's story about Clara defaming his sisters, Clark's mother, Catherine, and his younger sister, Ida, had only good things to say to the newspapers about Clara, and both appeared as character witnesses at her trial. The McKay-Ford family rented a shack adjacent to the Clarks on Jameson Avenue from 1888 to February 1892 (possibly the old stables) and likely exchanged domestic work for accommodation. Clara lived in the

Clark house for at least a year during that period, sharing a bedroom with Ida. Judging by Catherine's and Ida's interviews after Clara's arrest, Clara was treated almost as part of the family rather than as a tenant or servant.

Clara was even closer to another large family, the Crosiers, who lived on Camden Street in the emergent garment district at King and Spadina. Mary Crosier was Irish Protestant, forty-seven years old, and had eleven children with her invalid husband, William, aged sixty-one. The household was so large that there were two dinner shifts: 7 p.m. for the younger children and 8 p.m. for the older children and adults. At the preliminary hearing, when asked to describe who was there when Clara came to call on Saturday, October 6, Crosier replied:

Crosier: The family.
Dewart: Name them.
Crosier: Margaret, Sarah, John, Joseph, Caroline, Edith, Emma, Rachel and Anna. [*The court erupted in laughter.*]
Dewart: That is all?
Crosier: Well, my husband.

Everyone, including Clara, laughed.

Crosier met Clara when they were both working at the Temperance Coffee House in the Ward in 1891. She somehow found a room or at least a bed to rent to Clara for several months before her mother's death. Like Catherine Clark, she became a friend as well as a landlady. Clara was a regular dinner visitor during the six months preceding her arrest, partly because Crosier washed her laundry (Clara had no access to facilities in Chloe Dorsey's boarding house). Crosier also borrowed money from Clara.

The Crosiers were working-class. Her husband was a day labourer when he could find work, and she took in washing and sewing and occasionally cleaned middle-class houses, just as Jessie McKay had done. Two of the older daughters, Margaret

Mary Crosier at Clara's preliminary hearing

and Sarah, worked at home as seamstresses, and the oldest son, George, was a labourer in the nearby Gurney Foundry Company. Clara seems to have liked living with large families; and both Catherine Clark and Mary Crosier said she doted on children and was, in turn, loved by them. However, these white women's benevolence never extended to offering space so that her two young daughters, Flora and Annie, could live in the same home as their mother.

Clara had another friend, Eliza Reed, who lived as a boarder with the Dorseys and worked in the restaurant. Eliza and her sister, Hannah – aged twenty-six and twenty-eight, respectively, at the time of the murder – had been working there since 1890. Eliza's eight-year-old daughter, Eva, lived at the Dorseys as well.

There is little information on Eliza. She provided an alibi for Clara and was one of the first to congratulate her when she was acquitted. Her family came from an agricultural part of West York, peripheral to Toronto, that had a large Black population, and her father was listed as being born in the United States (her mother was from Ireland), so the Reeds might have been mixed-race.

According to *The Mail*, Clara went to Chicago when she was fifteen and soon thereafter became pregnant with Flora. Clara returned to Canada with her child, and they both lived with Jessie McKay, "who from the kindness of her heart, to shield Clara from her betrayal, always palmed off Flora as her own daughter." But the same newspaper also cited "a gentleman who is an active worker in an Episcopal Church" in the West End, surely Charles Ingles, as saying that Clara "became entangled with a young man who seduced her," at age sixteen in Toronto, and "the product was Flora." Shortly after the birth, according to the same source, Clara went to St. Paul for two or three years to earn enough money to support her family. Several newspapers searched the records of the Burnside Lying-In Hospital, the most common place for unwed mothers to give birth in Toronto, for the years 1879–87, to obtain a record of the birth and parentage of Flora and Annie, but to no avail. Given that Clara was resident in Toronto in the early 1880s, she likely left to seek her fortune in the United States (with at least some time spent in St. Paul) soon after being released from her sentence (in 1875, when she was thirteen years old) and returned pregnant with Flora in 1879.

Why would Clara go to find work in St. Paul? By the mid-1870s, Toronto was part of the international economy. The global Long Depression began with the collapse of speculative banks in central Europe in 1873. It spread to New York City and then to Canada, where the impacts were felt until 1896. By the end of the Long Depression, one in five Canadians had moved south of the border, either temporarily or permanently, because US industries, protected by tariffs and fuelled by high immigration in the years after the Civil War, were hiring more people and paying higher wages. The expansion of the continental rail network allowed easy movement within and between the two countries. Work visas were unnecessary, and citizenship had little effect on the prospect of finding a job. In fact, some of the loudest complaints about foreign workers in the latter half of the nineteenth century came from Americans upset about Canadians accepting lower wages and being brought in as strike-breakers. By 1875, the combined population of the Twin Cities was considerably larger than Toronto's – 200,000 to 60,000.

Minneapolis–St. Paul had been on the side of the Union during the Civil War. After the war, a relatively small influx of African Americans moved from the south and east. They made up much less than 1 percent of the population, perhaps five hundred to one thousand people in the 1870s and 1880s, about the same number as Toronto. But like Toronto, the Black community had an activist bent, eradicating segregated schooling in 1869, assisting a Black architect in a lawsuit against a hotel that denied him accommodation in 1887, and forming a chapter of the Afro-American League (forerunner of the National Association for the Advancement of Colored People). In St. Paul, as in Toronto, churches helped develop a sense of community. Black Episcopalian, African Methodist Episcopal, and Baptist churches were built by the early 1870s.

Clara told Charles Ingles that she'd tried and failed to find work as a tailor in St. Paul. When she dressed as a boy, she "found it easier to obtain employment and get higher wages." She joined the choir of the Episcopal Church as a tenor. As the minister prepared Clara for confirmation, he "found that this zealous boy was a girl."

A similar but more disturbing story has Clara moving to Syracuse, New York, when "she was scarcely more than a girl." She secured employment as a tailor, but her "masculine air and physical strength" caused people to think she was a man. Clara was arrested for masquerading in female attire to escape arrest. From

Syracuse, she went to Rochester, where "with their usual far-seeing acumen the detectives" again arrested her. She was subjected to an assaultive examination to determine her gender. Clara decided she might be better off masquerading as the man she was presumed to be. She bought "a suit of male attire" and left for St. Paul, where she lived and worked as a man for two years and had "a better success in that role than as a woman."

Clara was said to have taken various jobs while she lived as a man in the United States. In particular, people said she worked as a taxi driver and hostler at a livery stable. These were jobs often performed by Black men without higher education, men who couldn't get jobs as clerks or in factories because of discrimination. The most intriguing rumour about Clara came from *The Globe*, which said she'd "secured work in a drug store, learning the business." There were a few Black pharmacists, just as there were a small number of Black doctors and dentists in the United States, but they had to fight hard to practice. With only six years of schooling, it is unlikely that Clara, even passing as a man, would find this kind of employment.

Charles Ingles told one more story about Clara's time in St. Paul:

> By great industry and careful economy she'd managed to save up a sum amounting to several hundred dollars, which she kept in her trunk. At last she was determined to return and put into execution her plan to take her adoptive mother to live with her in a home of her own and of setting herself up in business in a small way. She went out to buy her ticket, but during her absence her trunk was broken into and stolen, and were never recovered, and all her bright hopes were shattered. She was nearly heart-broken, but with characteristic energy and force of character she said little, and set diligently to work again to try and replace the sum that was lost.

If Clara lived as a man, she was hardly unique. Both women and men relished the opportunity to reinvent themselves as they travelled to the American frontier. Horace Greeley, an American journalist, was the popularizer of the phrase "Go West, young man." In 1859, he interviewed people who'd taken his advice, including those who'd been disappointed in their quest. He dined with one of them, a young clerk who'd gone bankrupt in Colorado's gold diggings and was returning home to Indiana. The next morning, the train conductor informed Greeley, to his astonishment, that his interview subject and dinner companion had been a woman.

Similarly, Mary Johnston moved from Canada to California in 1890 and became Frank Woodhull by putting on a man's suit of clothes and learning to "walk, talk and work like a man ... ever since then life has been so much more easy and pleasant." Other women said that safety while travelling was a good reason to live as a man. In 1896, a forty-year-old named Georgie McRae spoke about riding the rails through states and territories in men's clothes.

Clara, too, told a story about posing as a detective to obtain free rides on trains. She carried a revolver to look appropriately tough. Mrs. Lansell, one of Flora's employers, said Clara had told her she'd worked as a detective in the United States and solved some big cases: "If a man ever insulted me, I would shoot him without hesitation." Regardless of whether her disguise as the first Black detective in North America worked (there was an African American police constable, James Shelton, in Chicago from 1871, but Black police wore plain clothes, patrolled Black neighbourhoods, and didn't get promoted to detective), the story fit with others she told the Crosier family: "They had all heard her stories of her adventures in male attire, of having travelled around the country by beating her way on freight trains, and of other escapades."

The newspapers loved gossipy stories about women who "got away" with male impersonation. The *Chicago Tribune*, the source for the appalling story about Frederick Douglass's interracial marriage in 1884, was remarkably blithe about cross-dressing four years later. It used the example of a recorder (US magistrate) in Kansas City who'd dismissed a case where a woman was dressed in men's clothes, to argue that "while the law is not against it, the police are," even if she is going "quietly along the street interfering with no one." In 1892, the same newspaper giddily described a same-sex marriage among "show folk." When Annie Hindle, the celebrated male impersonator, got married for the third time in Troy, New York, it reported: "She became, not the wife, but the husband of Miss Louisa Spangehl, who lives in Troy and is not on the stage. The ceremony was conducted in all good faith by the Rev. GG Baldwin, a Baptist Minister, and there is no reason to dispute his assertion that at the time of the wedding he believed Miss Hindle to be a man ... Once she was a bride, and twice she has been a groom. Once she had a husband and twice she had a wife. Once she was a widow, once a widower and now she is a husband again."

Sarah Bernhardt, the renowned actress of the late nineteenth and early twentieth century, regularly played male roles such as Hamlet. In 1882, she appeared in a play called *Fedora*, whose lead character, Princess Fedora Romanoff, wore a "man's hat" with a wide soft brim and a crease in the top. Women and men soon began wearing fedora hats, especially women's-rights activists. Even when Clara wasn't wearing men's clothes, she had a favourite fedora, which hadn't yet replaced bowlers and flat caps as the most popular variety of men's hat. Clara argued – before and during her trial – that women had a right to wear men's clothes without being accused of being less of a woman for it. She used the example of Vic Steinberg, a *News* reporter who had her own byline and often went undercover, including attending a baseball game and a tavern while dressed as a man.

It's impossible to know whether Clara identified as a man or was attracted to women. The notion of gender dysphoria – emotionally and psychologically identifying as a gender different from what your body indicates – wasn't discussed in mainstream white society until the late twentieth century. Lesbianism was sometimes openly hinted at (as in the cases of Annie Hindle and Florence Hines, both "show people"), but, in general, cross-dressing, homosexuality, and transgender identity were conflated. Clara said she wore men's clothes to earn more money and to feel safer and freer in public spaces. This "progress narrative" was applied to women who transgressed gender lines in the nineteenth century. From over a century's distance, we know only two things with certainty. One, Clara saw herself as the primary breadwinner of her family in a way that was gendered as male at the time. Two, Clara preferred the company of women.

Flora testified to being fourteen ("soon to be 15") when her mother was arrested in November 1894, and *The Telegram* noted that Flora's birthday was December 24, 1879. That means that Clara gave birth to Flora not long after she turned eighteen.

Charles Ingles, Catherine Clark, and Mary Crosier all agreed: Clara didn't like to talk about the circumstances leading to Flora's birth. After her arrest, Sergeant Reburn visited Clara more than once in jail "to get her to admit to Flora's parentage. Her invariable response: 'What has that to do with the case? No one has the right to ask me that. I won't tell you. There is no need to mix that up with the case.'"

The newspapers implied that Flora's father was white and that Clara's daughter was the result of seduction ("a faux pas" is how Reverend Ingles referred to it, insisting that she wasn't "dissipated"). As was the case with Clara, who was the subject of fetishist scanning for "Negro" features, Flora's appearance fascinated newspaper reporters. *The Globe* described her as "a bright, good looking girl, well grown for her age, and showing only slight traces

Flora McKay at Clara's preliminary hearing

of coloured blood in her veins, although bearing a resemblance to her unfortunate mother." *The Mail* said she was "olive complexioned with dark eyes and masses of dark wavy hair."

Clara lived in Toronto during the first few years of Flora's life, but not in the same home as her daughter and mother. After five years of short-term renting in Cabbagetown, Jessie McKay finally found a home she could live in for longer than a year or two. This was 23 Gloucester Street, just off Yonge Street, and Jessie and Flora would live there from 1879 to 1886, when it was torn down. In the 1881 census, Clara is not listed, but two-year-old "Florence" and Jessie are. Jessie's profession is listed as "nurse," and an annotation explains Flora's presence: "she takes children in the house." The home was another single-storey shack, twenty-two by eighteen feet, and, like the house on James Street, it was the cheapest on the block. Jessie rented from her next-door neighbour John Stitt, who is listed as a "porter," a common profession for Black Torontonians.

Clara spent her daughter's first three years working as a domestic servant. These were not happy times for her. Her first of two dismissed charges of drunkenness was in April 1880, four months after Flora was born. In 1882, she worked as a servant at the prestigious Jarvis Street home of barrister Thomas Rolph, who lived with his mother, wife, and infant daughter. The following year, she worked for Henry Taylor, a merchant tailor, at a slightly less prestigious address on St. James Street. The second charge of drunkenness, in August 1883, bookends this period in her life.

If Clara was getting drunk (these arrests might have simply been racist harassment by police), it wasn't her typical behaviour. She was praised by friends after her arrest as "a quiet, well-behaved girl, hard-working and steady, and devoting the whole of her earnings to the upkeep of her foster mother and her daughter Florrie." She didn't waste money on drink (Clara was described by most of her friends as "temperate") and didn't rely on public charity. Clara, to her friends and supporters, represented a subset of the Decent Poor People trope – the Good Negro Citizen.

Jessie and Clara had a mutually beneficial relationship with their parish. *The Globe,* whose suspicion of Anglicans was second only to its hatred for papists, reported that although Clara and her mother "passed as Presbyterians," Jessie used to wash the surplices for St. Luke's Church to pay for a pew and that Clara (more likely Flora) had attended St. Luke's Sunday School, "her demeanour [race] attracting no special notice."

St. Luke's Anglican Church was a curious spiritual choice for the McKay-Ford household. Established in 1870 as a High Anglican alternative to St. Paul's in Yorkville and located north of present-day Wellesley and Bay Streets, it largely served the wealthy families who lived on Queen's Park Crescent. Jessie and Clara probably became congregants after 1879, when Jessie moved to 23 Gloucester Street, two blocks from the church. St. Luke's was known for its choir, and perhaps Jessie and Clara were attracted by the lavish scale and musicality of its services and ceremonies. *The Globe* described a Christmas tree presentation at the Sunday school in late 1871: "The presents with which the tree was adorned were beautiful and evidently very costly ... Dr. Davies delighted the assembly with a large number of magic lantern scenes, and Miss Brokavski and Monsieur Pernet, who were present, kindly sang several songs."

Moments of spiritual succour and genteel entertainment were welcome breaks from the unpleasant realities of working as a servant. Domestic service was the most common form of paid employment for women. In 1891, 41 percent of all waged women in Canada were employed as servants. Servants were expected to do the most back-breaking household work: cleaning floors and stoves, washing clothes, hauling fuel. For this, live-in domestics received room and board and a low wage. At the end of the nineteenth century, female servants were paid between eight and fourteen dollars a month, as compared to between ten and twenty dollars a month for a male servant. What is worse, lack of privacy while living in someone else's home made women vulnerable to sexual assault by employers, their male relatives, or hired men working in the same or nearby households. In 1889, the Royal Commission into the Relations of Labor and Capital cited a report from Manchester, England, which stated that 60 percent of prostitutes in that city had been in domestic service, where they were "led astray." This is an ironic counterpoint to the argument that institutions such as the Girls' Home and Magdalen Asylum were "saving" women from prostitution by providing them with positions as servants. C.S. Clark quotes "one lad of 18" who boasted "that there had not been a maid in the past five years with whom he had not had improper relations."

By 1884, Clara had left Toronto again, this time for Chicago. She testified at her trial that she'd married in Chicago in 1885 and had lived with her husband for a year. She told the cook at the Gladstone Hotel near Parkdale, when she worked there, that her husband in Chicago had been a white man and she'd had two children with him, who were now deceased.

Chicago would have been Clara's first experience living in a city with a critical mass of Black people. Chicago was a much larger city than Toronto or St. Paul, exceeding 1 million people by 1890. Between 1870 and 1900, its Black population grew from four thousand to thirty thousand. Racism in housing, employment, and police violence was as vicious in Chicago as it was in St. Paul or Toronto, but the economic opportunities in this burgeoning capital of the Midwest would have appealed to Clara.

By 1887, her marriage was over, and her second daughter, Annie, had been born. Sarah Crosier testified at the trial that Clara said she'd given birth to two girls and often referred to Flora and Annie as her daughters. But according to Catherine Clark: "The child spoken of has no relation to Clara or Flora. Her name is Annie Mitchell and has a fair complexion. She is about three years younger than Florence [Annie was seven years younger than Flora] and has a sister living with an uncle. Her mother was a relative of Mrs. McKay and was deserted by her husband or died. She left to find work in the United States and died soon afterwards of a rapid consumption."

Following Clara's arrest, D.M. Kennedy of Petrolia in western Ontario wrote *The Mail* to say that a maid named Clara Murphy, "who answers exactly to Clara Ford's description," had worked for her for a few months in 1887. Murphy told her that she'd travelled a good deal. Kennedy wrote: "She was a good worker and could do any kind of work. She was strong and muscular. At last she got reckless in her company, so we had to let her go."

The man who fathered Flora and the possibly apocryphal husband in Chicago were the only sexual relationships spoken about in relation to Clara. All her confidantes stressed that she travelled to support "her adopted mother and her child[ren]." Both Catherine Clark and Chloe Dorsey said they'd tried to push Clara toward potential marriage prospects but that Clara resisted these efforts. Clark explained where Clara's priorities lay: "Many a time when I have suggested to her that she should get married the poor thing has told me that the great dream of her life is to save enough out of her small wages to buy a little home on the instalment plan where she might take her adoptive mother and care for her until her death."

The move to Parkdale was intended to fulfil Clara's great dream: a home for her family and a business of her own. Instead, it turned into a nightmare.

SEVEN

BAD
FENCES

Lakeshore Boulevard, winter 1889. The Carswell estate and Dean's
Boathouse are visible just to the right of the tree.

Clara longed to have her own secure family home and business, but her life was nomadic and insecure. In her late twenties and early thirties, she found it harder to find work in Toronto, and her home life disintegrated.

Clara preferred tailoring to being a servant. It paid better and gave her more autonomy. Samuel Barnett, her employer at the time of her arrest in November 1894, told newspapers that she'd worked for him twice in the past and provided "a very positive character" for her in terms of being "always industrious and quiet, never missing time and often working after hours," until 9:00 or 10:00 p.m. She was "one of the best tailoresses he had in his establishment," and her earnings frequently amounted to seven dollars a week. According to Barnett, she'd not taken a holiday or absented herself for one day during his employ, nor did she seem to have anything on her conscience in October and November. Barnett particularly enjoyed Clara's quietness and devotion to the task at hand, saying that they'd been known to work together "all day without exchanging more than half a dozen words outside of absolutely necessary conversation. He said that several girls of not very good character tried to quarrel with Clara. He thought it was because she had nothing to say to men, and seemed to value her reputation and hold herself aloof from loose girls. Then by way of feminine revenge they invented all kinds of yarns about her."

Furthermore, testified Barnett, "her habits are temperate, and she cannot be induced to drink even a glass of beer." He allowed under cross-examination that "she had a temper" but pointed out:

SAMUEL BARNETT.

Samuel Barnett, Clara's employer

"We all got tempers, ain't we? I got as much as she has." Barnett reiterated at the trial that Clara "kept herself somewhat aloof from her shopmates and seldom talked about her circumstances." In fact, when the police detectives came to her workplace on November 20, Barnett referred to her as "Clara something or other."

The newspapers referred to Barnett as the "Jew tailor," and most of Clara's former employers and coworkers in the garment trade who testified – Benjamin Vise, Jenny Bloom, and Benjamin Polakoff – were Jews who lived in the Ward. Clara worked off and on for Jews from the time she and Jessie moved to Macaulaytown in 1867 until her arrest in 1894, almost thirty years later.

The emergence of the garment trade as an alternative to domestic service or marriage for young women sparked a moral panic in late nineteenth-century Toronto. Paid work combined with independent living weakened patriarchal control over women's leisure, earnings, and, it was feared, sexuality. Working girls often dressed in flashy, immodest clothing and mingled with male workers and lodgers with bad language and manners. It was feared that delayed marriages would lead to "race suicide" in Toronto, one of the most ethnically homogenous cities in North America. By 1901, there were 123 women to every 100 men, and those in the paid labour force were hypersexualized in newspaper portrayals, partly because their pay was so minimal it was hard to imagine them surviving without bartering sexual services. C.S. Clark noted that ads for bookkeeper or cashier positions promised only $2.50 to $3.00 per week: "After paying her board out of that amount, was the young lady expected to prostitute herself to wear clothes?"

Clara was part of a growing army of female workers. In 1881, the Toronto garment industry employed two thousand women, out of a total female paid labour force of six thousand. Over the next decade, the number jumped to forty-five hundred women working in over one thousand small businesses. Although unions feared women would replace skilled male labour, the Knights of Labour helped organize the first all-women's local for tailoresses in 1886. Of the 1,800 witnesses who appeared before the Royal Commission on the Relations of Labor and Capital, only 102 were women.

There were two major concerns about garment work. The first was the practice of sweating. The three oldest Crosier girls and their mother "sweated" at their home. Piecework could pay as little as four dollars per week in the late 1880s, which would not pay for room and board. The second was the practice of paying entry-level seamstresses nothing while they "apprenticed" and then letting them go at the end of their "training period." In January 1894, *The Star* ran an exposé on this practice, saying that young women and girls were expected to work for nothing or very little for the first month or two: "After that, they receive from $1 to $1.50 per week for a few months, until they get up to $2, and then, unless they are exceptionally good hands, and do not stand out for too high wages," they are let go, to be replaced by the next generation of "learners." In fact, the exposé continued, what is "wanted principally is plenty of strength and power of endurance to withstand the long and tedious work at the sewing machine." With custom work being replaced by ready-made, it was increasingly difficult for a skilled tailor such as Clara to be hired for a living wage.

Given the insecure and cyclical nature of the garment industry, Clara was often forced to take on waitressing and cleaning work in hotels and to look beyond Toronto for employment. Aside from her waitressing work at the Temperance Coffee Palace, where she met Mary Crosier in 1891, she moved back to Chicago and worked as a waitress at the famous Palmer House Hotel from December 1892 to February 1893, and then she travelled to Cobourg, east of Toronto, where she worked at the St. Lawrence Temperance Hotel from February to April. She worked as a barmaid at the Gladstone Hotel, a tavern on Queen Street adjacent to Parkdale, in July 1893, and from October to December 1893 she worked as a chambermaid at the Rossin House Hotel in downtown Toronto.

Even with her varied employment and travels, Clara always returned to her mother and daughters. Jessie McKay had managed the dual demands of mothering and paid labour by bringing Clara along when she cleaned people's homes, by doing washing and sewing piecework at home, and by pushing Clara into the formal labour force at the age of twelve. Clara managed by relying on her mother to take care of Flora and Annie. After a relatively stable period on Gloucester Street and in the Clarks' servant quarters, Jessie's declining health put pressure on the family. In early 1892, after their eviction from Jameson Avenue, Jessie rented a house on Pearson Avenue in North Parkdale. Clara and the children lived with her: the assessment record lists five people, two of them school-aged (the fifth tenant is unknown).

Jessie moved one more time, to Fern Avenue in North Parkdale, and Clara spent some time there alone after Jessie entered
the Home for Incurables in mid-1893. Flora became a servant to
the Phyalls at the Magann estate, just to the west of the Westwoods, and Annie was sent to the Girls' Home. Clara could not
take Annie to work with her, let alone travel to the United States.
When a friend spoke to Clara about living alone, Clara told her
"she was not afraid of any man, and she slept with a revolver
under her pillow."

One of the tragedies of her life was that Clara was portrayed
as a good daughter but rarely as a mother, good or otherwise.
During the trial, Flora was sometimes called a friend of Clara's,
sometimes just "the child" or "the girl," and sometimes "Jessie's
adopted daughter." When Flora testified, she called Clara by her
name and never called her "mother." To maintain the vital cur-
rency of respectability, Clara had to pretend that Flora and Annie
were not her daughters.

Flora seems to have worked with the Phyalls at the Magann estate in Parkdale from mid-1893 to the summer of 1894. Then she
worked for the Lansells on Spruce Street in Cabbagetown before
finding two successive positions in downtown boarding houses in
the fall. Although Flora and Clara lived apart, Clara often visited
her daughter. When Flora was dismissed by the Lansells, she left
her clothes, and Clara went there several days afterward to collect
them. Clara said the Lansells were right to dismiss Flora, who
was "never to stay out late and she lied to me." Similarly, when
Clara visited her daughter at the boarding house run by Harriet
Phyall, she told Phyall to keep a close eye on Flora and not to let
her stay out late. Clara must have remembered her two arrests for
vagrancy at that age and how hard it was to maintain respectability and stay safe as a Black girl.

Although Clara and Flora lived apart, several people, including
her employer Samuel Barnett and landlady Chloe Dorsey, remarked

on Flora's frequent visits to York Street. Flora told the police she often went to the theatre with her mother on Saturday nights, and she told her fellow servants at the Phyall's that "her mother had always acted kindly towards her and gave her good advice." But the same article – printed in the newspaper most sympathetic to Clara, *The Telegram* – pointed to a fraught relationship between mother and daughter: "Like Clara Ford, Flora possesses considerable temper, but it is evinced more in sulkiness and moroseness than by any tiger-like displays of ferocity. She does not appear to have the affection for her mother that most children have. You could not say she was very fond of her, but she seems willing to obey her."

Clara worked so her children could have a less peripatetic and healthier upbringing than she'd had. She contributed to her mother and children's rent and living expenses, first in the northern and more salubrious part of the city and then in the western suburbs. Jessie had lived in at least seven houses during Clara's childhood, always soon-to-be-condemned shacks in slums. Jessie, financially supported by Clara, rented the same house for the first seven years of Flora's life, and the Ford-McKay household held on to that shack in waterfront South Parkdale for as long as they could: almost four years.

Parkdale would have been cleaner and greener than Toronto, rents would have been cheaper, and there would have been less development pressure to tear down the substandard accommodation that was the Ford-McKays' only option. On the other hand, there was a cost when Clara worked downtown: a five-cent streetcar ride or a three-mile, one-way walk if that was too dear.

It seems the price Clara paid for semi-decent accommodation, fuel, and food for her family was absenting herself from her children's upbringing. Female Black servants who migrated from the Caribbean to Toronto in the latter half of the twentieth century and onward lived a similar life. To some extent, Clara's infantilization – papers called her an "ignorant and helpless female" and no match for the wily police – depended on divorcing her image from the reality of her being the mother of two. Of course, the use of the term "girl" to describe Clara was an expression of racism. But the journalistic emphasis on Clara's friendships with older mothers – Catherine Clark and Mary Crosier – suggests that Clara was seen more as a daughter than as a mother. Unable to acknowledge her children, Clara was denied an identity as a mother and an adult woman.

At some point during the time the McKay-Ford family lived in Parkdale, Benjamin Westwood heard that Clara "liked to sit on the steps from the boardwalk to the lake" next to the Westwood boathouse. During the trial, five stories emerged involving Clara, and they all related to incidents in or near the Parkdale waterfront.

In the first, Clara's confession, she said that during the summer of 1894, when she no longer lived in Parkdale, Frank had thrown her down at the waterfront and tried to rape her. She fought him off and vowed revenge. Racism played a role, according to Clara. Frank and other Parkdale boys used to harass her for being Black. His father told a *Mail* reporter that "Frank may possibly have exchanged a bit of 'chaff' with her at various times," and *The World* referred to Frank "tantalising" Clara with racist insults. In a second story linking Clara and Frank, Gus Clark contended that Frank had told *The Telegram* in August 1894 that Clara was in Parkdale dressed as a man and tried to get the police to arrest her. A Black woman who sometimes wore man's clothes "didn't belong" in Parkdale.

A third story dated from the time Clara lived in Parkdale, specifically the two and a half years (from September 1889 to February 1892) when she and Frank were next-door neighbours. At the trial, Clark's brother-in-law, Christian Dorenwend, painted Clara as an aggressive troublemaker who had written Catherine anonymous letters slandering her two eldest daughters under the pseudonym "Jim Hardy" in May 1890. In this version of events, the "Westwoods' Frank," thirteen years old, was twenty-eight-year-old Clara's informant and friend; at the trial, it was suggested that they became lovers in 1890.

A fourth story – also attributed to Gus Clark and Christian Dorenwend by *The World, The Star,* and *The Mail* – had the opposite slant. In it, Clara got angry on that evening in May 1890 because the Westwood boys had insulted the Clark girls. First Bert and then Frank were dragged over to the Clarks' veranda, where they strenuously denied making improper accusations. *The Star* added that Frank also made insulting remarks to Flora about her mother's morals: "That night [Clara] vowed revenge" and for "four years brooded over the insult" before exacting retribution.

The fifth story was the most implausible. In it, Clara and Frank became lovers after Clara left Parkdale, in 1894. They'd had assignations in the boathouse in the summer of 1894 and Frank didn't return Clara's affections. Clara became jealous, either because Frank paid attention to other women, because he wanted to break off the affair, or because he was revolted by her approaches. She flew into a rage and shot him. A variant on this story, also told at the trial, didn't involve Frank but established Clara as an immoral and violent Jezebel with marital ambitions above her station. In this story, Clara and Gus Clark were having an affair, and Clara threatened to shoot Clark if he didn't marry her.

These stories of an affair between Clara and Frank or Clark ring false, not because of the age, class, or race of the two people involved. According to contemporary reports, Clara was considered very attractive, and there are certainly many examples of cross-class nonmarital sexual relationships. As the age of consent was twelve, and seduction was seen only as male-on-female predation, Clara would not have broken any laws in seducing a thirteen-year-old in 1890, let alone an eighteen- or twenty-three-year-old in 1894. No, a consensual affair is unlikely simply because Clara disliked both men intensely.

In conversation with his friend and bar buddy John Miller, a re-porter for *The Mail,* Gus Clark provided the following story – full of unbelievable details – about Clara's time with the Clarks:

> In 1885, early in the year, when the Riel Rebellion was in full swing, I went up to the Northwest with the Royal Grenadiers, to which regiment I belonged to for quite a long time. I came back to Toronto when the others did, but in April 1889, with my father, who is now dead, my half-brother Charles, and my brother-in-law Mr. Brewer, I went west again, this time to Saskatoon, where I thought of mak-ing my home. Before I left on this second occasion, Mrs. McKay had moved into the little cottage behind my father's house, and with her came Clara Ford, Flora McKay, and an-other little girl, whom we all called Annie McKay and who was quite young then and so far as I knew, had no coloured blood in her veins. When we went away to the North-West, Clara came to live with my mother and sisters and little brothers. Even in those days she used to dress up in men's clothes, and she had, not one revolver, but two, one I re-member was pearl-mounted. She lived under our roof for about a year, and we all got to know her very well. She even-tually returned to her foster-mother, Mrs. or Miss McKay, and later on they moved to the north part of Parkdale.

At the commencement of the Northwest Resistance, Clark had just turned fourteen and was probably too young for military glory, although it's possible that his half-brothers, Frank and Charles, volunteered. In April 1889, John Clark was a month away from his death from kidney failure caused by Bright's Disease, which he'd suffered from for five years. The Clark men, without their father, likely returned to pursue their land claim in 1889. Gus Clark, eighteen, would have just been released from his first stint in prison for burglary. Following his departure, either to prison or out West, Clara moved from the servants' quarters into the house. Catherine Clark must have needed help with her dying husband and assistance with the younger children. According to *The World,* she considered Clara "as good as a man in the house" in terms of chores and protecting the family by driving "stragglers from the house."

Catherine Clark's four stepchildren had already made their way in the world. Of her biological children, the two oldest daughters, Eva and Carrie, aged nineteen and sixteen at the time of their father's death, were already being courted by their future husbands. Clara shared a room with the third daughter, Ida, who was fourteen.

Ida Clark told *The Mail* reporter John Miller that one night they'd

> heard a noise and we both thought a man was trying to break in. I knew Clara had a revolver and I asked her: "Clara, what would you do if you saw a man breaking through the window? Would you shoot him?"
>
> "I don't think I could bring myself to shoot" was Clara's reply.
>
> "But what if you were sure he meant you harm?"
>
> "In that case, I would wait until he got in the room, and then I would shoot him in the leg or arm. But" – and I remember these words distinctly – "I don't think I could ever go on living if I shot a man."
>
> "And this is the girl," said the young lady with a fine contempt, "who is supposed to have shot Frank Westwood and then gone on without betraying that in the slightest difference in her manner or way of living."

While this story may be as suspect as the one told by her brother, it suggests that Clara had a relationship with the Clarks that went beyond being a servant.

When Gus Clark returned to his mother's home in early 1890, the trouble began. Clara left the Clarks' house and moved back in to the shack behind it with her mother and children. One night, in May 1890, according to Clark:

A few friends had gathered at my mother's for the purpose of spending the evening, when my brother-in-law [Christian Dorenwend, then engaged to Carrie] heard a noise outside on the verandah, and went outside to see who was there. He found Clara there, and she appeared to be in a very bad humour about something, and she came inside and created a very unpleasant scene. She applied some improper remarks to my sisters, which were resented, of course. She then laid the blame on one of the Westwood boys, but first Bert, and then Frank, denied her statement that they had been the originators of the objectionable comment, and Clara appeared very incensed at Frank.

The Westwoods had moved into their Lakeside Hall in late summer 1889, a year after the McKay-Fords began to rent from the Clarks. Flora – who, at nine, was two years younger than Willie and two years older than Emily – became the Clarks' schoolmate in the newly opened Queen Victoria School.

The incident described above appeared to be related to two anonymous letters addressed to Catherine Clark, signed "Jim Hardy," and postmarked May 16 and 18, 1890. The letters were saved for four and a half years by Christian Dorenwend and given to the police at the time of Clara's arrest. The letters were read by the judge at the trial but suppressed as evidence because they slandered white "ladies." However, excerpts were obtained and published in *The World* during the trial.

The first letter accused Carrie Clark, then sixteen, of being attracted to thirteen-year-old Frank: "Ask Westwood's Frank. She is crazy about him. There is no young lady in the village who will be seen with her." The second also cited Frank: "Young Westwood told me this week that two young women [presumably Carrie and her nineteen-year-old sister, Eva] ... were asking their hired man to take them to the theatre." According to Judge Boyd's trial notes, the first letter went even further, saying that "C is a regular whore. She used lust ... by talking before all the boys: ask Westwood's Frank." Dorenwend had found out that Clara was the author of these letters and confronted her. She didn't deny being the author and claimed that every word was true. The letters would be used in the trial to suggest that Clara and Frank had an intimate relationship from the time he was thirteen.

However, Gus Clark's story suggests Clara was angry with Frank for denying he was the originator of the rumours when confronted on the veranda. Clark and Dorenwend said Clara and her family were asked to leave their shack at this point, in May 1890. But the family lived there until early 1892. Clara continued to have good relations with Catherine Clark, who categorically denied that Clara had slandered her daughters, let alone killed Frank:

> Poor Clara. I cannot tell you how deeply I feel for her. She is just one of those people who think they have not a friend in the world, although she has far more than she thinks. I cannot believe for one moment that she will be proved to have committed the crime. During the three years I was acquainted with her I have seen her do a hundred unostentatious acts of kindness. She was passionately fond of animals and of children. It is a gross libel on her to say that she was dissolute or immoral, and that she had a loose tongue. I have never known her to utter a word to which exception could be taken.

Catherine's twenty-year-old son, Cass, who comanaged the CPR Hotel with his mother at the time of Clara's arrest, confirmed that "nothing but the most pleasant relations existed during the four years Clara lived behind the Clark house" and that they lived there rent-free in return for cleaning and doing the laundry.

The two anonymous letters were used as key evidence to prove that Clara had had a relationship with Frank. It's hard to know what to make of them, particularly since the full text and context are unavailable. Frank seems to have gossiped viciously about the Clark girls, just as he passed on vicious gossip five years later to *The Telegram* about Clara's cross-dressing. It's unclear why Clara would convey that gossip via anonymous letters to Catherine Clark, even if she was angry about being forced to leave the Clark house when Gus Clark returned. Perhaps the letters were written by Frank himself, or, if they were written by Clara, they might have been a way to cause trouble for Frank. Clara is plausible in the role of angry defender of Catherine Clark and her daughters, railing at the Westwood brothers on the veranda. It's easy to believe that Gus Clark resented Clara acting as the "man of the house."

Parkdale's assessment records provide another, somewhat startling, commentary on the relationship between the Westwoods, the Clarks, and the Ford-McKays. Benjamin and Clara Westwood testified at both the preliminary hearing and the trial that they knew Clara Ford by sight but had never exchanged words with her. At the preliminary hearing, Clara Westwood deposed that "when [the McKay-Fords] first moved to Parkdale, she had heard the children tell of a coloured girl and heard them tell little stories about her. The prisoner was afterward pointed out to her by the children." Flora confirmed at the trial that she knew Willie and Emily fairly well and Frank a little.

In Parkdale's first assessment in 1879, John Clark is registered as having subdivided his large waterfront property into six lots and constructed his house on the northernmost part of the estate. These lots didn't sell, and by 1884, Clark is listed as a "gentleman" rather than a "customs official," dependent on property sales and any pension for an income for himself, his wife, and thirteen children. He owned a horse and had a stable in which a groom lived. By September 1891, the "stable" belongs to Benjamin Westwood's enlarged estate, subdivided from the Clark property and with a new fence enclosing it. The Westwoods have nine people living on the property, six between five and twenty-one years of age. The Westwood household consisted of Benjamin and Clara Westwood, their four children under twenty-one, and a live-in servant. It's possible that the two other schoolchildren were Flora and Annie and that Jessie and Clara were left out of the count, Clara because she was travelling and Jessie because she was ill.

In the following year, 1892, the Westwood estate had only seven residents (four of whom are between five and twenty-one, that is, the Westwood children). Clara and her family were likely renting from the Westwoods by 1891, not the Clarks, and evicted by them in early 1892, possibly while Clara was travelling. In contrast to most newspaper descriptions of the Ford-McKay household, Dr. Adam Lynd (who knew everyone) testified at Clara's preliminary hearing that he knew Clara from having attended Mrs. Mackay, who "lived behind Mr. Westwood's house, about 300 feet away."

In 1989, a century after the fact, Frank Jones of the *Toronto Star* published an account of the Clara Ford trial. A reader, Lorraine Parker, sent photos of Lakeside Hall taken in the 1920s, when the house was owned by the Penman family, for whom her aunt and uncle had worked. (Lakeside Hall was torn down in the 1950s to make way for the Gardiner Expressway.) Parker said Clara Ford and her family had probably lived in a small frame cottage, reached by a pathway behind the kitchen. So, the Westwoods' testimony that they knew Clara only by sight and had never spoken to her appears to be as specious as Benjamin Westwood's initial inquest testimony that he'd shot at stone hookers in September 1894, not at Gus Clark trying to break into his boathouse.

Clara returned from one of her work trips in February 1892 to an unpleasant surprise. Early one morning, according to Harriet Phyall, "Clara arrived [at the Magann house, where Harriet, and possibly Flora, worked] ... drenched to the bone and half-starved at my door and asked for something to eat. She had arrived from the States and found the cottage abandoned. She was worried the old lady was dead and had slept on the floor. She said very little about her wanderings in the States. She said she had had a rough time of it, and indeed she gave every evidence of it."

Even without the possible landlord-tenant dispute, news-papers hinted that Clara and her family knew the Westwoods well and were subjected to considerable racial harassment from them. After Clara's arrest, *The Star* alleged: "In Parkdale, there is a story that Frank made slighting remarks to Flora about her mother's complexion." A story in *The Mail*, inaccurate in several details, is also worth dissecting. Dixie Rice was the younger sister of Frank Rice, who, with Willie Westwood, saw the suspicious piano delivery man on the day of the shooting. She and her cousin Maud Winkler, both friends of Emily Westwood, said they walking home arm in arm from Queen Victoria School on Friday, two days before the shooting when they saw Clara in the company of a younger girl (Annie, aged seven) walking down Jameson together. Dixie saw Clara point toward Mrs. Westwood, who was standing at her front door; Clara frowned and muttered something. When Dixie suggested approaching Clara and her daughter, Emily said Miss Ford was dangerous and carried a revolver.

Clara and Flora were both living and working in central Toronto by October 1894, and Annie was living in the Children's Home. Clara worked long hours and was unlikely to have ever walked either of her daughters home from school. What this story suggests, however, is that Clara and her daughters were highly visible subjects of malicious rumour in Parkdale. And it points, again, to the bad relationship between the Westwoods and their former neighbours. In the same article, John Harvey Hall, a CPR train conductor and South Parkdale resident, said he knew Clara by sight, and he knew that a newspaper had published a story about Clara, a woman in a man's clothes. He told his daughter, a friend of Flora's, not to spend time with the daughter of a woman with that reputation.

When Clara was arrested, one of the possible motives was revenge for the story published in *The Telegram* on August 27, 1894, six weeks before Frank was shot.

Dressed in Male Attire/A Young Lady Promenades in South Parkdale/Police Are Inquiring
The residents of South Parkdale are discussing the actions of a young lady of that neighbourhood, who has been masquerading in male attire. Last evening, shortly after the Parkdale Methodist congregation had dispersed, she was noticed on Spencer Avenue, dressed in a light suit of clothes, with a straw hat, and carrying a cane. Her hair is dark, short and curly, but her feet – they are genuine Chicagos. The masquerader has a decidedly girlish expression, and if it were not for this her identity would remain unknown. The police of No. 6 division are inquiring into the matter.

There are certainly hints that Frank may have been the source, particularly the mention of Parkdale's Methodist congregation. While the race of the cross-dressing "young lady" is not provided, the "dark, short and curly" hair provided a clue to those who knew Clara by sight, and the reference to large "Chicago feet" (a trope of the time) was a thinly veiled reference to Clara's supposedly masculine characteristics and may have had a racist undertone as well.

Clara felt discriminated against in Parkdale, where her "dusky skin and wild pranks made her rather conspicuous." She told a neighbouring friend, who might have been either Catherine Clark or Harriet Phyall: "It's easy enough for folks to get along when everything is all right about them. If only I had a fair chance, I know I could have done well, but they never give me a good word." Clara was uncomfortably visible and vulnerable in Parkdale. In 1893, five years after she moved to Parkdale, she moved back downtown.

In the months before her arrest, Clara returned to her childhood neighbourhood, once known as Macaulaytown but by the 1890s known as the Ward. Living as a boarder with Chloe Dorsey and her family was a step down from renting a home but a common situation for working-class people. Lodgers testified at Frank's inquest, and Jessie McKay herself had been a boarding-house landlady.

C.S. Clark had much to say about living in a boarding house in the 1890s, and none of it was good. The rooms were too cold in the winter and had bedbugs in the summer. Breakfasts consisted of thick lumpy porridge and thin, hard toast followed by bacon and liver that had been "left out in the sun for a week then baked for an hour or two." Lunch was invariably soup made of leftovers from the dinner before, while dinner was almost always served cold, with tea that had been boiling for three hours.

The expenses that Clara saved by not taking the streetcar or paying for heating and cooking fuel were surely spent on meals and laundry. Although there was a Chinese laundryman, Charles Lee Ting, next to Rebecca Alexander's second-hand store on York Street, Clara found it either cheaper or friendlier to have Mary Crosier wash her clothes. Clara had no capacity to cook for herself, although Dorsey provided two or three meals per day as part of the rent.

Vic Steinberg, a pioneering female journalist for the *Toronto News,* offered a woman's perspective on the perils of boarding houses. On an undercover assignment, Steinberg posed as a down-on-her-luck female lodger. For four dollars a week (keep in mind Clara earned six to seven dollars a week, at best), Vic got a twelve-foot-square room in a "worn out house on Sherbourne" in central Toronto. The clean but "bare and dreary" room had "a small simple bed in one corner, a dressing table in another and a washstand in a third." The food, while better-sounding than C.S. Clark's fare, was plain: pork chops, potatoes, corn, bread, rice pudding, and tea for lunch, the main meal; unidentifiable cold meat, a little pickle, more bread, and "jelly cake without any jelly" for dinner.

Steinberg was sitting in the parlour one day after lunch, reading the morning papers, when a male resident came in, placed his arm affectionately around the back of her chair and asked, "Would you like to take the air today?" She suspected that "the little man has been drinking something stronger than seltzer." She left the room. Several female residents watched in sympathy.

At the Dorseys', Clara had little privacy and felt threatened by male residents. Chloe Dorsey's son George was told by his sister Mamie "not to enter her room to sweep because Clara did not like people in her room," and Dorsey herself said that Clara's revolver, which she kept under her pillow, was "protection against insult or assault, and on one occasion when a boarder in the house attempted to enter her room he was threatened with serious results unless he desisted."

The Dorseys were at the centre of the Ward. The sizeable clan – John, Chloe's future husband, and his four younger brothers, Henry, Benjamin, Romeo, and Rodney – arrived in Toronto in the early 1850s as refugees from Maryland. John and his brothers plied various building trades: John was a moulder, Benjamin a housepainter, and Romeo a plasterer, all in or near York Street. Henry and his wife, Mary, also ran a York Street grocery store and restaurant with a lodging house above. John's first wife died in childbirth in 1862, and the following year he married Chloe Hickman, who took responsibility for her three young stepchildren. Chloe, thirty-three years old at the time of the marriage, worked at her father's grocery store and was part of a Black women's benevolent society that taught Black immigrants from America literacy skills in the evenings. Chloe eventually ran her father's grocery store,

MRS. DORSEY

Chloe Dorsey, Clara's landlady

which expanded to include a restaurant managed by her son, also named John. By 1871, John Sr. and Chloe lived with six children and a Black maid named Josephine Skelton, with whom they later had a massive falling-out.

The Dorseys had frequent run-ins with the law, either as victims or defendants. In January 1874, John Dorsey was fined one dollar and costs or twenty days hard labour for drunkenness. White men charged with the same offence usually got ten days in jail, without hard labour. Later that year, Chloe unsuccessfully took a man named Robert Rennie to court for forging a cheque with her signature. In July 1879, Josephine Skelton was convicted of "insulting" (i.e., assaulting) Chloe and sentenced to one dollar and costs or ten days in jail. Two months later, John's son William was shot by a man named Wesley Collins, who then shot at a police officer who intervened. In 1882, Josephine Skelton assaulted John. In 1887, Sarah Dorsey, John's oldest daughter, was convicted of larceny and sentenced to six months at the Mercer Reformatory – again, a harsher sentence than usual for theft. York Street was a rough part of town, but the Dorseys received particularly harsh treatment by the police and courts.

The Dorsey clan were political activists within the Black community who fought for equal rights in Toronto and across North America. In 1874, Henry Dorsey gave a "stirring speech" at a meeting held at the African Methodist Episcopal Church "for the purpose of expressing indignation and protestation against the outrages and cold-blooded murders perpetrated against the coloured citizens of the United States." The White Leaguers, a paramilitary wing of the Democratic Party in the South, were shooting African Americans attempting to vote. Those at the Toronto gathering resolved: "We the Coloured Citizens of Toronto ... feeling ourselves closely identified with the coloured citizens of the United States ... view with regret and indignation the recent outrages ... by monsters in human shape." They pledged to provide "material aid if required" to their American brothers. In 1882, Henry, Benjamin, and Romeo Dorsey were among the prominent Black citizens who held a party for Delos Rogers Davis to honour his becoming one of the first Black Canadians called to the bar. On August 1, 1894, the sixtieth anniversary of Emancipation Day, the abolition of slavery in the British Empire, "a very large number of colored citizens went off on an excursion to Berlin [Kitchener] organized by the Oddfellows" under the leadership of Benjamin Dorsey.

The Globe happily covered these congratulatory events, which showed Canada's moral superiority to its southern neighbour when it came to dealing with "the Negro problem." In 1888, it provided extensive coverage of a case of African Americans seeking political refuge in Toronto. In December 1887, Adam Samuel Morse, an eleven-year-old Black child, was on a streetcar travelling between Savannah, Georgia, and the suburb of Warsaw when the conductor, a man named Alexander Barbee, "squashed" him down on the seat, threatened to throw him out the window, and tried to punch holes in the boy's hand with a ticket puncher. When Adam Junior got home, he told his father, who spoke to Barbee, his neighbour, about why he'd assaulted his son, apparently not for the first time. Barbee used "offensive epithets," and Morse hit him, once with his open hand and three times with a walking stick. Before Morse could be arrested for attempted murder, with the possibility of "the chain gang" or being lynched, he fled with his wife and three children to Canada.

The State of Georgia sent a detective to arrest Morse. William Murdoch represented Morse in a trial for attempted murder that was also an extradition hearing. Following a successful appeal for funds by the Black community, several white philanthropists, including the editors of *The Telegram* and *The Globe,* helped pay for his legal representation. Murdoch contended that Morse's reaction was proportionate to Barbee's assault on Morse's son and, furthermore, that returning Morse to stand trial in Georgia would be a denial of the former slave's right to a fair trial. Murdoch argued that Black men accused of assaulting white men in the South were either killed on the spot or had a "99 out of 100 chance of confronting a jury from which men of African tincture have been excluded." Southern prisons were "9/10s coloured," and chain gangs were "quarry slaves." *The Globe* supported Murdoch's contention that impartial justice wasn't possible in the South.

The verdict was guilty, and Morse was ordered to be extradited to stand trial in Georgia. But after several weeks of heated campaigning by both newspapers, Judge McDougall ordered the decision reversed on a technicality. A massive public celebration was held at the African Baptist Church. On the speakers' platform were Romeo, Rodney, and Henry Dorsey. The Reverend J.O. Robinson, a renowned Black preacher from Hamilton and publisher of the *British Lion,* a Conservative newspaper, spoke "without any of the peculiarities of pronunciation usually ascribed to his race" of how "the desire was to get [Morse] a fair trial and not to protect a criminal." He continued, "I was born under the British flag and never knew the horrors of slavery. But my father left Kentucky at the age of 15 with a revolver and a dirk, determined to die before he returned to that country ... We know the value of the British subject under that great flag."

Murdoch, Morse's lawyer and a Conservative candidate for the riding of West Toronto, spoke and was "a lion of the night." Conservative Senator John Macdonald, a successful Toronto businessman, said that "Canada is like an ancient city of refuge, pledged to protect those who landed on her shores with all her men and all her means. He was not going to say that Georgia would have treated [Morse] with injustice, but he was saying that they would not get that chance." Macdonald planned to stake the Morse family funds to establish themselves in Canada: "Morse should show his gratitude to the many friends who had helped him by his industry and by showing himself to be a peace-loving and law-abiding citizen." Reverend Oliver of the African Baptist Church had the best line of the night: "I thank [Morse's] friends, both black and white, for a white man is just as good as a black man ... if he behaves himself."

Two months later, a two-paragraph story ran in *The Globe* with no follow-up. Reverend Robinson tried to check into the Queen's Hotel and was told the last room was taken. Robinson then tried to order dinner but was told he would not be served there. "Do you decline to entertain a respectable Negro gentleman in your hotel?" Robinson asked the manager. Mr. Richmond said yes, adding that the presence of Black people would "cause distress" to other guests. Robinson went to the prominent law firm Blake, Kerr, Lash and Cassels and filed a suit for five thousand dollars against the hotel. If anything happened with that lawsuit, *The Globe* didn't say. C.S. Clark referred to the incident ten years later in *Of Toronto the Good*. In the book, he writes that the Queen's Hotel "had an unpleasant experience with a man they declined to accommodate" who "got into quite a rage." The lawsuit, in the end, was never "threshed out." Toronto wasn't the haven of racial equality it pretended to be.

Chloe Dorsey had a good impression of her lodger. According to Chloe, Clara "never stayed out late and was very hard-working and industrious and earned good wages." Clara often worked overtime, and Dorsey, who had a favourite chair by the stairs leading up from the restaurant to lodgings, made sure she ate before she went to bed. She knew about Clara's revolver and her men's clothes. She characterized Clara as a "man hater" who "was never seen in the company of men" and was "known to reject the advances of men in the street in no gentle manner." She concluded: "She was a daring girl and peculiar in some of her habits, but I think harmless."

For an intensely private person who dreamed of owning her own suburban home and living with her family, life in a downtown boarding house must have been a disappointment. Clara still attended St. Mark's Church in Parkdale on Sundays, walking both ways as the streetcars did not run on Sundays. Ida Clark remarked on Clara's "extraordinary passion for the lake," where she "was known to remain ... from early morning to the end of light, seated at the edge of the water," reading. Clara continued this habit during the summer of 1894. In her confession, she said that one afternoon in July or August 1894, Frank "caught her round the waist and tried to throw her on the ground and take improper liberties with her." At her trial, she said she didn't visit Parkdale after mid-August. The lakeshore views and breezes were no longer hers to enjoy.

EIGHT
HOURS

Police arrest a man for drunkenness, Queen Street, 1916

When the police arrived at Clara's workplace, they were having a good day. The next few hours convinced them they were having a spectacularly good day, one that would successfully resolve the mystery of Frank Westwood's murder and prove their prowess as exemplary detectives. In retrospect, however, this was a day that the Toronto Police would rue for years to come. Clara's treatment on the day of her arrest – during which police questioned her relentlessly, without an attorney or other support person present and before making an arrest – would justify her acquittal, and her case would continue to be a flashpoint in debates on the rights of accused persons for the next half century.

When Alex Smith was arrested for the Priestman "murder," he was tricked into entering a cab with another police officer, who handcuffed and arrested him and put him in jail. Brutal as this behaviour was, it was correct procedure, according to English common law. From the sixteenth century onward, concerns about extracting false confessions under torture had led to a set of unwritten rules about the right to silence. This meant protecting those suspected of a crime but not yet formally charged from incriminating themselves through lies or intimidation by authorities. These rules were encapsulated in an 1870 decision by the English chief justice Alexander Cockburn: "You may ask a man a question with an honest intention to elicit the truth and ascertain whether there are grounds for apprehending him; but with a foregone conclusion of arresting him, to ask him questions for the main purpose of getting anything out of him that may afterwards be used against him, is a very improper proceeding."

At the time of Clara's arrest, the right to counsel – that is, advice from a legal professional – wasn't yet entrenched as a right, and retaining counsel following an arrest was a privilege limited to those who could afford it. Lawyers were rarely called into police stations to represent the accused, unless asked to do so by the person charged. A journeyman lawyer such as William Murdoch might arrive at Magistrates' Court every morning, and perhaps one accused person in twenty could afford to hire him.

So, in Clara's case, it wasn't unusual to question a suspect without counsel, but it was extremely unusual to question one for so long before their preliminary hearing with a magistrate. In *Of Toronto the Good,* C.S. Clark gave the example of an eighteen-year-old named James Bailey who said he was induced to plead guilty to rape against Maudie Tyrell, a girl under the age of fourteen. He claimed that, after arrest, the detective told him that if he pled guilty, he would be let off, but if he continued to protest his innocence his punishment would be terrible. Bailey was sentenced to five years and fifteen lashes at the Magistrates' Court, but the Ontario Court of Appeal set aside Denison's judgment on the grounds that Bailey hadn't been allowed to consult with his mother during the interrogation. *The Telegram* wrote: "Col Denison is generally right, but the case in point is proof that he is not above trifling away a prisoner's liberty and ruining his life in order that he get through a day's worth of work before 11 am."

Barrister James Knowles wrote to the *Toronto News* after Clara's arrest to argue that the police had acted inappropriately in questioning her before arresting her and bringing her to Magistrate's Court, where she could hire a lawyer:

I was informed by one of the police that Inspector Stark and Sergeant Reburn had expressed their determination that no lawyer should see the woman till they were through

with her. Is this just? Several of our judges have emphatic-
ally disapproved of any questioning on the part of the detectives whatever.

Only last Quarter Sessions a young woman, charged with
larceny, swore that two local detectives threatened her with
four years in Kingston if she didn't give evidence against a
man with whom she was jointly charged of crime. They, of
course, denied the allegation, but in spite of the fact that
they swore to her confession, the jury acquitted them both.

The truth is that the detectives of Toronto, all men void
of education or exceptional ability, men who have begun
life on the policeman's beat and have gradually risen to
their present positions, who are petted and extolled by the
newspapers till they are spoiled ... They run the court, and
with the magistrate their word is conclusive ... What right
has a detective, even though he be a sergeant or an inspector,
to constitute himself a prosecuting attorney, and out of
court, secreted from the public eye, and without even allowing a helpless women the common privilege of legal advice, usurp the office of the Crown Counsel and then hold
himself forth as a miracle of astuteness?

To be fair to the police, they were used to dealing with Magistrate Denison, who had no interest in the rights of "the criminal
class." They were also the recipients, on November 20, of a fast-
paced and escalating series of admissions from Clara's friends
and family and the suspect herself. After six weeks of unrelenting
criticism from the newspapers for their inability to find Frank
Westwood's killer, after watching lead after lead disappear, they
were getting all the answers they'd been hoping for.

But had Clara been a white working-class man, such as Alex
Smith, or a white middle-class man, such as Gus Clark, the police would have respected her rights by arresting and then formally cautioning her before leaving her alone until the next day's

appearance before the magistrate, especially considering she was a person suspected of a crime punishable by death. Arthur Conan Doyle, who was briefed on the Westwood case by *World* reporter Hector Charlesworth the day after his public lecture on November 26, opined: "The system of closeting a prisoner with an officer and cross-questioning her for hours, savours more of French than English methods of justice." It was characteristic of late nineteenth-century social norms that the question of "fair play," especially for an accused woman, would help decide a case, even as Clara's claim of sexual assault was removed from consideration.

Eight hours passed from the time Detectives Charley Slemin and George Porter started to question Clara and her alleged confession to Reburn, and during those eight hours, the police grossly underestimated Clara. They were certain that if it was their word against hers, they'd be believed. They were wrong.

The police had talked to Gus Clark and Christian Dorenweld the Thursday before, and they wanted to question Clara. The only clue Clark could give them as to Clara's whereabouts was that her daughter Flora had previously worked for Harriet Phyall in Parkdale before they'd moved downtown. The police used a street directory to locate the Phyalls at a boarding house on Jarvis Street. They were lucky. Flora had recently left domestic service at another boarding house to work once again with the Phyalls.

Arriving at about 2:00 p.m., Slemin and Porter spoke to Flora "alone in the parlour." Harriet Phyall said they gained entry by saying that "some money had been left to [Flora] and her sister, Clara Ford. I know that this could not be true, since poor old Mrs. McKay, with whom I was well acquainted, had died penniless." The detectives' main goal was to find out where Clara lived and worked. However, they also asked Flora whether she knew what Clara had been doing on Saturday, October 6. Flora responded in a suspicious manner, as she described at the preliminary hearing:

Flora: I said that I had been at the theatre to see The Black Crook with Clara.

Crown Attorney Curry: Did you know why they were asking you?

Flora: I did not know they were detectives. I am fourteen years old.

Curry: Were you frightened?

Flora: I was not frightened, but it thought it was strange. They said they knew I was not there [at the theatre] ...

Curry: Why did you lie?

Flora: [*After hesitating*] I said it because I thought they might think that Clara killed Frank Westwood.

Curry: Why did you think that?

Flora: Well, it just came into my mind. I don't know why.

Flora told the detectives that she'd met with her mother at her place of employment, Mrs. Watson's boarding house, the night before the shooting. They'd agreed to meet at 7:30 p.m. the following night at the corner of Bay and Queen Streets to make the 8:00 p.m. curtain at the Grand Opera House. But Clara didn't show up, and after twenty minutes of waiting, Flora went to visit Harriet Phyall, for whom she'd be working as of the following Wednesday.

The Saturday after the shooting, Clara visited her daughter at the Phyalls' to see how Flora had settled in and whether she was "going out at night." Flora was busy serving dinner, and while Clara waited for her to finish her work, she and the Phyalls chatted about the Westwood case (they all, of course, knew the victim). Clara remarked that it was odd that Percy Clark had been born the same day Priestman died and had been buried the same day Frank was shot.

When she had a few private minutes with Flora, Clara told her to say, if asked, that she'd been with her mother at the theatre the week before. Clara said she'd actually been in Parkdale, and it might look bad if anyone knew she was there on the night of the shooting.

Flora eventually admitted all this to the detectives, after an hour of questioning.

The officers were delighted that this highly incriminating evidence had fallen into their laps. Slemin and Porter told Flora not to talk to anyone else and that they'd return later.

Then they took a ten-minute walk to Clara's workplace, where they identified themselves to Clara as police detectives, said she was under suspicion of a serious crime, and told her she had to go with them to police headquarters to be questioned by Inspector William Stark.

At the preliminary hearing, Slemin deposed: "I asked her first whether we could see her room." Clara led the detectives next door and upstairs to her room at Mrs. Dorsey's. Asked whether she had a man's suit, Clara hesitated for a moment, then took out her keys and opened her trunk. Slemin said he'd take the jacket, vest, and pants to the station. Then they asked her if she had a revolver. She unlocked another trunk and said: "Oh, it's the Westwood case you mean."

When William Murdoch asked at the preliminary hearing whether she'd been cautioned at this point, Slemin answered: "She was not yet under arrest."

At the time, Slemin confirmed to Clara that she was suspected of a "very serious crime," while neither confirming nor denying it was the Westwood case. "We said we had threshed out hundreds of clues and they had led us here." (It was actually one conversation with Gus Clark.) The .38 revolver, the same calibre of gun that had shot Frank, was empty. When Slemin asked if she had cartridges, Clara produced four instead of the usual six. She kept them in a kerchief separate from the gun. She said she hadn't used the revolver since the spring, when she'd fired two shots at ducks on Lake Ontario. She told them she could prove she'd been at the Opera House the night Frank had been shot. The detectives, of course, knew better and were delighted that she'd brought up the Westwood case unprompted.

After weeks of frustration and misdirection, the case was coming together faster than the two detectives had dreamed. On the way to police headquarters, located four blocks east on Court Street, near Church and Adelaide, Porter walked beside Clara, and Slemin followed behind, carrying her suit bundled up with some string and the revolver in his pocket. At headquarters, Clara waited in a room with a police matron while Sergeant Henry Reburn, the second in command of the detectives, was briefed by Slemin and Porter on the events of the day. Then they asked Clara about one more item of clothing. Did she, by any chance, own a fedora? Clara said she'd owned one but had left it with her friend Mary Crosier. Slemin and Porter went to fetch the hat, and Reburn, whom the detectives considered the best at the art of questioning, took over the interview. It was a little after 5:00 p.m., almost two hours after Slemin and Porter first spoke to Clara.

Reburn had his own office where he interrogated Clara alone for an hour in his slow and deliberate way. Clara talked about her alibi and received the first of what would later be considered essential reminders of an accused person's right to silence. Reburn cautioned that she was under suspicion of a serious offence and that anything she might say would be taken in evidence against her. But she still wasn't formally placed under arrest or told that she had the option of remaining silent.

At the preliminary hearing, when Murdoch asked Reburn why this hadn't happened, Reburn said that she'd been "cooperating at that point and had she resisted any questioning or tried to leave she certainly would have been placed under arrest." From Reburn's perspective, it was obvious she was in police custody and had been adequately cautioned. At her trial, Clara would argue that she was too frightened to not answer the questions of these powerful white men.

Clara told Reburn that although she'd lived next door to the Westwoods, she hardly knew Frank, only the two younger Westwoods, who were closer in age to Flora. Besides, she told him, she had an alibi: she'd seen *The Black Crook* with Flora, and when they left the theatre, it was 10:30 p.m., according to the Wanless Jewelry Store's clock on Yonge Street. (Recall that the inquest established that the show ended at 10:55.) Reburn called Sergeant Porter into his office and asked Clara where this "Florrie" lived so that they could ask her to corroborate the story. Clara had no idea the detectives had already spoken to her daughter, and she didn't know the exact address of her daughter's new workplace, so she sent them to "Jarvis Street three doors north of the Unitarian Church."

During the preliminary hearing, while Reburn testified, Murdoch objected twice to Denison about entering evidence gathered before Clara had been arrested or cautioned. Denison quashed the objections. And, from the police's perspective, they hadn't lied to Clara about checking her alibi with her daughter; they had simply tried to orchestrate a voluntary confession by confronting Clara with her lies.

When Flora arrived at the station, Reburn asked Clara whether she would like him to send out for dinner. It was now 6:00 p.m., and he told her she was required to stay until she "spoke to Inspector Stark." Reburn told her he always went home for dinner, but instead of leaving the station, he and Stark questioned Flora in the matron's room while Clara ate in Reburn's office, not knowing her daughter was in an adjacent office being questioned.

Meanwhile, Slemin found another evidentiary bonanza at the Crosiers. After obtaining the fedora, Slemin asked Mary Crosier whether she knew of Clara's whereabouts the night of Saturday, October 6. Mary certainly did – that was the night her friend had acted so strangely. Clara had come to the Crosier home around 8:00 p.m., she thought to pick up the laundry she'd left the previous week. Although Crosier had been Clara's friend for three years as well as her landlady for several months, it was only the second time she'd seen Clara suffering the effects of "drinking a little." In fact, Crosier smelled the liquor on Clara's breath when Clara explained she was going to Parkdale to fetch Flora for the theatre. Crosier pointed out it was too late to catch the show. Clara ignored her and laughed. She said she could hardly take the laundry to the Opera House. As Clara put on her cloak to leave, at about 8:45 p.m., Mary's oldest daughter, Margaret, caught sight of a revolver tucked into Clara's vest. Margaret said she'd never seen Clara with a revolver before.

The following Monday, when Clara came by to pick up her laundry after work, Crosier mentioned that morning's headline. Clara glanced at the paper and said, "I knew him. It was a good thing I wasn't in Parkdale that night or I would be a suspect." Two days later, on the day the papers reported Frank's death, she once again visited with Mary and discussed the case. She talked about living near Frank and said that whoever shot him "would have to know the area well, since to get out of there in a hurry you would need to cross a fence and go through some brush."

Slemin didn't need to hear more. He told Mary Crosier and her oldest daughter, Margaret, to accompany him to the station.

At 7:00 p.m., after dinner, Clara was taken to Inspector Stark's office. She still hadn't been arrested. Reburn told her that Slemin had returned with a statement from Mary Crosier that Clara had been at her home on Saturday night and not at the theatre. Clara called Crosier a liar and was cautioned not to say more. Then Reburn brought in Flora, who reiterated that Clara hadn't shown up on Saturday night. Clara got angry with her daughter, saying that she could prove she'd been at the theatre and that her daughter "was forgetting or slow." Reburn cautioned her a third time at that point. Mary and Margaret Crosier were ushered into the room, and they repeated their story in front of Clara.

By then, reporters had noticed a parade of frightened-looking girls and women being brought into the station and began to ask questions in the outer offices of the police headquarters. Clara was moved to the more private police commissioners' meeting room in the corner of the building. According to Reburn's testimony at the preliminary hearing, he was lighting the gas light in that room at around 10:00 p.m. when Clara said: "It is no use misleading you any longer. I don't care. I'll deserve what I get but if you had had a sister treated like that, you would do the same thing."

"What do you mean?" Reburn asked.

"I shot Frank Westwood."

After a moment of silence, Reburn asked, "What did you do it for?"

Clara told him that even after she'd moved to central Toronto, she liked to sit on Sunday afternoons by the lakeshore at the foot of Jameson Avenue. One evening, in "July or August, [Frank] caught hold of me round my waist and tried to knock me down and take improper liberties with me; and I promised to get even with him then." She added that Frank and his friends had often harassed her: "They had been teasing me, you know, the way they tease coloured people."

Reburn didn't ask questions about Clara's accusation of sexual assault, such as the date, whether anyone had witnessed the assault or its aftermath, or the names of the other young men who'd insulted her. Instead, Reburn turned to the specifics of Frank's murder. Clara provided a detailed description of what happened after she left the Crosiers' house:

I went from Camden Street to the first street west, then along King Street past Gurney's foundry [at King and Bathurst], then along Dufferin Street to the dock there [which was used heavily during the Exhibition but deserted three weeks after it had ended]. I took off my skirt and cloak [and placed them under the dock]. I went along Dominion Street to Jameson Avenue, coming out by the rail station. I saw three boys there; one of them might have been Frank.

I went down Jameson to the east side [across the street from the Westwood residence] where it was dark and the lamp was between us. I saw Frank enter the gate. I went along the picket fence to a point I could get through and stood under a tree near the lake. I stood for 20 or 30 minutes under the tree until the lights went out and then rang the doorbell. A light went on in the hall. Frank Westwood came to the door and I shot him. I didn't intend to kill him and never dreamed I would.

Then I ran down and out the same hole in the fence to the boat house and along the commons until I got to the place where I had left my clothes. I went along the waterfront, past the Old Fort, then up Bathurst, and along King back to York Street.

Reburn asked, "Do you think Westwood knew you?"

"I don't believe he did." She added, "I'm sorry I killed him but a man who would do that deserved it."

Reburn told her that if she'd shot him at the time of Frank's attack it might be different, but afterwards, she had the courts to appeal to. Clara responded:

"You know my colour; they wouldn't believe me."

Reburn then called Inspector Stark into the office, and Clara repeated her statement to him, adding that she'd not meant to kill Frank, only wound him. The confession wasn't written down by a stenographer (in fact, Reburn was absent during most of Clara's statement to Stark), let alone signed by Clara. Again, this measure wasn't considered necessary at the time, but reliance on the memories of the police officers would return to haunt them.

Clara was – finally – formally arrested for the murder of Frank Westwood at 11:40 p.m., more than eight hours after the police had shown up at the tailor shop. She asked to see Flora again. She told her daughter that she'd confessed and that Flora could now tell the truth. The police escorted Clara to a cell downstairs, and Flora spent the rest of the night in the matron's room. She returned to the Phyalls in the morning. After breakfast, Clara, accompanied by Reburn, took a short journey along the underground passageway between the holding cells and the courtroom and ascended the ladder into the Magistrates' Court.

NINE

MONSTER

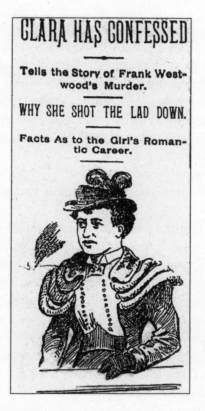

Clara's confession was an open secret from the first

The morning newspapers reported the arrest, and crowds gathered on Adelaide Street at dawn, hoping to catch a glimpse of Clara at Magistrates' Court. Reburn descended to the cells after breakfast. Clara seemed resigned to her fate. "My time is short," she said. Reburn, an experienced veteran of Denison's brand of justice, wanted Clara to have a sporting chance. Even though Clara hadn't been offered the possibility of legal advice to that point, Reburn suggested she see a lawyer.

"A lawyer wouldn't do me any good."

"You didn't intend to kill him and if you are found guilty, you'll be hanged."

Clara told him she knew the solicitor John Hoskin from her mother's days of being his laundress. Reburn replied that she'd be better off with a younger, more experienced criminal lawyer such as William Murdoch. He sent a message to Murdoch, but Clara did not get to speak to him before her case was called.

At 11:00 a.m., Clara took her place in the dock accompanied by an intense murmuration of voices. Newspaper illustrators pulled out their sketchpads. Journalists dipped their pens into ink. The consensus was that she was fashionably dressed – dark green dress with a black vest, fur-trimmed coat, stand-up white collar, black tie. She wore a dark fedora trimmed with ribbon and a feather, presumably retrieved from the Crosiers. She hadn't dressed for the occasion; she was still wearing her work clothes. She showed no signs of nervousness or embarrassment but gazed at the magistrate as he read the charge.

"Are you guilty or not guilty?"

The silence was oppressive. No one was prepared for what followed.

The answer came, clear, low, unfaltering. "Guilty."

Spectators looked at each other in surprise. The magistrate paused and looked at the prisoner. Murdoch rose and hurried over to whisper something to her.

Denison repeated the question.

"Not guilty," she replied in the same clear tone and with no sign of emotion.

Denison should not have asked for a plea – by law, Clara could not plead guilty to a capital crime, punishable by death.

Denison asked Murdoch whether he was ready to proceed. Knowing that committal to trial was a foregone conclusion, Murdoch agreed. But Crown Attorney James Curry, like everyone else in Toronto, was gobsmacked by the shocking new development in a case that had seemed dead. He requested a week's adjournment, which Denison granted. Clara was ushered out of the courtroom ten minutes after she'd entered it, and a dozen reporters sped off to be the first to publish the latest nugget in what had suddenly turned into a journalistic pot of gold.

Over the next week, all seven newspapers scrambled to provide information and insights about the "mulatto man-woman," as *The Globe* called her: who she was, what her life had been like to that point, how she might have been connected to Frank Westwood, why she might have shot him. From the first, the confession was an open secret, and everyone assumed Clara would be convicted. Fantastical rumours about Clara – not only that she'd lived as a man in the United States but also that she was a serial killer who'd murdered Joseph Priestman as well as Frank Westwood – were published.

Then, as now, there was a desire to put people into narrow moral boxes. Frank Westwood and Gus Clark, as middle-class white men from good families, would have typically filled the Good Citizen box. White middle-class men remained in that category so long as they held a job, didn't drink intemperately (or at least not in public), and abjured sex outside of marriage (or at least didn't get caught). Or they could go wrong, like Clark, get arrested, break their mother's heart, and go west to redeem themselves. It was easy enough for those with race, gender, and class privileges to climb back into the Good Citizen box, even after straying outside it. Witness Frank's brother Bert, who'd seduced his neighbour Maggie but then did the right thing in marrying her when she became pregnant.

The boxes for working-class Black women such as Clara Ford or Chloe Dorsey were much more restrictive. Because the poverty of most Black women forced them into paid labour, it was nearly impossible for them to fulfill white womanhood's mission of being an Angel in the Home, like middle-class Maggie Westwood. To qualify as Good Negro Citizens, they had to be pious, invisible, and impassive in the public sphere, never seen drunk or otherwise behaving in a disreputable manner. They had to maintain their sexual "purity" before, during, and after marriage, with consequences far more severe than their male counterparts if they strayed. They would have to contend with limited work choices, longer hours, and considerably worse working conditions than white men, for a wage that didn't cover both food and rent. They had to be continually stoic in the face of racist and sexist slurs and the threat and reality of attacks. They were public property, to be scrutinized, commented upon, judged, laughed at, and insulted. If sexually assaulted by white men, they wouldn't be believed. If poverty led them to sell their bodies or commit petty crimes, they'd receive less mercy in the courts than working-class white women.

There were two boxes for Black Canadians who failed these tests, particularly those charged with crimes: the Brute and the Pitiable

Colonized Subject. Stereotypes of Black men as threats to white female purity were as common in nineteenth-century Canada as they were in the United States. In 1861, after England abolished the death penalty for rape, John A. Macdonald, then joint leader of the united colony of Canada, posited lynching Black men as an alternative in Canada, "on account of the frequency of rape committed by negroes, of which we have too many in Upper Canada. They are very prone to felonious assaults on white women; if the sentence ... were not very severe there would be a great dread of the [white] people taking the laws into their own hands."

As the Dorsey family experienced, Black people were more likely to receive harsher sentences than their white counterparts. Sometimes, Black adults were portrayed by white lawyers as ignorant children, as Pitiable Colonized Subjects, to avoid the death penalty for capital crimes. In 1914, Frank Smith, charged with murder, was portrayed as "a child of nature ... docile, except in enraged moments, possessing a number of the characteristics that have made his race faithful under oppressive circumstances"; and in similar circumstances, Levi Steward was characterized as a "stupid ignorant mulatto of a very low mental type" by his lawyer in 1900 as part of a plea for clemency. While these pleas for pity worked to save the lives of individual Black men, they made it harder to advocate for Black people's rights.

Newspapers soon put Clara in one of three boxes, and sometimes in multiple boxes at once. One of the remarkable aspects of the media reaction to Clara's arrest was that newspapers moved breathlessly from one stereotype to another, from one wild rumour to a completely contradictory one, often within a single article.

The first trope, typical of coverage in *The Globe* and *The Telegram*, was the Tragic Mulatto Girl, a variant on the Pitiable Colonized Subject. In the nineteenth century, fictional stories of girls with white slaveholder fathers and Black enslaved mothers, girls who "belonged" to neither race, were common (as was the reality of mixed-race children begotten from the rape of Black women by white slaveholders). Even if "her heart was pure, her manners impeccable, her language polished, and her face beautiful," the Tragic Mulatto Girl was marred by self-loathing. She "pitied or despised blacks and the 'blackness' in herself; she hated or feared whites yet desperately sought their approval. In a race-based society, the tragic mulatto found peace only in death." *The Telegram*, as part of its project to defend Clara, cited Chloe Dorsey as saying Clara was sensitive and highly strung and that "she would not associate with the negro class in which she was usually assigned membership. She felt herself above them, and she found that among such people as she felt a desire for companionship with, she was rather looked down upon and subjected to many little cuts and insults which grievously wounded her. Small wonder if she became, in a certain degree, reckless and while holding aloof from both classes indulged in some '*decidedly peculiar pastimes*' [cross-dressing] of her own."

This allegation was false. We know that Clara was a good friend of another Black woman who boarded with the Dorseys, Eliza Reed. Rather than feeling trapped between multiple identities – Black, white, female, and male – Clara made both Black and white female friends and moved comfortably and fearlessly between gender and racial identities, however uncomfortable that made others.

Hector Charlesworth, as part of his project to vilify Clara and provide a motive for murder that didn't include sexual assault, wielded the Tragic Mulatto Girl trope in a particularly vicious way:

Ushered into the world by whom she knew not, she has been buffeted about with no more comprehension of cause or reason than has a dog; nay, not so much, for she knew not friends from foes. As she grew older she realised that it was to the presence of African blood in her veins that many of the rebuffs she received were due. She brooded over this fact and the untold, untellable suffering and misery which people of her color had suffered in the past. There is the tale of some chivalrous young Frenchman who so heated his indignant blood with the perusal of Spanish cruelties that then and there he sallied out to avenge the crime of past generations on the offspring of the evildoers. Such a wild impulse may have stirred in Clara Ford.

The Tragic Mulatto Girl trope was subverted in several pioneering works by Black women, the most famous among them *Incidents in the Life of a Slave Girl,* published in 1861 by Harriet Jacobs. In this thinly veiled autobiography, the ability to "pass through" whiteness (that is, appear to be a white woman) helps the heroine escape from slavery. By disrupting both racial and gender stereotypes, Jacobs appealed to multiple audiences at once. But perspectives such as hers were still exceptions. In general, Tragic Mulatto Girls were treated as objects of pity, not as autonomous subjects who could create bridging narratives by using their connections to multiple worlds.

In this strand of reporting, Clara is treated as little more than a child (or in Charlesworth's reckoning, as sentient as a dog). She is victimized by Frank, the police, and society in general. Her intelligence is erased. The detectives' disinterest in following up on the motive of sexual assault was mirrored in the public's reticence to discuss the topic. Clara and her lawyers would eventually transform this Pitiable Colonized Subject trope into a courtroom tale of how Clara got tricked by the police into making a false confession, a tale that ignored the motive provided in that confession. William Murdoch, who met with his client for the first time for an hour after her appearance in Magistrates' Court, began laying the groundwork for this approach immediately. He explained away her man's suit, which was already common knowledge, by saying that Clara's "strain of negro blood precluded her from associating with white people and she would not mingle with negroes. Subsequently, she is a recluse and some-times for recreation wears men's clothes." He characterized her initial plea of guilty as a "slip of a tongue" from a "nervous girl."

The Globe, despite its sympathy with the Westwoods and its immediate characterization of Clara as a "mulatto man-woman," was the only newspaper to treat Clara's stated motive seriously. However, the newspaper infantilized Clara and robbed her of agency. The Globe's description of Clara as she appeared in the dock emphasized her youth: "She is a tall, fine-looking woman, with neat, well-cut features, and but for her swarthy skin and short, curly, woolly hair, has few of the physical characteristics of the negro race ... When registered at police headquarters, she gave her age as 33 years, but no one would suppose from her appear-ance that she was more than 25."

Unlike newspapers that repeated the canard that Flora McKay was a "sister" or "friend" of Clara's, The Globe and The Telegram ac-knowledged from the first that Flora was Clara's daughter. This fact was incorporated into the evolving narrative of her so-called tragic life. To build up this box, Clara had to be depicted as having only "lapsed once." Then, repentant, she forever shunned men. In this version of her life, Annie, Clara's younger daughter, is erased.

On November 24, before the confession was discussed in court, The Globe published a summary of its main points. According to the article, the information didn't "come from the Crown." A mem-ber of the police, possibly Reburn, leaked the confession, includ-ing Clara's stated motive, which had "startled the officers of the law." In The Globe's words: "One Fall evening Frank had seen her on the lakeshore near his residence and attempted a criminal assault on her. Her strength stood her in good stead and she threw him aside, but she vowed revenge." The Globe cautioned that Clara's story was "without corroboration and of course, must remain so." It argued that the alleged assault "does not provide sufficient mo-tive for so awful a revenge." But The Globe did, uniquely, empathize with Clara's stated perspective as someone who felt continually attacked by both individuals and institutions as a Black woman: "To one who felt, as she is known to have done, that she never received a fair play in the battle of life, the outcome of an appeal to the courts, where only her word would have been against that of her assailant, might have appeared too problematical ... Such an occurrence would have assumed momentous import."

In the same article, *The Globe* speculated that Frank had recognized his attacker but "knew he could not divulge her name or direct suspicion to her without having made known the lapse from respectability and decency accredited to him by his family and friends. It is possible, too, that he felt he owed an atonement to the woman, whom he'd insulted, and determined that ... at least he would not be the means of bringing her to justice. Perhaps a mix of these two."

This theory actually helps explain why Frank might have mentioned Gus Clark, and then David Low, as his possible assailants, despite originally describing the assailant as a middle-aged, heavyset man with a moustache. *The Globe* was wrapping the case up in a trite melodramatic narrative, albeit one that fit some facts: the assault on Clara triggered a full-fledged psychic breakdown in the beleaguered victim that led her, three months later, to shoot Frank Westwood. *The Globe* applied the same "unwritten law" standards it had used to justify revenge killings by male relatives of female victims to Clara's case.

The Globe was roundly criticized by other newspapers for publishing Clara's story of sexual assault. On November 27, *The Globe* published a partial apology, saying, "We made an error in commenting rather than simply publishing the statement." The paper recognized that the story made "an unwarranted reflection upon the dead," but it argued that other newspapers had reproduced portions of the confession leaked by the police and, in Solomonic fashion, said it was best to "suspend judgement on the whole case until the facts are known, that can be known, neither judging that the victim was a criminal in intent, nor that the prisoner slew him without cause."

So the Tragic Mulatto Girl trope was in place from the first.

Clara was also portrayed as a dissolute and continually enraged Angry Black Woman by reporters and the Crown. This trope, still going strong in the twenty-first century, characterizes Black women, particularly those who have achieved some success, as "aggressive, unfeminine ... overbearing.... bitter, mean ... hell raising ... ill tempered, illogical, overbearing, [and] hostile." The Angry Black Woman drives away men by "emasculating" them with her savage wit. Another trope is the Jezebel, the Black woman of excessive sexual appetite who seduces men to their doom. Because these two tropes were used together in describing Clara, perhaps Angry Black Mistress better captures how she was portrayed, as a seductress with a child out of wedlock who'd given in to her "ungovernable" temper and murdered Frank out of jealousy.

Newspapers stressed Clara's alleged overreaction to harassment. For instance, Clara had a history of being the recipient of nasty remarks from white people on Toronto's streetcars when she commuted to and from Parkdale. During one incident, reported by *The Mail* the day after her arrest, two young men had insulted Clara on the streetcar. She got off with them and "in true pugilistic style" punched one. An "Extra" edition of *The Star* amplified the story that same evening: "Clara Ford is an immensely strong woman and is known to have exhibited her strength by knocking down two men."

Similarly, several newspapers said she'd threatened to shoot another man, identified only as "Anderson." *The Empire,* for instance, said Clara "at times has exhibited terrible ebullitions of temper and has threatened the lives of at least two persons," including the mysterious Anderson. Clara's main defender, *The Telegram,* finally got to the bottom of that story:

Much has been said about her threatening to shoot a man named Anderson who had a tailoring establishment on Queen Street West. In 1890, one Jacob Breslau started a similar business on the flat below him. Jacob didn't make the business, so he tried to make some arrangement with Mr. Anderson, subletting space for himself, two girls (one of whom was Clara) and the man who did his pressing. Wages went into arrears and Clara heard he was planning on leaving for New York. Breslau (not Anderson) said she threatened him with a revolver. Others there said that Clara "showed temper" but did not display or even mention a revolver. She went to the police station in Parkdale and swore out a warrant for his arrest and to avoid trouble, [Breslau] settled her account in full.

In other words, Clara took legal action against a Jewish employer over payment of her wages, and the media then turned her actions into a motiveless armed threat against a Protestant man.

Clara was said to have threatened many people with various weapons. The Breslau story pops up in another guise in *The Mail*: "Clara worked 5 years ago as a tailor with a man named Brissell (a Jew near King and York). He accused Clara of ruining a coat and the heated argument ended with Clara grabbing a pair of shears. Brissell ran out of the shop." The same paper, on the same day, reported that "the other girls were afraid of her" at Chicago's Palmer House Hotel because she carried a revolver. By the next day, this rumour had been upgraded to Clara attacking "a man at the Palmer House with a razor she drew from her stocking." *The Empire* said that Clara had tried to strangle one of the Clark sisters in a dispute over money. Hands, razor, shears, gun ... Clara was embodied as a trigger-happy weapon.

Clara was also characterized as hypersexualized. The day following her arrest, *The Star* alleged that Clara had gone to Manitoba to "hide a difficulty [pregnancy] caused by Frank Westwood." *The*

World went further, arguing that Clara and Frank "had been intimate" when she lived as his neighbour and that when he eventually rejected her, "the girl deliberately killed young Westwood for revenge." Thirty years later, when Hector Charlesworth wrote his memoirs, his disgust hadn't yet cooled: "Enamoured of his good looks [Clara] pestered [Frank] with attentions at which he naturally revolted."

The Empire provided the most elaborate description of Clara as the Angry Black Mistress:

> Police say she became infatuated with Frank two years previously. She followed him about and courted his attention in every possible manner. There is nothing to show Frank reciprocated. In fact, the detectives have evidence that his affection was centred upon a most respectable young lady living in Parkdale. Six months ago she went to this young lady's house and threatened that if she did not give Frank up she would kill them both. The young lady and her mother went to the Westwood home. The police say that Frank met Clara a day or two later and told her that if she bothered the young lady any more he would have her arrested.

If the police ever had any evidence of this incident, it wasn't brought up in either Clara's preliminary hearing or the trial.

Frank's family and friends insisted that any suggestion that Frank had either assaulted Clara or been her lover was false. Benjamin Westwood spoke to several newspapers after Clara's arrest, saying he was "confident his dead son never wronged her." Ed Lennox insisted that his best friend was "not intimately acquainted, nor had anything to do with her, although he'd probably just known her enough to speak to." The police official in charge, Inspector Stark, who'd initially told the press there was a woman involved in the case, now supported Frank's family. He told *The Globe* that the police "had no reason to believe that the deceased youth had ever wronged her, or that she was known to be jealous of him."

The Westwoods and the police preferred the murder to be treated as the crime of a maniac, without a motive. Every story about Clara resisting men who publicly harassed her pathologized her. In the first days following her arrest, Clara's cross-dressing was combined with these outrageous stories of self-defence to characterize her as a Monster. The Monster brings together the Black Brute trope with homophobic pathologizing. In the late nineteenth century, homosexuality was beginning to be discussed as a threat to families and society. Clara's murder trial coincided with Oscar Wilde's second trial for sodomy and gross indecency. Because Clara occasionally dressed as a man, it was assumed she inhabited some nether zone between the two sexes. She was then characterized as a person of such perverted instincts that she'd attack an innocent boy out of sheer madness.

In contrast to *The Globe*'s description of a girlish beauty, *The Mail* emphasized Clara's masculine features at her first court appearance: "The accused is rather stoutly built, but not inclined to embonpoint [large breasts], with large, bony hands, square, dark, determined face, olive complexion, and a pair of dark, flashing eyes. Her lips and cheeks are covered with a faint dark down, and her bearing is rather mannish." *The Star* went further in the quest to gender Clara masculine: "Two pairs of men's suits were found in her room and many articles used by men. She is what is usually called a 'mannish woman,' only more so, for she smokes a pipe and shaves. Her appearance is so masculine that many observers thought she was a man." The *Star* repeated rumours that Frank Westwood wasn't the only man she'd shot, that Joseph Priestman was also her victim, and alleged: "She drinks bullock's blood which

CLARA FORD.

CLARA FORD.

Mannish Clara and Girlish Clara

she obtains from a butcher in the north part of the city." In an alternative universe, a smarter reporter might have looked at Clara's working-class Scottish mother and wondered whether she occasionally bought blood from the butcher to make blood pudding.

The Mail felt it had the inside track on the case, as it had been sitting on the story for a week after Gus Clark drunkenly spilled to their reporter John Miller. It threw every rumour, however implausible, it had gathered over the previous week into its coverage. It reported that Clara showed "an abnormal tendency to indulge in pursuits generally followed by men. She dressed in men's clothing, she shaved, she smoked, she carried a revolver, she was an expert in the gloves [that is, a boxer], she played the cornet and the kettledrum and displayed a curious taste in literature by reading works related to love and murder."

But wait, there was more: "She currently is reported by the Parkdale children to drink a quart of warm blood every morning, going around heavily armed on all occasions, with the strength of any two or three men." In the Monster version of events, Clara murdered Frank because he told *The Telegram* that Clara wore men's clothes. As *The Mail* itself admitted, this was a thin motive for shooting a man, "but those who think or speak in this way forget that they are dealing with an abnormal character. Clara Ford is no ordinary person."

The World's two-page, two-day feature on "the real motive" for Frank's murder, which ran on November 22 and 23, made *The Mail* seem sedate. Charlesworth began with a bold rush to judgment: "*The World* refrains from asking anyone to condemn Clara Ford before her trial ... [yet] it seems to be the fact that Frank Westwood was shot at the door of his father's house by the mulatto woman, Clara Ford." But why? *The World* wouldn't entertain the notion that Frank Westwood had sullied himself by sexual relations with an older mixed-race woman. Instead, it would delve into "what the medical authorities call *homo-sexuality* – in other words that she was suffering from what is called sexual perversion."

Charlesworth referenced Richard von Krafft-Ebing's *Psychopathia Sexualis,* translated into English in 1892: "The books which are authorities on the subject cite any number of cases of men who thought themselves women, or wished to become women, and of women who desired to be considered as men. Women who are affected this way show an intense desire to be considered masculine. There is no doubt as to the sex physically, but the perversion is on the mental condition. Such women go about in male clothing. They prefer masculine work, and show an unusual skill in it. They eschew female occupations, and often show a weakness for smoking and spirits."

Clara was being described as transgender rather than as same-sex attracted, although *The World* had also upgraded *The Telegram*'s August story of Clara wearing men's clothes to say that "complaints [were] made to police that a colored girl in male garb had stopped different young women in the streets." Of course, there is no way that this diagnosis could be seen as anything other than pathological:

With this perverted condition there often go pronounced outbreaks of passion and jealousy, which drive the unfortunate victim at times to crime ... It may be mentioned that it is a coincidence borne out by authorities that sexual crimes are progressively increasing ... A medical man stated last night that if it was so that young Westwood had in any way interfered with Clara Ford in her masquerading as a man, to her, sexually perverted as she appears to be, it would be an interference with what she considered one of her dearest pleasures, and it would create in her a feeling of jealousy and rage sufficient to instigate the murder of the young man of itself and requiring no other incentive whatever.

The next day's article delved further. Although Clara appeared normal to hundreds of people with whom she came into contact, Charlesworth contended that "alienists and those who are the highest authorities in Psychiatry are easily able, with this knowledge in hand, to account for her conduct and for the crimes committed by these peculiar people." Charlesworth's expert racist gaze had already diagnosed Clara's ancestry: "A strong dash of negro blood in her, being probably a quadroon or nearer akin to the black. Her curved nose shows the white strain, while her restless eyes and sensuous mouth tell of her African origin. Her complexion is between a chocolate and an unhealthy yellow."

He now subjected her gender to the same scrutiny. Her "perversion ... is organically manifested in the shape and size of her feet and hands, the set-up of her body and in her chest development." Her every movement displayed gender trouble: "This girl Ford got on and off streetcars like a man and was a by-word to all the streetcar drivers and conductors in that respect. She smoked, she chewed [tobacco], she drank, she swore, she spit, she shaved, she kept a razor and carried it ... was an expert shot ... was soldier-mad and on a day when the volunteers and soldiers turned out like yesterday she would follow them all over the country, climb fences, and run after the bands and uniforms."

Charlesworth characterized Clara as boyish, and in a set of images that Frank's friends would hardly recognize, he said she was part of his "gang":

> When they were about the barns playing, this is four years and more ago, when she was nearly 30 years of age and they were in their teens – she must have indulged her mannish proclivities in their presence. They knew of her love for revolvers and her dexterity in handling them ... It may be that she tried to rival them in smoking and in the conduct and language of boys. She was certainly more vicious than they. They simply in a way grew up with her. None of the older people about the place seemed to have had a distinct idea of the girl's character. It was only gradually that one and then another thought something was wrong, but went no further ... She was a kind of outcast, who romped with the boys, was now and then in some of the houses, and who all the time was carrying on a peculiar double life.

But Clara didn't belong, Charlesworth continued: she didn't belong with white men, women, and children and certainly not in a suburb. Her very presence in Parkdale was grounds for suspicion: "This girl could not keep away from Parkdale ... Many people in Parkdale believe that this girl knows something of the Priestman homicide, while occurred in that suburb seven years ago."

Clara was also innately violent, due to her homosexuality: "Another characteristic of these persons ... is that they revel in blood. This woman constantly went to slaughter houses for bullocks' blood and drank it, and delighted to dip her fingers in it, and at times to write with her blood-dipped fingers on the boards words like 'murder' and similar import."

When news of Clara's confession was confirmed at her preliminary hearing, *The World* falsely crowed that it had been the only paper to provide accurate coverage of this fact. It smugly reminded their readers: "If it's so it's in *The World* and if it's in *The World* it's so."

The Star also felt questions of motive didn't matter when dealing with a Monster. Yes, it argued, "there is a story that Frank made slighting remarks to Flora about her mother's complexion" and for "four years [Clara] brooded over this insult." But that was an absurd reason to shoot a man, it contended, unless Clara was insane, and Clara must have been insane to plead guilty in her first court hearing: "There are several experts who think that Clara, like the sexually perverted Chatelle, said 'I am guilty, go on and get it over with.'" *The Star* (and *The World*) referenced a contemporaneous murder case in Listowel, northwest of Toronto. A thirteen-year-old girl, Jessie Keith, had been murdered in September 1894 by a sixty-year-old French Canadian rough sleeper named Amadée Chattelle, who was allegedly wearing women's stockings as he committed his crime (he admitted to stealing a suitcase with women's clothing, but he argued he planned on selling it). Chattelle conducted his own defence and was promptly found guilty and hanged.

The newspapers quickly moved away from any suggestion that sexual assault or racial harassment had played a role. In fact, according to *The Star,* the police were so confident, they didn't need to use the confession. By Friday, *The Globe* was reporting that the police were "resting on their oars." Inspector Stark had been seen meeting with Hartley Dewart, who would be prosecuting the case, along with Detectives Slemin, Porter, and Reburn. There were "satisfied looks on all faces as they emerged from the office," and the day "was observed as a holiday in the police department."

For one week, from the arrest on November 20 and her appearance before Magistrate Denison the next morning to her preliminary hearing one week later, Clara Ford was on the front pages of every Toronto newspaper, with their stories reprinted in American and English newspapers. On November 26, *The Mail* devoted a half page of an eight-page newspaper (four pages were advertising) to rumours about Clara's antecedents and life. Clara's parentage, Flora's parentage, Clara's possible time living as a man in the United States, and her "character" all received extreme scrutiny. But something odd began to happen, as reflected in and moulded by *The Mail*, *The Globe*, and *The Telegram*. As more interviews took place, the public's "revulsion of feeling in favour of the accused [became] very pronounced."

In other words, newspapers began to paint Clara in a sympathetic light. If she worked hard, and took care of her mother, and felt genuine "repentance" for the "misstep" that had produced Flora; if Annie wasn't her daughter; and if Clara rarely drank or stayed out late, then surely she could not be a Monster or even an Angry Black Mistress. Perhaps she *was* a Tragic Mulatto Girl or even a Good Negro Citizen who'd been tricked by the police. Interviews with Catherine and Ida Clark, Mary Crosier and her children, Charles Ingles, and Chloe Dorsey painted a collective portrait of a hard-working, intelligent, generally abstemious woman. Moral complexity wasn't a strong suit in nineteenth-century Toronto. If Clara was likeable and economically productive, perhaps she was innocent.

The Telegram refused to believe Frank's possible role in its article about Clara masquerading in male attire could be considered a motive for murder: "What is the strong motive? ... telling of escapades in male dress [was] hardly a sufficient incentive." As was the case with other newspapers, there was a level of fetishization in their description of Clara's appearance at her first appearance before Magistrate Denison. But to Charles Clark, the reporter assigned to cover the case: "Her appearance is decidedly reserved and lady-like, and her face possesses an air of refinement and indicates a strength of character and mind beyond the ordinary.

She does not look the type of woman who would plan deliberate murder as revenge for a boyish trick." Furthermore, he argued, Clara's initial plea was made in a very soft and quiet voice. It might have only *sounded* like "guilty."

The following day, *The Telegram* threw shade on the latest theory, namely, that Clara had thrown herself at Frank and, when rejected, vowed revenge: "It seems rather a curious idea that a woman of thirty-three should fall so violently in love with a boy of Frank Westwood's age." On Friday, in an editorial titled "Fair Play, Gentlemen," *The Telegram* hinted that *The Star, The Empire,* and *The World* were being positively American in their rush to judgment. As it had with the Morse case in 1888, it brought up the spectre of lynching in an effort to appeal to Canadian moral superiority: "Newspapers that work up evidence that justifies them in convicting the young woman now under arrest upon the charges of murdering young Frank Westwood are to be congratulated upon the possession of a merciful impulse that keeps them from immediately proceeding with the execution of the prisoner they have already condemned." *The Telegram* rejected many of the monstrous rumours developed by its circulation-hungry rivals: "She is an unusual girl. The crime was an unusual crime. These two considerations tell against her in the public mind."

Charles Clark, Clara's journalistic defender, followed Sergeant Reburn to the Don Jail. There, the reporter was allowed to view a discussion between the detective and the prisoner from a distance and interview the matron and Reverend Ingles, who'd recently spoken to Clara. According to the matron: "She is an exemplary prisoner and seems most obedient. She has been perfectly cool and unconcerned from the moment she first came under the wall and heard the iron doors clang and the bolts shoot behind her, and between her and freedom ... Since she entered Castle Green [the Governor of the Don Jail was surnamed Green, and this was a wordplay on the nearby estate Castle Frank] she has hardly spoken a dozen words ... It is hard to believe her a woman capable of killing Frank Westwood."

Clark said Clara spoke clearly and calmly in her interview with Reburn, which lasted ninety minutes. When Reburn questioned her about whether she was Flora's mother, "she laughed and her laugh carried a genuine tone of amusement with it":

> Carefully was every question asked – just as carefully was it answered. Her interrogator was a man skilled in dealing with criminals. The woman was endowed with a shrewd mentality of a masculine nature, and supported by the natural instinctive reasoning of a woman. Sometimes a swift retort would rise to her lips, then again with her subtle swiftness of thought she would lead her questioner to an inference astray from the track. She displayed a judgement in her answers that would have done credit to careful advice from a solicitor. Indeed she was throughout so completely non-committal that she must undoubtedly have been advised not to say anything ... [Reburn] is probably less sure about it than he was before his visit.

Then it was her lawyer William Murdoch's turn. He only stayed a half hour, so "perhaps he was a better listener or a better questioner."

The *Toronto News* also counselled against a rush to judgment, arguing that Clara's arrest and alleged confession were just a little too convenient for the beleaguered police: "The flexible minds of some detectives whose chief object in life is to rise by hook or crook to the zenith of fame" might unfairly condemn the "friendless negress." It argued that "what the general public want is to see this poor, unfortunate, colored human being given a fair and square show ... there appears to be a fluttering of sympathy in her favour."

By Wednesday, November 28, and the preliminary hearing, Clara Ford had transfixed an entire city. The crowds at the inquest and Clara's first court appearance paled in comparison to the scene at Magistrates' Court at 8:00 a.m. Special constables tried to ensure that no one gained admission except newsmen, witnesses, and those who had business in the court, but they eventually had to give up. The "doors were thrown open, and the crowd surged in." It was so crowded that the windows were opened: "Stray flakes of snow drifted in at the western window, and floated in a kind of aimless, irresponsible way down upon uncovered heads, and flocked the blue helmets [of the police constables] that rose here and there prominently above the general altitude."

Denison found himself "supported on the bench" by Mayor Warring Kennedy and Alderman James Boustead, who usually left him to run the court as he saw fit. As was the case at the inquest, both Toronto and York Crown attorneys, James Curry and Hartley Dewart, showed up. Neither would take the one seat available, so both stood awkwardly until a special constable secured another chair. Every time a witness was called, the special constables had to push spectators aside to allow them access to the box. A drawing in *The Mail* captured Denison's discomfort – and Kennedy and Boustead's avid enjoyment – at the circus.

The crush at the bench. From left to right: Magistrate Denison,
Mayor Kennedy, and Alderman Boustead.

In contrast to the chaos around her, "the accused came up to the steps [of the dock] apparently as calm and unconcerned as if she was going for breakfast." Occasionally, Clara showed some emotion. She smiled when Flora and the Crosiers tried to put their incriminating evidence in the best possible light, "but the greater part of the time she sat with half-closed eyes and languid mien, with absolutely no expression of interest or anxiety upon her dusky features." *The Star* leaned heavily on subhuman, African metaphors to describe Clara's stoic expression: "Like the lion subdued after years of clubbing, she sat looking straight ahead, not defiant, but still resolute."

After a week of wall-to-wall newspaper coverage, there were few surprises at the three-hour hearing. Clara and Benjamin Westwood were the first two witnesses, and they repeated the tales they'd told at the inquest, as did the omnipresent Dr. Lynd. Slemin, Flora, the Crosiers, and Harriet Phyall told their damning tales. Gus Clark wasn't called, nor was his mother, Catherine.

Finally, the moment everyone had been waiting for: Reburn repeated the events of the previous Tuesday leading to Clara's confession. The "densely crowded court" listened "in breathless silence" as the "weird, tragic and almost pathetic recital created a most profound impression ... So terrible and minute a confession has seldom if ever been heard in a Canadian court of justice, and a feeling almost akin to awe oppressed the listeners as they drank in sentence after sentence of its appalling narrative." Even Reburn was affected by his recitation of the questioning and confession. He stopped to compose himself when he described bringing Flora into his office to confront her mother.

Charles Clark from *The Telegram* kept his eyes on Clara: "As Reburn spoke, Miss Ford's lips tightened ... At first she looked at the Sergeant but gradually her gaze wandered ... until she seemed to be gazing out the window into the dusk of the fall twilight." Benjamin Westwood kept his eyes on Clara, but the reporter saw sorrow rather than anger in his face. Perhaps, like Clara, he knew that the day wouldn't decide anything.

The rest was anticlimactic. The police had gone over the route described by Clara and found a loose slat in the Westwoods' fence. It took them just under two hours to complete the round trip from the Crosier house on Camden Street to Parkdale and then back to York Street. Aside from vainly trying to block the confession, Murdoch held his fire. Denison didn't hesitate to commit the prisoner for trial at the next Assizes, on the charge of the murder of Frank Westwood.

A GREAT TRIAL — AND ITS AFTERMATH

Journalists and newspaper illustrators alike clung
to Clara's every word during her testimony.

TEN

THE
FORCES OF
THE LAW

Don Jail shortly after completion (circa 1864)

On December 8, 1984, a week after she testified against her mother at the preliminary hearing, Flora visited Clara at Don Jail, where Clara was being held until the Assizes, the travelling court that adjudicated serious crimes, in mid-January. Flora had been "let go" by Harriet Phyall, and the fourteen-year-old didn't know where she'd sleep that night, but she didn't mention that to her mother. Flora sat on a chair in the corridor and talked to her mother through the bars, as a *Star* reporter looked on.

They also didn't discuss the case. Clara seemed to be in the best of spirits (or was at least trying to appear that way) and told her daughter stories about fellow prisoners who scrubbed the floors and made the gloomy corridors and cages more habitable. She said she listened to their gossip but rarely spoke to them. The matron brought her books, and she read them. The reporter noted that her "dusky face" looked fuller and brighter than on the evening of her committal. According to *The Star*, "the lines that had marked her face as she listened to her daughter's damaging testimony had disappeared. The dazed expression in her eyes had given way to an expression of intelligence, if not confidence." They concluded that "she appeared to be a person of strong character. If she was guilty of shedding blood, she must have had a motive to justify the deed to her conscience."

As one 1920s description of the trial phrased it: "All winter the dusky woman remained in her prison on the banks of the Don River." One of the odd aspects of Toronto was that the Central

Prison, just east of Parkdale, was where most of those convicted for petty offences were found. The much more innocuous-sounding Don Jail, east of Cabbagetown, was where the most serious criminals were incarcerated and where public executions took place.

A sensible betting man would have taken odds on Clara having one of those public executions by the end of 1895. She'd confessed and entered an initial plea of guilty. The evidence appeared conclusive: she'd had the means (men's clothes and a revolver with the same calibre as the one that had shot Frank) and the opportunity (the kind of intimate knowledge of Lakeside Hall that allowed her to stealthily approach the victim through a hole in the fence). She'd provided a motive that fit well with the public's initial hypothesis that a wronged woman had been involved somehow.

She could plead insanity or throw herself on the mercy of the court, but these choices were risky. There was no question that Clara would be charged with a hanging offence, the premeditated murder of a promising young man. Of the 750 executions between 1860 and 1962 (when the last executions occurred before capital punishment was abolished in Canada in 1976), only thirteen were women. Clara, a Black woman charged with murdering a wealthy white boy, would be a prime candidate to join this exclusive club. Black people, along with Chinese and Indigenous people, who were found guilty were executed disproportionately, especially when the victims were white. Irish Catholics convicted of murdering Protestants were also unlikely to receive clemency in nineteenth-century Ontario. All but one of the first twenty-three people hanged in British Columbia were First Nations men convicted of murdering white settlers. Louis Riel was the only man in Canadian history to be executed for treason, and eight of the nine other executions associated with the 1885 Northwest Resistance were Métis or First Nations men. In Ontario, three women were executed during Clara's lifetime: twenty-seven-year-old Irish Catholic Mary Aylward, who, along with her twenty-nine-year-old husband, Richard, was convicted of murdering her

Protestant neighbour in Belleville in 1862; Phoebe Campbell, who was executed in London for the murder of her husband, Richard, in 1872; and Elizabeth Workman, who was executed in Sarnia in 1873 for the same offence.

While Phoebe Campbell was found guilty of a "Postman Rings Twice" affair-with-the-hired-man husband poisoning (the hired man testified against her and escaped punishment), Elizabeth Workman's case had elements that Clara would have found disturbing in relation to her own predicament. Workman, who lived in the village of Mooretown, near Sarnia in western Ontario, was unhappily married to a much older man, a drunkard who beat her regularly. She cleaned and did laundry for a Black barber named Samuel Butler, which got the neighbours gossiping, especially when he visited the Workmans' home with a bottle of whiskey in hand. Workman was accused of beating her husband to death with a mop handle. The most damaging testimony came from her eight-year-old son, Hugh. When arrested, she didn't have the money to pay for a defence lawyer, and the man hired by the county to defend her had less than a day's preparation. Although she was found guilty, the jury recommended mercy. Unfortunately, the petition came before John A. Macdonald, a man unlikely to approve of a woman who'd supposedly conspired with a Black lover to challenge not only male authority but also white purity.

Class mattered too. Clara might also have been aware of George Bennett, who was dismissed from his position as a printer at *The Globe* in March 1880 for drinking on the job. He returned to confront publisher and politician George Brown. He walked into his office carrying a clutch of papers that contained accusations against fellow employees and a gun. During a scuffle, his revolver fired a shot into Brown's leg. Brown died three weeks later from blood poisoning. Bennett was hanged at the Don Jail in July and, like several other executed inmates, was buried in the same exercise yard where Clara walked each day. Bennett's execution suggested that in a case where a poor person attacked a rich one, lack of intent to kill wouldn't help to mitigate a sentence.

Clara might not have known the story of Mary Aylward, who was executed not long after Clara was born, but it, too, had parallels with Clara's and the more recent trial of Adam Morse. All three involved an accused person who lashed out against racist discrimination. Aylward and her husband, Richard, migrated to Canada from Ireland in the late 1840s, only to face considerable anti-Catholic persecution in eastern Ontario. In March 1862, soon after the birth of their third daughter, the couple were the victims of a hate-fuelled beating in their home. Their relationship with their Protestant next-door neighbours, the Munros, was strained.

The proximate cause of the fatal dispute seemed trivial: the Munros' chickens had foraged in the Aylwards' newly planted wheat field in May. When Mary went over to complain, William Munro hurled stones and racist terms at her. Several days later, he came onto the Aylwards' property and told them that his wife had heard a gunshot and accused them of shooting his chickens. Richard took out a rifle, the two men wrestled, and Mary attacked Munro with a scythe. Munro returned home and died several days later of his wounds.

That Mary had recently gotten the scythe sharpened, before harvest season, was accepted as evidence of premeditated murder. Although the jury found the couple guilty "with a strong recommendation for mercy," the judge was inclined to use the luckless couple as a cautionary tale of not fighting back against your more socially privileged harassers. Five thousand people attended the public hanging of Mary and Richard Aylward in Belleville in December 1862. As was common in executions of the time, their necks were not broken, so they died of slow strangulation, struggling in their nooses for several minutes.

By 1890, a "professional hangman" was hired to take a more scientific approach to executions. Not long after this seven-hundred-dollar-a-year appointment was announced, Hector Charlesworth interviewed the hangman, John Radclive, and found him packing his ropes and weights for a trip to the West, where he was to "hang an Indian" (Sumah, executed on January 16, 1891). Radclive explained that he'd developed his technique for breaking necks while hanging Chinese pirates when he was a sailor: "If they're heavy, I drop 'em; if they're light, I jerk 'em up." He pointed at Charlesworth and indicated the spot on his neck where he'd place the noose. "Now you, I'd jerk you up."

Radclive was a neighbour of Clara's. He used his new civil-service salary to purchase a house on Fern Avenue in North Park-dale. But he was never able to separate himself from the brutal work he did. He drank a bottle of brandy after every hanging and died of cirrhosis of the liver in 1911.

If Clara was distressed at the thought of a rendezvous with her former neighbour Radclive, she didn't show it. In fact, several observers remarked that she seemed healthier than ever and in good spirits. Perhaps her food and living conditions were better in prison than in some other places she'd lived during her travels. Even before her preliminary hearing, on November 26, *The Mail* had commented on Clara's "remarkable astuteness in giving hints" to her defence lawyer William Murdoch. Clara was a Good Negro Prisoner from the first: "She is no trouble to the officials, and never speaks unless when spoken to. She does not converse with the other prisoners."

Two days after Clara was committed to trial, on December 1, 1894, *The Telegram* began its campaign to prove Clara's innocence. Charles Clark opened with the results of the paper's investigation into Clara Ford's "alleged confession": "People generally do not seem to take very much stock in the confession as promulgated by the detective department. Interest in the case has reached a point where some investigation by unprejudiced persons seems almost necessary. If the words which Detective Reburn put into the mouth of Clara Ford were spoken by her it was under circumstances to say the least most extraordinary."

Clark then set the scene two weeks earlier, the day Clara was arrested: "A young woman is working industriously in the shop of her employer, where she is known as a hard-working, business-like, lady-like employee." Two detectives arrive and "ransack her room, dive into her trunks and then give her to understand she is wanted for some crime." Then, at "the detective department she was closeted with the detectives and chased around from one room into another to avoid newspaper men. No chance is given her to get any advice. Six hours she is kept under examination, first by one man then by another ... Six hours of detention in the detective department, six hours of quiz and question, six hours alone with men whose daily bread is derived from the conviction of criminals, is enough to drive a strong man to say almost anything. What a woman would say under such circumstances is hard to tell."

After making the case for a coerced false confession, Clark questioned whether "Clara's midnight journey" along the dark Toronto waterfront had even been possible. Regarding her walk to Lakeside Hall, how could she have removed her skirt at the foot of Dufferin Street, opposite the entrance to the Exhibition Grounds, without being witnessed by a resident or passer-by? "John Chambers lives just north-west of that entrance. There is a patrol box and a gas lamp." Why would she remove her clothes there?

Clark continued. Dominion Street, along which Clara had allegedly approached Lakeside Hall, had many empty lots, but David Kennedy, who lived at Spencer and Dominion, had two guard dogs, which he kept loose at night, that were "looked upon with respectful awe by prowlers." If Clara evaded them, she would have

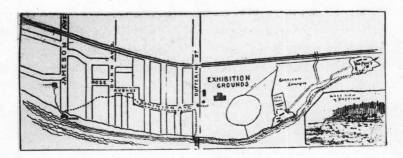

Clara's alleged route

passed under the streetlamp on the east side of Jameson directly opposite Lakeside Hall (where the Card children, with the Wesley sisters babysitting, had awaited their mother's return). Another streetlamp stood on the west side of the street near the boat-house: "The hole in the picket fence is right next to the boat house. Anyone going through the hole would have to walk along the edge of the wharf, outside the fence and up a high terrace."

Even if Clara had approached Lakeside Hall, waited inside the fence, shot Frank, and returned to her clothes under the dock without being detected, there was the question of her return journey along the waterfront, past the New Fort. Clark – accompanied by his editor, George Barnett, and an illustrator – followed the route on December 1, two months after the shooting, when ice covered "six inches of water." When they passed the New Fort, they encountered a twelve-foot-high cut-stone fence that touched the Exhibition fence adjacent to the water. They couldn't get around it in the dark. Furthermore, "the Harbour Master's records state the water is now eleven to twelve inches lower than it was two months ago." If Clara had splashed through a foot of water, the sentry stationed directly above the fence would have heard.

Finally, Clark assessed the "murdered boy's" claim that "his assailant wore an overcoat and had a moustache." The Crosiers said Clara had been wearing an Eton (a short, form-fitting jacket) and, underneath that, a close-fitting vest, where she allegedly stashed her revolver. The suit of men's clothes produced in Magistrates' Court included a jacket, a vest, and trousers. The jacket would not fit under an Eton, let alone an overcoat. No fake moustache or overcoat was ever produced.

What *The Telegram* – and the Toronto Police – never investigated was whether Clara had tracked water or been seen carrying a bundle of men's clothes back to the Dorseys'. Even if Clara had managed to enter the Dorseys' undetected after midnight (Chloe Dorsey insisted that she'd had the only front door key and had locked up at 11:00 p.m., with Clara in her room), she would have had wet boots. Of course, it's also possible that she told the truth about the shooting but lied about her route home. She might have walked through the deserted Exhibition Grounds or simply retraced her steps along King Street. But why would she lie about the route? *The Telegram* increased the public's sense that the case wasn't as open and shut as it appeared.

The Star, which had characterized Clara as a deviant maniac only two weeks before, accepted Clara and Murdoch's interpretation of events, one that *The Telegram* article supported: Clara had been manipulated by brutal police detectives into a false confession. It characterized her as a weak, pitiful female, whose "hysterical utterances ... in the detectives' sweat box were but the echo of questions put to her." After all, formally cautioned or not, "the girl had been on the rack for six or seven hours before she made the fatal admission," and there was "certainly strong evidence that the unfortunate young woman was subjected to a trial few men could stand firm under."

But *The Star* tried to have it both ways in the same article. It claimed that certain unnamed newspapers (*The World*) were arguing that Clara had also killed Priestman, based on "flimsy evidence" that at the time of Priestman's death, she was "living with

Mrs. McKay within a couple of blocks of the scene of the tragedy ... the mother of an illegitimate child, and was practiced with a revolver." Repelled by "those whose morbid cravings conjure up fancies as wild as they are absurd," *The Star* then used another column of text to repeat the tale of Priestman's "murder" before self-righteously concluding that those who condemn Clara "are mentally gazing through spectacles that are glazed over by unjustifiable suspicion."

The following week, *The Star* reported that a servant named Lizzie Dewar, who'd come to Toronto two years previously, had read all she could about the Westwood case, to the point that she was "crazed about Clara." She'd gone to Murdoch's office to tell him she had vital evidence and then on to West Lodge Avenue in Parkdale, where the Catholic Magdalen Asylum was located, to fetch it. The police arrested her, and she was "awaiting examination." (This may have been the Libby Black who eventually testified.) Meanwhile, the usually sober *Globe* ran a "story," almost certainly an advertisement, that "Clara Ford's Head" had been examined by world-famous phrenologist Dr. Cavanagh of Elm Street. The outcome of the examination would not, unfortunately, be provided without a consultation fee.

The most bizarre story that ran as the Winter Assizes and Clara's date with justice approached was a rumour that Flora's real mother wasn't Clara and that she had no "African blood." Catherine Clark had already attempted to "rescue" Annie from the "taint" of mixed-race ancestry. Now Flora was being "saved" from Blackness.

The source of the rumour was *The Empire*, which would go bankrupt in a few weeks and be absorbed by *The Mail*. *The Empire*, which carried the most unlikely rumours in the wake of Frank's shooting, reported it had received a letter, dated January 10 and addressed to Flora, from an "Eliza B. Matheson of Madford, Manitoba." "Miss Matheson" was described as "the niece of old Mrs.

McKay who raised both Clara Ford and Flora McKay and other children," and she claimed to be Flora's mother:

> Dear Flora,
> I had given up ever hearing from you when your letter came. I hope you don't have to work hard.
> I read about Clara in the paper and was horrified to learn that she was charged with such a horrid crime, if she did do it.
> I read in the papers that you passed as her daughter. Did you call her your mother?
> Oh Flora. It made me so angry when I read that. She is not your mother; surely my aunt told you that.
> Dear Flora, I pity you, being so young and alone. Pray to God, Flora, and ask His help to keep you from evil. Try to do what is right and you will get through. You may have a good, happy home yet if you are careful and good.
> Now dear, as to that money; if you have any, keep it yourself and put it to good use. Mother and Alix and all are well. Try to do what good you can, and be sure you do not get into bad company, as you will soon be a woman now. I should like it if you would continue to be a good girl and have luck and do well. May God bless you and keep you from all the evil and temptation of the city.
> Now I will close for this time, and don't do as you did before, but write and tell us everything you can. I will look for a long letter and full particulars.
> Now I shall say good-bye. May God bless pray and guide you in the path of truth and righteousness.
> From your friend, Eliza B Matheson

In a story similar to one told about Clara, it was said that "Mrs. McKay said she had a secret to impart but the friends of the dying woman would not allow her to talk."

What is certain, *The Empire* claimed, was that

there is no negro blood in Flora McKay's veins. There are certain marks by which negro blood may be detected, even in the remotest degree, by experts. The half moons on the finger nails of a person possessing negro blood are pink, not white, as is the case with a white man. The ball of the eye of the negro has a blue tint, which is a certain sign.

On Saturday evening a lady and gentleman who were born and raised in New Orleans, and before the war were slave owners, made a thorough examination of Flora's fingers and eyes, and declared that she had not a drop of negro blood in her. The lady seemed inclined to think her of Spanish origin, and this drew from the girl that her real name was Dolores Flora McKay. Dolores is a Spanish name. When asked why she had not always called herself by that name, she said that the school children made fun of it.

Flora was said to have written to Mrs. Matheson asking for particulars of her birth and parentage and expected an answer within the week. Unsurprisingly, there were no further reports of a response having been received.

This story seems to be a variant of the "white slavery" moral panic discourses rampant in 1890s Toronto, which centred on stories of "innocent white girls" trapped in the lures of "non-white" schemers, in this case, Clara. There were no suitably aged Mathesons in the 1891 or 1901 censuses for Manitoba who might have been Flora's "real mother." Perhaps someone sent a false note. It's more probable that the entire story was a manufactured "fake," intended to fit into the heavily racialized narratives of illegitimate motherhood common at the time.

As it transpired, the most important thing Clara had on her side – and it turned out to be a valuable weapon, indeed – was the perverse and highly gendered sense of chivalry that permeated society. Perhaps the best way to enter this worldview is through *The Black Crook*, the play Clara said she attended with Flora the night of the murder (and the play that Emma Card, who testified at the inquest and would also appear at Clara's trial, definitely attended that night). If *The Creole Show*, despite its racist stereotypes, represented the future of musical theatre, *The Black Crook* represented the worldview it rejected.

The Black Crook is said to have been the first Broadway musical. It was certainly the biggest hit of the nineteenth-century musical stage, performed continuously by up to thirty road companies for at least three decades after its premiere in 1866. But there is a good reason why Gilbert and Sullivan's operettas dating from the same era are still performed whereas few people have heard of *The Black Crook*. It stinks.

The story behind *The Black Crook* is more interesting than the play itself. William Wheatley, the manager of Niblo's Theatre on New York's Broadway, had to fill a 3,200-person theatre with a mediocre melodrama. A fire had destroyed the nearby Academy of Music, leaving a troupe of dancers unemployed and some handsome stage sets without a home. *The Black Crook* phenomenon was born by adding one hundred underdressed "ballerinas" in flesh-coloured tights to the musical interludes in a play with a dreadful plot and execrable dialogue. Billed as an "extravaganza," tickets came at a premium.

In the play, the evil Count Wolfenstein, wishing to win the hand of lovely young Amina, makes a deal with her evil foster mother. Amina's boyfriend, Rodolphe, is captured and placed in the clutches of Hertzog, a nasty crook-backed master of black magic (hence the show's title). He tells a minion: "Track yonder knave ... Seize him, but let no eye see you. Place him in the secret vault beneath the eastern wing. Once there – you know the rest."

The ancient Hertzog stays alive by providing the Devil – known as Zamiel, the Arch Fiend, with a fresh soul every New Year's Eve.

While Rodolphe is being led to this hellish fate, he selflessly saves the life of a dove. The bird magically turns into Stalacta, Fairy Queen of the Golden Realm. Her delighted fairy maidens hold a dance to celebrate, after this immortal fragment of dialogue: "Mistress, but now the light in yon great sapphire died out and stains of blood flushed in the face of the pale moon. You have 'scaped some deadly peril."

The grateful Queen whisks Rodolphe to safety in fairyland before reuniting him with his beloved Amina. The Fairy Queen's army then battles the Count and his hideous horde. The Count is defeated, Satan's demons drag the magician Hertzog down to hell, and Rodolphe and Amina live happily ever after, with Amina revealed (of course) to be a rich heiress kidnapped as a child. Happy dancing ensues.

The Black Crook takes four centuries of nuanced characters and poetic discourse developed in the theatre and ignores them. Instead, it returns to the tropes of the medieval passion play, in which wholly good people battle wholly bad people described as "Black," and a *deus ex machina* descends from the heavens to save the day. Virtue is rewarded, evil vanquished. There is semi-nudity for the gentlemen and romance for the ladies. It was a play for a society that believed in progress and the end of history, for people who still worshipped an interventionist God. Most of all, it was a play for people who believed that bad people bore physical marks of their degenerate natures (from a hunched back to marks on their fingernails), industriousness was next to godliness, respectable white boys such as Frank Westwood could never sexually assault a woman, and hard-working women such as Clara Ford could never murder a man. *The Creole Show* was a masterpiece of nuance in comparison.

The "code of chivalry had a revival in the late 19th century." Trials played out as tournaments, where brave barristers donned robes and jousted oratorically while a judge looked on from an elevated stage and stepped in to ensure that virtue was rewarded and evil punished. This drama would only be heightened when a woman's life hung in the balance, although it would be difficult to fit Clara into the costume of a demure and submissive maiden.

E.F.B. Johnston, who took over as Clara's lead barrister in January 1895, had no difficulty seeing himself as a knight in shining armour. Born in Scotland in 1850 as the son of a modest farming family, Ebenezer Forsyth Blackie Johnston, known to his colleagues by his middle name "Blackie," was a brilliant but egotistical show pony. Called to the bar in Guelph, where he was president of the Liberal Club, he was named at the young age of thirty-five as deputy attorney general for Ontario. But much as Johnston loved politics, he loved fame and money more. In 1889, he prosecuted William Harvey for the murder of his wife and two daughters in Guelph. Harvey pled insanity, and four alienists (as psychiatrists were then called) testified that he had no memory of the day and suffered from delusions. Johnston successfully argued that Harvey's actions – luring his older daughter from school into the house, where his wife and younger daughter already lay dead, then trying to track his son down in Toronto – showed *compos mentis* rather than delusional thinking. After this well-publicized trial and Harvey's hanging, Johnston returned to the bar and was appointed a Queen's Counsel (an honour that denoted an especially gifted barrister).

Johnston's specialty was cross-examination. As he once explained in an address to the Ontario Bar Association, "Counsel must prevent a witness from leading him off in an unplanned direction, begin cross-examination on a point only if he had a good chance of gaining it, and attack his witness at the weakest point at the opening." Toward the end of his career in 1915, his fees were so high that the Manitoba government hired him simply to cross-examine the main witness for the defence, presumably because they could not afford to retain him for the entire trial.

Johnston's great love was art. His personal collection was famous, and he was a central figure behind the creation of the

F. B. JOHNSTON, Q.C.

E.F.B. Johnston, the debonair show pony
who led Clara's defence

Toronto Art Gallery. All this beauty required a steady influx of cash. He was on the board of several large companies and always had his eye on the next big case that would improve his reputation as one of Canada's top barristers. Hector Charlesworth said that Johnston's technique was to never meet with his clients, since their stories might change the direction of his defence. Instead, he "would get facts from solicitors and then work out a plausible alternate scenario." Charlesworth contended that Clara Ford was Johnston's only exception to not meeting with a defendant, partly because she was a test case in the accused acting as a witness in their own defence.

Until the early nineteenth century, plaintiffs and defendants could not be witnesses "in their own cause," the assumption being that they'd lie on the stand. Gradually – with the United States taking the lead, Canada lagging behind, and England at the back of the pack – courtroom procedures changed to support the accused's right to speak in their own defence. The Canada Evidence Act, 1893, provided that "every person charged with an offence, and the wife or husband, as the case may be, of the person so charged, shall be a competent witness, whether the person so charged is charged solely or jointly with any other person." It would be risky to bring Clara to the stand, but it would be the only way to counter her confession, if it was admitted into evidence.

Where did Clara get the money to pay for the expert legal services of E.F.B. Johnston, Queen's Counsel? She'd been represented at her preliminary hearing by William Murdoch, the workhorse to Johnston's show pony. Murdoch specialized in relatively commonplace cases of theft and minor assault brought before a magistrate, and his most famous case before Clara's had probably been that of Adam Morse. Like Blackie Johnston, Murdoch was born near Detroit in 1852 in modest circumstances. He was called to the bar in 1876, and like all five key legal figures in Clara's case, he was politically active. He was a Mason and a member, of course, of the Orange Order. But unlike the lead counsels for both the Crown and defence, he was a staunch Tory. In the 1880s, he ran unsuccessfully against future Mayor William Howland in the South Toronto federal riding.

In the late nineteenth century, judges travelled, with other legal officers such as bailiffs and stenographers (as court reporters were then known), in a circuit around Ontario, trying the most serious offences. This was known as the Assizes, and they visited Toronto two or three times a year. On January 19, 1895, Clara's case came before the Winter Assizes.

Murdoch asked for a postponement of the case to the Spring Assizes in May. He argued that Clara had been unable to raise money to pay for her defence, since her friends were all destitute.

This meant that Murdoch could not question witnesses who allegedly saw her at the Opera House that night. By this time, Murdoch, in consultation with his client, had solidified the story of Clara being "harassed [by the police] to the extent that she was suffering from hysteria and made statements that were totally untrue." Justice Street denied this request for postponement. However, two days later, another judge named McMahon heard the news that Johnston had been brought in to lead Clara's defence. He granted a postponement so that the distinguished Queen's Counsel could acquaint himself with the case. Bringing Johnston in instantly elevated Clara's trial from a simple one-day affair to a potentially complex and precedent-setting case.

The circumstances under which Johnston became Clara's lead barrister are mysterious. At the trial, Johnston argued that he'd volunteered to take on the case *pro bono* because he was certain of Clara's innocence. This seems unlikely: the very day Clara was acquitted, there was an appeal for her defence fund. Clara's public lecture after the trial was advertised as a way for her to raise money to pay back her lawyers. But even with fundraisers, Clara could never afford Johnston's fee. This was no Adam Morse case, with newspaper owners and prosperous merchants subscribing to an African American's defence to prove a point about Canada's moral superiority.

There are four possible reasons Johnston decided to lead Clara's defence in January 1895. Johnston said it was the altruistic pursuit of justice. Less generously, the case would be an opportunity to show off his pyrotechnic courtroom skills and improve his marketability to wealthier clients. However, it's difficult to imagine the defence of an impoverished mixed-race client charged with the murder of a rich white businessman's son being an ideal calling card. Johnston might also have decided to attach himself to Clara's case once the possibility emerged that he'd be at the Spring Assizes for a decidedly larger purse – the Hyams twins. A final possibility is that his retainer was paid by someone with considerable wealth and a desire to avoid reputational damage to his family. Benjamin Westwood springs to mind.

Perhaps the only barrister with a more impressive reputation than Blackie Johnston was the counsel hired to lead the Crown's case. According to Hector Charlesworth: "In the 1890s, the man who dominated the Canadian scene as the most brilliant in his calling was Britton Bath Osler."

Unlike Johnston and Murdoch, B.B. Osler came from a distinguished family: his father was a notable Anglican minister, and his brothers included the famous medical researcher Sir William Osler, banker Edmund Boyd Osler, and the Honourable Featherstone Osler, chief justice of Ontario. A decade older than Johnston, Osler had also moved from a Liberal appointment as a Crown attorney to private practice, forming Osler, Harcourt and Hoskin (with John Hoskin, who had employed Jessie McKay as a washerwoman). Osler's first national exposure came in 1885 when John A. Macdonald hired him to secure the death penalty against Louis Riel. He then successfully represented the federal government in a lawsuit brought by the Canadian Pacific Rail company for unpaid bills related to the recently constructed transcontinental train line. Large corporations took note of his skills. As Osler, Harcourt & Hoskin's website now proclaims: "Almost from the start, the firm's clients included many of the country's largest companies and others that would grow to become leaders in key emerging industries including railways, banking and insurance, manufacturing and natural resources." Osler's corporate clientele provided him with huge billings – $26,110 in 1885 – at a time when Clara earned perhaps 1 percent of that amount.

Osler was described as "chivalric" for rescuing his wife, Caroline, and their maid from a gas explosion in their home, which left him with a badly scarred face and hands. Caroline was an invalid, although not because of the accident, as was said at the time. By early 1895, she was severely ill. Her eventual cause of death,

MR. B. B. OSLER, Q.C.

B.B. Osler, the romantic hero who was
considered the best lawyer in Canada

interstitial nephritis, was a kidney disease usually associated with
an autoimmune disorder.

When not engaged in his corporate law practice, Osler was
often hired to lead criminal prosecutions for the Crown; it was
said that "a prisoner had little chance of acquittal with Osler prosecuting." Charlesworth contrasted Osler's methods with those of a
baser practitioner such as Johnston: his cases "unfolded to the
jury in a lengthy series of questions, which he insisted that the
jurors must answer to themselves before rejecting the view for
which he stood. In criminal practice this type of argument is
usually met by *ex parte* appeals to the emotions, or by attempts to
confuse issues – the time-honoured method of the political platform. The task of creating confusion is not difficult to a resource-
ful pleader, given a jury of average fumbling mentality."

Osler generally won jury trials. His most famous criminal prosecution was that of John Reginald Birchall, a wastrel and confidence man from England who lured two men to purchase a farm with him in Woodstock, Ontario. They each agreed to pay him five hundred pounds. On February 17, 1890, Birchall shot and killed one of his partners and tried to murder the other. Because he was an English gentleman, the son of a clergyman, and had attended Oxford, the case aroused strong international interest. Osler's closing argument, reprinted in full in *The Globe*, did, indeed, consist of a series of rhetorical questions asked of the defence's evidence, demonstrating its logical flaws. Radclive, Birchall's executioner, gave Osler the highest accolade: "When 'e's on the case," he said, "I know that I won't be given the job of 'angin' an innocent man." Louis Riel might have begged to differ.

In Clara's case, Osler would be working closely with Herbert Hartley Dewart, who'd already represented the Crown during the inquest. Dewart was considerably younger than the other four lawyers engaged in Clara's trial. He was born in 1861, the same year as Clara. Like Osler, Dewart was the son of a prominent minister, a Methodist in this case. Edward Hartley Dewart was a leader in the temperance movement and a Liberal politician. He knew Benjamin Westwood quite well. Dewart Junior led the Young Liberals at the University of Toronto before being appointed as a Crown attorney for York County, at the age of thirty. At the time of the trial, he'd already begun a political career that would culminate in his leadership of the Ontario Liberal Party in 1919.

English Canada's two most famous criminal lawyers would face off against each other in Clara's trial, seconded by a less renowned but experienced barrister for the defence and an ambitious Crown attorney for the prosecution. Several judges were up to the challenge of refereeing this clash of titans. John Alexander Boyd wasn't one of them.

Boyd was similar in background and character to George Denison. Born in 1837 in Toronto, he was the son of a Scotsman who

CHANCELLOR BOYD.

Chancellor Boyd, the old-school judge for Clara's trial

was the headmaster of the prestigious private Bay Street Academy. At the age of twenty-three, Boyd wrote a strongly imperialist Canadian history textbook that would remain a standard until the end of the century. By 1876, he was a Queen's Counsel, and in 1881 he was appointed head of the Ontario Court of Chancery, a position he held for the next twenty-five years. He was an expert in property law dealing with estates and land rights. In 1885, he decided in favour of the Ontario government in the *St. Catharine's Milling* case, arguing that the Ojibwe Nation's treaty land rights could be redacted by the Crown at its pleasure. This decision, unsuccessfully challenged at the Canadian Supreme Court and England's Privy Council, is considered to have set back First Nations land rights claims for the next century. As an arbitrator, he favoured Osler's arguments in the dispute between the Canadian Pacific Railway and the federal government.

Chancellor Boyd didn't like, and wasn't an expert in, criminal cases. But his belief in his own abilities was supreme: "In his correspondence within the family, even on social matters, he often referred to himself as 'The Chancellor.'" I can imagine the magistrate and the chancellor spending long afternoons together over whiskey and sodas at the National Club, and their wives being just fine with them not being home.

In March 1895, in response to allegations about abuse in Ontario's prisons, a specially impanelled Grand Jury toured institutions. At the Don Jail, they inquired after the welfare of its most famous prisoner, Clara Ford. They reported that "her lower face had been swollen but it was improving," which sounds as though she'd seen a dentist. Clara "had a quantity of books, which she preferred to conversation" and "was very comfortable and treated with every consideration." Meanwhile, Flora, "the supposed daughter of Clara Ford is being kept in hiding by police," having proven "rather difficult to control" when she was working for the Phyalls. Flora was living at a shelter for "erring girls" on Agnes Street in the Ward. The manager of the shelter, Agnes McIntyre, was a part-time police matron.

By that time, a new murder mystery was dominating Toronto's headlines. Back in January 1893, a sixteen-year-old stock boy named William Wells had been found with his skull crushed in from a supposed industrial accident. His employers, twin brothers named Dallas and Harry Hyams, told the police that Wells had been trying to fix a faulty freight elevator when the two-hundred-pound weight fell on his head. Wells's body was released to his family in Pickering, east of Toronto. Exactly two years later, in January 1895, Hector Charlesworth and *The World* had a huge scoop: Wells's body was being exhumed, and the Hyams twins had been arrested for murder and were about to have their day in Magistrates' Court.

The Hyams twins case had many of the key elements guaranteed to engage Torontonians. Like the Priestman case, there was possible insurance fraud; like the Birchall case, wealthy confidence tricksters were trying to traduce vulnerable young men; and as in the Morse case, there was a clash between corrupt US law and Canadian moral superiority.

The Hyams brothers, from a wealthy New Orleans family, had arrived in Toronto with their mother in 1890. They set themselves up as commission merchants. Despite what appeared to be deep pockets, they were not successful; their stenographer later testified that only a few sticks of furniture and some bags of sugar were stored in their warehouse. They were deeply in debt to moneylenders.

In early 1892, the Hyams borrowed one thousand dollars from William Wells, orphaned heir of a prosperous farmer, and another thousand from his brother-in-law, with the condition that they both be taken on as intern commission merchants. Another sister of William Wells, Martha, visited and soon became engaged to Harry Hyams. Dallas Hyams convinced William to take out life insurance for thirty thousand dollars, payable to his sisters. Wells's loan to the Hyams brothers was returnable on January 14, 1893. He made arrangements with an uncle to make a down payment on a farm in Pickering, but he never showed up.

Two days later, the Hyams said they turned up at work to find Wells dead. The coroner, called to the scene, was so sickened by Wells's head injuries that he vomited. He quickly agreed that the elevator had caused the fatal injury and there was no need for an inquest. In May 1893, Harry Hyams married Martha Wells and obtained half of the insurance money paid out at William Wells's death. In late 1894, Harry persuaded Martha to take out $250,000 in life insurance. Thoroughly distrustful of her husband by then, she went to see a lawyer about a separation allowance. The lawyer contacted Hector Charlesworth, hoping a scandalous article would put pressure on the Hyams' millionaire uncle in New Orleans to settle quickly. By now, the insurance company, suspecting fraud, had hired a private detective, and Charlesworth soon had all the details leaked to him. He made the same agreement as had John Miller of *The Mail* when Gus Clark had drunkenly implicated Clara Ford: they'd give the police a week to arrest the suspects before publication.

Harry and Dallas's millionaire uncle immediately contacted Francis Wellman, the most famous criminal lawyer in the United States. Based in New York, Wellman was enmeshed in Tammany Hall crooked politics and was reputed to specialize in jury fixing, bribing jurors toward a favourable verdict. Wellman travelled up to Toronto, only to be told in no uncertain terms that he wasn't licensed to practise in Canada. He contacted Blackie Johnston and another well-known Toronto criminal lawyer named William Lount to represent the brothers in the Spring Assizes. He'd serve as the "consulting attorney."

By March, the Crown – recognizing that the murder trials of Clara Ford and the Hyams twins were garnering international interest – retained B.B. Osler as a counterweight. The Ontario justice system itself would be on trial. A two-round "battle royal" between Johnston and Osler was expected. By Monday, April 29, as the Spring Assizes set up shop in the Magistrates' Court, Clara's legal defenders assured *The Star* that their "case was ready." They'd not be pleading insanity on behalf of their client, and they planned to call multiple witnesses who would swear that Clara was at the Opera House the night of Frank Westwood's murder. But still, most reporters who arrived at the courtroom on Tuesday, April 30, expected Clara to be speedily convicted and sentenced to hang.

ELEVEN

WITNESS
FOR THE
PROSECUTION

Libby (or Lizzie) Black (or Smith)

The courtroom on April 30, 1895, was packed. Witnesses and gawkers sat cheek by jowl on the benches surrounded by as many people standing as the dismal court on Adelaide Street could hold. On special request, journalists and their companion illustrators occupied desks with inkwells in front of the benches.

In the morning, the court scheduled four cases to take place after the two "headline" murder trials: Arthur Dicks, charged with murdering his wife; Arthur Weighill, a Grand Trunk Railway stationmaster, charged with manslaughter in relation to a crash at Agincourt Station, east of the city; Fred Dwyer, charged with attempted rape (in nineteenth-century code "assault with intent to commit an abominable offence"); and two former City of Toronto aldermen charged with corruption.

Regina v. Ford was the first case after lunch. When Clara entered the docket, Charlesworth, always up for an attack, noted: "Jail life seems to have agreed with her. She is a good deal stouter than when she was arraigned in the Police Court."

The Globe reporter was more neutral. He found her "neatly dressed" in "the same black felt hat and feather, and black cloth jacket, trimmed with beaver edging" that she'd worn at her hearing. She did "not seem agitated, but stood up in a careless manner, entirely free from nervousness" when asked her plea. This impassivity, also remarked upon in her preliminary hearing, was considered unfeminine.

But Clara, a former servant, knew the value of not showing her emotions to people who controlled her fate. The courtroom grew silent. "Not guilty" she called out in a clear voice.

Justice was swift and unmerciful in nineteenth-century courts. Capital cases could be decided in less than a day. The newspapers talked of the "jurors' patience" in the Clara Ford trial, which took four and a half days from start to finish, with no day longer than six hours. Jury selection and opening remarks took up the majority of the first afternoon. The Crown presented most of its fifty witnesses on Wednesday, May 1, and Thursday, May 2. The defence took over after lunch on Friday, May 3. It had twenty-two witnesses of its own and concluded on the afternoon of Saturday, May 4. Final addresses by E.F.B. Johnston and B.B. Osler, along with the judge's charge to the jury, lasted until just after dinner on Saturday. The jury deliberated for an hour. They had returned to their homes and jobs by Monday, when the Hyams case began.

To those who'd been following the case since the initial inquest, much of the Crown's case went over well-travelled ground. There was no doubt about the means or timing of Frank Westwood's death. Flora and the Crosiers continued to reluctantly incriminate Clara. The only weaknesses in the Crown's case related to the circumstances of Clara's confession and its reluctance to discuss Clara's stated motive – revenge for attempted rape.

In the context of nineteenth-century norms, it makes sense that neither side was going to touch the allegation of sexual assault. Clara's lawyers likely planned to use her story to plead for mercy if she was found guilty, but to discuss sexual assault would be to expose a strong motive by a woman who didn't fit the narrow template for an "innocent victim."

In the Crown's case, it wouldn't want to risk the jury adhering to the "unwritten law" and acquitting Clara. From its perspective, the case was ironclad. In his opening remarks, Osler argued that the Crown didn't need to provide a motive. He would introduce strong ballistic evidence that Clara's gun was the murder weapon, that her clothing and knowledge of the Westwood estate had given her opportunity, and that she'd made a detailed and damning confession.

But if the case was ironclad, why did a surprise witness, Libby Black, appear on the second day? Caroline Osler was dying; her husband might have been distracted. His colleague Hartley Dewart might have been overly anxious about a conviction and perhaps too trustful of the police. In any case, this witness for the Crown damaged its case, and over a century later, Libby Black continues to be the most fascinating of the fifty witnesses who testified against Clara Ford.

To everyone's surprise, including her barristers, Clara took a keen interest in jury selection. She rejected the first of twenty-two men called over the next quarter hour to fill the thirteen seats (including an alternate juror). *The Star* sniffed that the "jury is composed entirely of farmers." Not true. It included five tradesmen from Toronto (the owner of a hardware store, a tailor, a shoemaker, a carpenter, and a wagon maker) and four tradesmen and three farmers from villages outside Toronto (a wagon maker and a weaver from Markham, a blacksmith from Newmarket, a painter from Aurora, and two farmers from Whitchurch and one from York Township). Judging from their names, they were of British Protestant origin, and judging from their professions, they were as likely to be sympathetic to Clara as a working-class woman as they were to those born into privilege.

According to *The Globe*, "The famous QC's 25-minute opening statement was, as usual, terse, clear, and simple." There'd been no eyewitness to the shooting, save the victim and his assassin. However, he argued, there was strong circumstantial evidence that, when taken together, proved beyond a doubt Clara was the killer. He would call witnesses to testify to Clara's state of mind and possession of a revolver on the night of the murder. Clara's poor effort to provide an alibi when arrested, he continued, merely indicated the premeditated nature of her cowardly crime. "Startling new evidence," he promised, would show that the German revolver retrieved from the prisoner had a fault and markings that matched the bullet. If the jury was "satisfied that the prisoner had fired the shot," they wouldn't need to look for a motive. However, the Crown would present "a witness who'd heard the prisoner declare that if the deceased and a certain other woman were seen together again there would be a shooting."

This last bit, the *Mail and Empire* remarked, was new and occasioned "much interest in court."

Finally, Osler advised the jury "that the confession had been obtained after every warning had been given the prisoner; that in the confession the girl had gone into minute details, and her statement had been tested as to fact since, with no discrepancies."

The witnesses called in the remaining two hours of the trial's first day had testified at the inquest and preliminary hearing. Clara Westwood, the first witness, spoke again of the night of the shooting and how her son was "in no [sexual] complication ... a good boy." Murdoch's cross-examination focused on the view into the parlour window, and "the wily lawyer" used the male pronoun when he referred to the assailant. *The Star* described Clara Ford's eyes following Clara Westwood until she "disappeared in the corridor."

Benjamin Westwood spoke again of his "harmonious family" and "exemplary son." Dr. Lynd confirmed that Frank's antemortem statement had been conducted when the victim was *compos mentis* and hypothesized that "mum's the word" probably referred to Frank's desire not to falsely accuse Gus Clark. Coroner Orr and medical examiner Dr. John Caven identified the bullet and described the wound. A police telephone operator placed the call from Benjamin Westwood as coming in just before 11:00 p.m. Neighbours confirmed that two shots had been fired approximately eight minutes apart. The defence didn't cross-examine

MRS. WESTWOOD.

Clara Westwood, reliving her son's last moments

these witnesses, but Murdoch did ask Temple Cooper and Ed Lennox, there to give an account of Frank's final evening, to confirm that they "might have heard something" against his character.

The second day began with the testimony of Flora McKay, the "little girl whose life is in some mysterious way connected to Clara Ford." Flora "wore a neat gown, and a childish hat," according to the fashion arbiters in the press, and she spoke intelligently and clearly, although "it was evident that she was suffering severe mental distress." Her testimony included the first mention of Clara's confession in the trial, and Johnston responded with the first of several attempts to have the confession blocked from consideration by the jury. Chancellor Boyd ruled, for the first of several times, against the defence, arguing that although British rulings didn't allow hearsay, the Canadian Supreme Court had ruled otherwise.

Johnston undertook Flora's cross-examination, which focused on the extent to which she'd been pressured by the police on November 20. She said her initial discussion with Slemin and Porter in the Phyall's parlour took two hours followed by two more hours being questioned in the station that evening. Asked whether she'd been pressed by Reburn to say anything about Clara that she didn't want to, Flora said she didn't remember. When asked why Flora had originally said she'd been with Clara on the night of October 6, she cried: "They have not got the thing down correct!" and began to weep. After a short recess to compose herself, Flora admitted that she'd been worried that the detectives considered Clara a suspect.

In the week following the shooting, Flora recounted, she'd had brief discussions with Clara during which they'd agreed that Gus Clark probably had something to do with it. In response to Johnston's questions, Flora was clear. Clara did not tell her she'd been in Parkdale on the night of Frank's shooting. Clara did not tell her to say they'd been together that night. She'd only seen Clara in men's clothes once, and she'd never seen her with a revolver. In response to Johnston's final question, Flora maintained: "I do not think she is guilty."

Then Harriet Phyall took the stand and swore that Flora had come to see her on the Saturday night before 9:00 p.m. She'd stayed for an hour. The cross-examination didn't shake her memory of the date.

Then five members of the Crosier family, like Flora, reluctantly repeated their damning testimony. They tried to put the best light on their evidence: they'd often seen Clara with a revolver, not only on the night of October 6; and Clara wasn't drunk, she'd only been "drinking a little." Under cross-examination, Mary Crosier stated that before Clara left her house, she'd refastened a garter, and she'd seen no trousers under her skirt. A small win for the defence.

The trial, dull to this point, featured some fireworks on the second afternoon. Detectives Charley Slemin and George Porter testified about the arrest and the evidence they'd found in Clara's lodgings. Johnston once again tried to bar testimony related to Clara's query as to whether she was wanted for the Westwood murder. He also argued that she hadn't been given an opportunity to refuse having her room searched. Chancellor Boyd once again ruled to admit the evidence but said that he'd reserve a judgment on Clara's statements on the day she was arrested until after the case was finished.

Johnston conducted an hour-long, hostile cross-examination of Slemin, calculating that of all the detectives on the case, he was the most likely to lose his temper in public. The gist of Johnston's cross-examination was that Clara had been *de facto* under arrest from the moment she'd been told she was wanted at police head-quarters at 3:30 p.m.; that Slemin hadn't warned her before she made statements; and that Slemin, living and working as he did in Parkdale, knew Clara and was prejudiced against her as a cross-dressing Black woman. Left unasked was Slemin's possible shield-ing of Gus Clark. Johnston made legitimate points, but Slemin wouldn't concede to any of them.

Rattling Slemin's cage was easy. When his responses were not demonstrably false, they were evasive, as when he denied questioning Clara in her room:

Johnston: Did you caution the accused before arresting her?
Slemin: She was not legally arrested, so a caution wasn't
   necessary.
Johnston: Did you ask her any questions?
Slemin: No, because ...
Johnston: At the Magistrate you said you did ask questions.
Slemin: I am not responsible for the manner in which your brief
   was prepared.

Johnston: Do you deny you asked her questions?
Slemin: Detective Porter did. I did not.

Slemin eventually conceded that, yes, he'd had a "strong suspicion" when they'd initially detained Clara that she'd be charged with murder.

Porter's testimony was much shorter, with a lighter cross-examination. But one piece of his testimony was seized on by Johnston: none of Clara's keys fit the Dorseys' front door lock. That meant that Chloe Dorsey would have had to let her in.

The second day ended with a body blow to the reputation of Detective Slemin. By extension, it harmed the Toronto Police and the case for the Crown.

Libby Black is a difficult person to track. Her given address in what was then the industrializing hinterland north of Bloor and west of Dovercourt does not correspond to any directory listing for "Black," and Magistrates' Court records show no cases under any variant of the name "Elizabeth Black." She may have had one or several aliases. Courtroom sketches suggest she wasn't a young woman and hadn't had an easy life. She was described as "a debauched looking female" in the *Toronto News.* She testified to having worked as a cook and a laundress in Toronto and the United States. The *Star* referred to her as "Lizzie Smith." If she was also known as "Lizzie Smith," then there is a long and distressing Magistrates' Court record attached to that name.

Lizzie Smith's first arrest was in 1875, but unlike Clara's sentence for vagrancy at roughly the same time, Lizzie was sentenced to the standard thirty days. In 1876, along with Mary Church, "keeper of a house of ill fame" where Lizzie was an "inmate," Smith was charged with robbing a man named George Lynd of ninety-two dollars. The following month, she was in court for "using insulting language." In 1880, Smith charged Jane Bullman, who'd employed her as a domestic, with assault. Bullman's husband, a

Grand Trunk Railway conductor, testified that Smith had been "greatly intoxicated" when she'd come to pick up her clothes from her former employer and there had been no assault. In July 1884, Lizzie Smith was indicted for smothering her newborn child on Edward Street in the Ward. She'd gotten pregnant by her employer and given birth in an outhouse, where neighbours heard her moaning. Several hours later, an infant's corpse was found in the excrement.

Infanticide cases were common in the times before safe and legal abortion and were generally treated with lenience, as an alternative to providing social and economic support for unwed mothers. While the verdict in the case was not reported, two years later, in October 1886, Lizzie was arrested along with several others in a house of ill fame run by William Berry on Centre Street in the Ward, and in August 1887 she was again convicted of being "disorderly." It's impossible to state that Lizzie Smith and Libby Black were one and the same, but this is the sort of criminal history that many impoverished women had in nineteenth-century Toronto.

Libby Black testified that "some time before June 26 ... around 9 pm," Frank, who was out walking with Clara Ford, spoke to her on Spencer Avenue in Parkdale. He asked her to wait until he returned while he continued a little way with his companion. A few nights afterwards, she was standing on the corner of Massey Avenue and King Street when Frank spoke to her again. A few minutes later, Clara Ford came up to her and told her not to speak to Frank again or "I will do for you."

Libby's profession would have been apparent to the jury. The corner of Massey and King, adjacent to the huge Massey Ferguson factory, was a favoured haunt of prostitutes. The implication was that Clara was a competing streetwalker. When asked how she knew that it was Frank Westwood, Libby said he'd given his name the second time he spoke to her and that she recognized his dark moustache from the first encounter. (Benjamin Westwood was brought back to the witness box the following day to confirm that his blond son had never had a moustache.) Murdoch, in charge of second-string cross-examinations, didn't even break a sweat when he asked what had caused her to come forward at this late date. She told him she was serving a sixty-day term for drunkenness, having been arrested for that offence "two or three times before," and that Detective Slemin had promised to put a good word in with the magistrate in return for her testimony. *The Globe* reported that the "witness, who was expected to give evidence of an important nature, failed utterly to strengthen the Crown's case." More than that, her testimony exposed the desperate nature of the Crown's attempt to portray Clara as the Angry Black Mistress who'd seduced Frank and then shot him out of jealousy. Even *The World,* which had confidently predicted before her testimony that Libby Black would illustrate the "story of a mulatto girl who'd been the plaything of an apparently respectable young man [who when] discarded by him for another, she deliberately shot down," found Black's "testimony totally unworthy of credence."

Christian Dorenwend was then called to comment on the relationship between Clara and Frank. The two anonymous letters dating from May 1890 were produced. Johnston and Murdoch examined the letters and consulted with Clara. Johnston's cross-examination stressed that the letters hadn't strained the relationship between Clara and Dorenwend's mother-in-law, Catherine Clark, and also that Frank had been thirteen years old at the time. Still, *The Star,* which had taken against Clara from the first, adamantly argued that these letters "proved an intimacy ... Perhaps afterward [Clara] possessed enmity against [Frank] for revealing her identity to Mr. Dorenwend."

On Thursday, day three of the trial, the newspaper coverage began to reflect the fact that, to borrow a metaphor from another case before the Assizes, the Crown's express train to the gallows had met with a switching error, and it appeared the case might be headed off the rails.

Caroline Osler died on the evening of May 2. Dewart tried to postpone the trial until the next week, when B.B. Osler could return, but Chancellor Boyd refused. Judge Street, who'd been chief justice of the previous Assizes, was scheduled to adjudicate the Hyams trial the following Monday. Boyd had other engagements, and the courtroom was booked. The trial must go on. Dewart took over as lead counsel for the Crown. Deputy attorney general John Robison Cartwright served as his second. Dewart had been involved in both the inquest and the preliminary hearing, so he presumably knew the case better than Osler. However, he was much less experienced than Osler in the art of cross-examination.

The day was supposed to begin with Gus Clark and David Low providing alibis to rule out other suspects. However, Clark hadn't yet arrived from Central Prison, where he was midway through a six-month sentence for burglarizing his mother's tavern. Boyd attempted to interject some levity: "Perhaps he has escaped!"

No such luck. When Clark finally appeared, in chains and with a scrubby beard on his usually clean-shaven face, "there did not appear to be any point to his evidence." Yes, he knew Frank Westwood. Yes, he'd an alibi. Yes, Clara Ford had lived "close by at one time." Similarly, David Low testified that he knew Clark and had an alibi. The defence team held fire for the next witness.

Sergeant Henry Reburn was called, and Johnston leaped to his feet to have the confession excluded. The chancellor was, by now, grumpy. To be fair to Boyd, Johnston was using objections to appeal to the jurors' sense of chivalry. Johnston argued that "the Crown needs to show beyond all doubt that this story was told voluntarily, and if the court has the slightest doubt that the confession was voluntary, it is its duty to exclude that evidence. As well as calling that questioning of prisoners and confronting them by other persons illegal, I would call it revolting to all ideas of fair play and justice." For a precedent, Johnston cited Ontario Chief Justice Armour's exclusion of Chattelle the child killer's confession, which didn't have an impact on the conviction.

Boyd agreed that legal opinion conflicted on whether evidence produced under lengthy questioning should be allowed and that England had a more stringent approach than Canada. But "he did not see why criminals should be surrounded by a special sanctity ... Prisoners should shut their mouths, but if they open their mouths there did not appear to be any reason why they should not be allowed to do so." He ruled that the jury could "hear the entire story before deciding whether it was admissible, adding that if [Boyd, as the judge] admitted it, and the accused was convicted, he would be willing to grant a reserved case for a higher court."

Johnston tried to shake both Reburn and Inspector Stark, who was called to provide his version of Clara's confession. Despite liberal use of the term "sweatbox" and a cross-examination called both "sharp" and "harsh" by newspapers, the two senior officers, less hot-headed than Slemin, could not be shaken. They'd changed minor details since the preliminary hearing, such as the time and location of Clara's dinner at the police station, but both were adamant that Clara had been cautioned no fewer than five times and that her confession had been made "without hope of release or fear of maltreatment."

Johnston focused his questions on the exact route Clara had taken on the way back. Was it, in fact, south of the Old Fort's high fence, along the Lake Ontario shoreline? Yes, the police had walked the route she described twice along the lakeshore in front of the Old Fort. Asked whether Clara had been questioned to obtain more details of Frank's alleged sexual assault, Stark said no, he "wanted to get at the facts, in order to clear up the mystery." Stark also said Clara had told him, in relation to the alleged sexual assault: "At that time, I told [Frank] I'd get even with him and now I suppose I have, even though I'll get life for it." No, the detectives hadn't bothered to interview anyone at the Opera House, after Flora McKay had denied that she'd been there with her mother.

After three days' testimony about the night of the murder and the confession, the final morning of the Crown's case, on Friday,

May 3, was given over to showing that Clara frequently carried a revolver and "had frequently declared that if insulted by a man she would use her revolver as a means of punishing her insulter." Five former tailoring employers or coworkers were called. All gave her an "excellent character for industry and steadiness," but they varied in how they described her temper.

"Samuel Barnett, the shrewd, good-natured Hebrew for whom Clara worked up to the time of the arrest," said that they'd talked about the Westwood tragedy on the Monday after the shooting, but she was "always telling him what occurred because he couldn't be bothered with the news." Benjamin Pollakoff and his employee Jennie Bloom had both seen Clara with a revolver at work at least once when she worked with them in 1893. The latter said Clara had told her that "a man tried to assault her the night before and as she had to pass the place that night she had the revolver to frighten him." Gussie Cohen, described as "a buxom lady covered in jewelry," said she'd laid Clara off three years previously, in 1892, because Clara had threatened to "do up" another female employee.

Benjamin Vise provided the most damaging yet unlikely story, dating from 1891. One day, Clara told him she was going to marry Gus Clark, who came from wealthy white parents. Vise told her that such a man would never marry her, a "coloured girl." Clara retorted: "If he does not, I will do him up as I did another man in the United States." Shortly after this conversation, her jacket fell, and a revolver rolled out. When Vise quoted Clara as saying that Gus Clark took her "buggy riding every night," Clara burst into laughter, the only time she changed her expression during the first three days of the trial.

The purpose of the final testimony was to match Clara's gun to the bullet. Forensic ballistics, the science of matching recovered bullets and their casings to the originating firearm, was still in its early stages as an evidentiary tool. In the late nineteenth century, with mass production of guns, bullets could be matched to a standard-sized firearm, but side-by-side magnification wasn't yet used. It wasn't until after the First World War that the "finger-printing" of tiny markings became commonplace.

Two firearms experts were called to the stand. William Elliot testified that he and his colleague George Oakley had attended a demonstration wherein Detectives Stark and Porter shot bullets from Clara's revolver from five feet away into a side of beef covered in an undershirt. The retrieved bullets' markings matched the bullet removed from Frank's body as well as defects in the gun. However, under cross-examination, Elliot said that "Clara's revolver was of a very cheap iron variety, cast in mould by the thousands. He had seen perhaps 30,000 of that kind of revolver in Toronto," many of them defective. George Oakley was more certain that Clara's revolver had shot Frank and that one chamber had been discharged recently. A member of the jury asked whether a demonstration could be provided to the jury. This was arranged for the following morning at 9:00 a.m., but "Mr. Johnston asked that no detectives be there at the test ... [as] he has developed quite an animosity towards detectives since the trial began."

With that: "This is the case for the Crown, said Mr. Dewart ... and the jury sighed unitedly." After lunch, the first witness for the defence would be Clara Ford.

THE
PERFORMANCE
OF HER LIFE

CLARA FORD.

The strain of the trial had begun to tell on Clara

On Friday, May 3, 1895, after a slow start in the morning, the trial reached its climax when Clara Ford took the stage after lunch. The courtroom was packed to the point of suffocation, and Clara wore a half-smile as she stepped from the dock and crossed the room to the witness box. Asked to take an oath, she kissed the Bible and then gazed out at the sea of faces before her. She leaned over the rail and asked William Murdoch to speak up, as she was a bit deaf. The room erupted in laughter.

Nearly two years earlier, in October 1893, Benjamin Westwood had attended a national temperance congress where the most popular and quoted speech was given by the Reverend J.H. Hector, "the negro orator." He was "happy to join the noble work of redeeming his country from the accursed drink traffic (Cheers). He was a Canadian, although he didn't look it (Laughter). But the light was poor and if they would look closely they would see he'd quite an English look (Renewed laughter) ... If [the delegates] did their duty [in advocating for a national prohibition referendum] the vote would be so pronounced that the politicians must give heed, and if they refused, the electors would so rip them up the back that the angels would not know them (Loud laughter)."

Measured cadence, self-deprecating humour, exaggeration, and earthy metaphor were all hallmarks of nineteenth-century Black oratory. It could be heard during the victory celebration for Adam Morse in 1888 and in Sojourner Truth's 1851 address at the Akron Women's Convention, which was as short and powerful as Lincoln's

Gettysburg Address. Despite her white mother and High Anglican churchgoing, Clara would have experienced this oratorical tradition during her childhood in Macaulaytown and her sojourns in the United States. Clara knew how to grab a hostile audience's attention and get it on her side.

Clara loved to tell tall tales, and she wielded another trope during her testimony – that of the Trickster. Joel Chandler Harris, a white journalist from the South, introduced the Uncle Remus stories in 1881. The stories appropriated West African legends of the God Anansi, a small, weak spider who turns the tables on his more powerful enemies. In them, Brer Rabbit uses cunning, guile, and quick-witted talk to bend social mores to his benefit. He also dresses up, including cross-dressing, to confound those who want to harm him. (He is the progenitor of Bugs Bunny.) Condemned today, like minstrel shows, for romanticizing the horrors of slavery and mocking African American speech patterns, Brer Rabbit stories were also about "slaves' experiences, dreams and hopes – the revenge of the small and weak against the powerful." Clara's light, comedic, and almost flippant manner on the stand followed a story-telling tradition that had developed over centuries to transform tyranny into analogy. The "he says and then I says" rhythm of it helped jurors identify with her tale of police oppression, a Tar Baby interrogation that threatened to stick to Clara. Through her testimony, she was trying to get unstuck.

Clara had to walk a fine line. She had to provide a convincing counternarrative to a seemingly voluntary confession to murder. If she sounded too intelligent or well-spoken, jurors might doubt she'd been intimidated or duped by the police into giving a false confession. Above all, she had to get jurors on her side and provide reasons to distrust the police version of events. Clara used every trick in her considerable story-telling arsenal.

According to *The Star*, Clara was "the second person charged with murder to avail herself of the recent changes that allow her to testify." The first, said the newspaper, had been the inaccurately named Charles Luckey, "the murderer of his father and mother who practically convicted himself." Luckey was charged with the triple murder of his father, stepmother, and stepsister in the tiny village of Newbliss, close to the town of Smiths Falls in eastern Ontario. Their three badly burned bodies were found after a mid-afternoon fire destroyed their farmhouse in October 1892. Two axes were found inside, and the house had exploded so dramatic-ally that the use of an accelerant was suspected. Luckey had just been released from Central Prison, where he'd vowed to return home and "settle some accounts." After being acquitted of his father's murder, he testified on his own behalf six months later during his second trial, in November 1893, for the murder of his stepmother. But he failed to convince the jury that he'd had a plausible reason to check into a hotel in Smith's Falls the day be-fore his family's death. The jury found him guilty, and he was exe-cuted. This was a chilling precedent for Clara.

There was, of course, a contemporaneous counterexample – Lizzie Borden, the axe-wielding accused parent killer who ap-peared to get away with it. Lizzie Borden did such a poor job pro-viding an alibi at the inquest into her father and stepmother's death in August 1892 that she didn't speak at all at her trial in June 1893. She put her trust, instead, in the best lawyers a rich heiress could buy. She never confessed, and jurors could not be-lieve that the genteel white woman they saw before them could have cold-bloodedly killed her stepmother with seventeen blows of an axe then waited ninety minutes for her father to get home and nap before butchering him as well. Clara had no race or class privilege to shield her. If she didn't explain the circumstances of her confession, she would head to the gallows.

William Murdoch, who Clara appeared to know better and trust more than E.F.B. Johnston, led her through her testimony. Clara started by setting the scene. She'd lived in Toronto for most of her thirty-three years, she was left an orphan as a child, and she'd earned her own living since she was twelve years old. She provided a long list of people for whom she'd worked and places where she'd lived. Then Murdoch guided her toward the day she was arrested. Clara told the courtroom that after a brief, awkward dialogue with Porter,

> this gentleman [*she pointed to Slemin*] comes up and says: "We want to see your room."
> I says: "What for? I haven't stolen anything."
> He says: "Well, we want to see it."
> We went into the room and Slemin shuts the door and puts his back against it. There is no other way out but through the window.

Clara painted a word picture of involuntary detainment that included two men trapping a woman alone in her room by blocking the door. This scenario transgressed nineteenth-century moral norms and acceptable behaviour for officers of the law. She also subtly signposted her ignorance of the detectives' intentions:

> Then Slemin says: "Do you have any men's clothes?"
> I hesitated a minute, because I was worried about who told them I had men's clothes, and then he asked me again, so I said: "Yes."
> Porter asked me whether I had ever been in Parkdale disguised as an old man or an old woman, and I said no. I went over to the small trunk and as I was stooping over, Porter asks "Do you have a moustache?" I looked him straight in the face and said no.

The courtroom burst into laughter. Clara was subtly alluding to the question of her "mannishness." She couldn't deny that she wore men's clothes, but she could normalize it as a quirk and imply that she thought the police were harassing her for it, not for the first time. If the jury was laughing with her, they might get on her side. Clara was also reminding the jury that Frank had described his assailant as a middle-aged man with a moustache.

Clara let the laughter subside then resumed her story:

> I got out the clothes and I put them on the bed.
>
> Then Slemin asks me: "have you got a revolver" and I says "yes" and then it struck me in a flash this was the Westwood tragedy they are after.
>
> I went over to the other trunk, and took the revolver out of the bottom, where it was wrapped in a white handkerchief, and four bullets in a bit of dress lining. The pistol had been there all summer, since before August, and the bullets had been there two or three years. I bought the revolver from a Jew on York Street for $1.50 [and he threw in the bullets]. I got it because I had been insulted on the street and wanted it for protection.

Clara didn't address Gus Clark's allegation that she'd owned two revolvers in 1890. She implied that she never loaded her gun. Most of the jury members would have owned a revolver, and many would have been sympathetic to owning a gun for protection. When Murdoch asked if she'd ever used the revolver, Clara replied: "The only time I had used it was a year ago last April when I fired at two ducks on the [Parkdale] lakeshore at Dominion Street. I don't know why, just for devilment."

Murdoch brought her back to events in her "little room" on the afternoon of November 20:

> Then Slemin put the clothes in a bundle and the revolver in his pocket and said Inspector Stark wanted to see me at the office. I had no idea I was under arrest.
>
> I says "what does he want me for?"

He says "He just wants to talk with you."

So we started out, me and Porter in front and Slemin
about a block behind. When we got to the office, they took
me through into Reburn's room.

The *Mail and Empire* subtitled the next part of her testimony "In
the Toils." It said Clara "described with vivacity and acuteness" the
detectives and the station, causing considerable laughter in the
court at the "piquancy" of her details. Clara used the opportunity
to provide the jury with the detailed alibi she'd given the police,
and she began the process of making Reburn out as a villainous
and unprofessional officer:

Reburn looked me up and down as if he'd snap my head off,
and asked me my name and where I lived. He didn't sound
at all like he did yesterday, but gruffer and snappier.

Then he says, "Where were you on the night of October
6?" and I says "At the theatre."

He says "How were you dressed?"

"I had on a green skirt and waist, a green corduroy vest,
white collar, cuffs, and tie, this jacket and a straw hat."

"Who was with you?"

"Florrie McKay."

Then he says "You was seen up in Parkdale that night."

If Reburn said that, he was lying. The police detectives hadn't
yet interviewed the Crosiers, who, in any case, lived two miles east
of Parkdale. Clara was describing police who would stoop to lying
(as Slemin had in suborning perjury from Libby Black) in their
pursuit of a conviction. She continued:

I says "I wasn't, and whoever says they saw me there was
telling a lie."

He says "Do you know Frank Westwood?" and I says "No."

Then Reburn says "What were you doing round Parkdale that night?" and I says "I wasn't there."

Then Reburn says "When were you last in Parkdale?" and I says "On the first or second Sunday after Civic Holiday, which I think was about the 15th of August."

Then Inspector Stark comes in and stands round and he says "What were you doing wearing men's clothes?" and I says "I don't know that it is a harm to wear them" and he says it's against the law and I says "Well if it is, how about Vic Steinberg who goes to a baseball game in Hamilton wearing men's clothes and writes it all up in *The News*?"

Then he doesn't say anything but kind of smiles and strokes his moustache.

Clara got a laugh there, too, but she was beginning to run the risk of sounding too sassy. Murdoch guided her back to her alibi:

Then he and Reburn go out and talk and then Reburn comes back and says "Where did you meet Flora McKay?"

I says "On the corner of Bay and Queen and we went to the Opera House [which was on Bay and Adelaide, two blocks south] and she waited in the corridor while I got the tickets. I got two 35 cent tickets, and we went up in the balcony and gave our checks to the usher and he took us to our seats."

Reburn says "where did you sit?" and I told him "Three or four seats from the stairs on the left-hand side." He asked what Flora wore and I said a light dress and cape and a Tam-o-Shanter hat and I told her she should have worn her jacket and she said she didn't need it.

We stayed the play out and then went to walk on Yonge and it was either five minutes before or after half past 10 on the Wanless clock.

Here, Clara contradicted the testimony of the Opera House manager at the inquest, who said that the play ended at 10:55 p.m., which was just after Frank was shot. However, Dewart never picked up on this contradiction in his cross-examination. Clara continued her detailed alibi:

We went past Simpsons and then I bought a *World* and then we walked on Queen Street West. I asked her whether she knew that Percy Clark was dead. I had seen it in the *Telegram*. She said "no" and I said she should go see Mrs. Clark.

Then we went down Bay [Street] and I dropped her off at Mrs. Watson. I didn't go in because it was late but I told her to tell Mrs. Watson she had been to the theatre with me and that was why she was late. I then went home and when I got into Mrs. Dorsey's, it was just a quarter to 11.

Having run through her alibi, Murdoch asked how the police reacted to it:

Reburn didn't say anything but he went out and talked with Stark and then asked me where Flora lived. I didn't know the number but I did know it was on Jarvis, just one or two doors past the Unitarian Church.

Porter and Slemin went out and I was in Reburn's office. I don't know what time it was, but it was getting dark.

Then Reburn took me into Stark's office and I was set down facing the light. Inspector Stark and Sergeant Reburn sat opposite me, and the sergeant said: "I know you are making it all up" and I says "No I ain't, I'm telling the truth."

"Well," he says, "you needn't get saucy about it" and I says "Well, I've a right to speak up when I'm telling the truth."

Clara provided vivid details of a gruelling examination by two men against one woman. She could not see their faces because light shone in her eyes, but they could examine her every expression. She tried to exert her rights but had to answer the same questions over and over.

Murdoch asked Clara whether she believed she was under arrest. Clara answered: "I saw that they didn't let me alone for a minute and I was being watched, but I didn't dream I was under arrest." For her, she explained, this kind of police harassment was routine and didn't necessarily mean she was in peril. She expected to be released imminently, after two hours of questioning: "Inspector Stark asked about my nationality [she told him she was half Spanish, which was duly reported in the newspapers the following day] and where I had lived in Toronto and he said I'd only be here a few minutes longer. Reburn then took me to the matron's room and said he would get me some supper. He left me there and I heard the bolt slip into the door. I was left there alone for an hour or so and then Mrs. Smith [the police matron] came in [with food]."

Clara colourfully described her sense of not knowing what was going on. Locked up for an indefinite amount of time, she knew she was in over her head.

At around 7, near as I can reckon, Reburn came back in and asked where I had worked, which I told him.

Then Reburn asked me when I started wearing men's clothes and I said at Mrs. Crosiers in Brockton and the last time was about a year ago. I was asked about my fedora hat and I told him I gave it to Mrs. Crosier for her boy Jack. I gave the detectives Mrs. Crosier's address on Camden [the Crosiers had moved from Brockton to Queen and Spadina in 1894] and saw them go out again.

Clara's version of the interrogation continued. She told the court it entered its fifth hour with the same questions and a continual refrain – her being told she was a liar:

Then Reburn asked me again about the Opera House and said: "You weren't there at all; the little girl says so." I says: "My god, if she says that, she is telling a lie."

Then he said again "Do you know Frank Westwood?" I says "No I don't."

"Never mentioned his name?"

"No."

"Never seen him at Mrs. Clark's?"

"No."

Reburn took a letter out of his pocket, holding it with both hands, like I was going to snatch it.

He says "You didn't know I had that?" and I said "No, I didn't"

"You wrote that?"

I said "I don't know whether I did or not."

He showed me the words "Westwood's Frank" and I saw the name "Jim Harding" [sic] at the bottom and then I knew where it came from.

It was only at that point, Clara testified, that she realized that Gus Clark or his sister Carrie had kept the anonymous letters for four and a half years and that they'd gone to the police with them. She didn't deny writing them. Using Frank's name as a source of gossip, she argued, didn't mean she'd had an ongoing relationship with him, and the anonymous letters hadn't affected her relationship with Catherine Clark. However, at this point, Clara realized the detectives were preparing a case against her for Frank's murder.

The *Mail and Empire* called the next section of Clara's testimony "Forcing the Confession":

> Slemin comes in and says that Mrs. Crosier saw me that night and I was drunk.
>
> I said "Well, she lies. Bring her here to face me."
>
> Then Mrs. Crosier and Maggie come in. Mrs. Crosier was looking at the floor and had a very long face. She looked scared.
>
> They say I was there that night and I said it was a lie.
>
> Reburn said "Shut up."

In Clara's account, Reburn switched at this point from "bad cop" to "good cop":

> Then Reburn took me to [the commissioner's room] and shut the windows and the blinds. He told me to sit down and he sat down beside me and said "Clara, if you don't tell it will be the worse for you. If you were my own sister, I could not wish you more out of this hole."
>
> I said I didn't know anything about it.
>
> He said "Only tell me what your motive was. Say he insulted you. There's $500 or $600 offered for this" [an Ontario government award for information on Frank's murder] and he winked at me. He said that if Frank Westwood had insulted me nothing would be done to me. "No one will know to the contrary. He is dead and he won't come back again. If you confess you will be a free woman and walk the streets again."

The Globe reported that her testimony caused a "sensation in the courtroom." Clara's myriad details were building a picture of a forced confession through lies, deception, and threats by powerful white men.

Clara waited for the hubbub to subside then recounted the climax of her tale:

> Then Reburn looked at his watch and said it was either a quarter to or a quarter past 11, and he had no more time to bother with me.
>
> He said "Clara, you are in a net and you can't get out." He was walking up and down the room.
>
> I said I had nothing to tell. That was true.
>
> At last I got so confused, seeing as they were blaming me for what I hadn't done, and that they said they would let me go if I confessed, that I said I had done it. I told him how I was dressed, and as he'd said I had the hat on, I put it in, and about being in Mrs. Crosier's, just as she'd told them. I thought it might as well fit her story.

Clara said that the route she'd described was similar to walks she'd taken to Parkdale.

Until that point in the interrogation, Claire testified, she hadn't seen Flora. When she was brought into the room, she told Flora she'd just made an "alleged confession." She asked Flora if she didn't remember being at the theatre on October 6. Flora answered, crying: "I wish someone would say they saw us at the theatre." The police, according to Clara, had so frightened her daughter she couldn't think straight.

Then Stark came in, and Clara repeated her false confession. In Clara's version of events, Stark told her what to say, and she simply agreed. Stark told her: "'So you and Westwood quarrelled in the hallway. He tore your coat and then you shot your revolver.' I said 'yes.' He said 'Well, there is nothing they can do to you for that.'"

Reburn said he had to lock her up overnight. On the way, he said: "Now stick to this story. Be sure you don't alter it." He took her down to a cell and gave an order that no reporter could see her. He told her she would be let go in the morning, which is why she said "My time here is short" the following morning. "And what did he mean by telling me that lie?" Clara asked. Murdoch said: "Never mind, go on. Were you at the Crosiers on October 6?"

Clara said she wasn't, but she did pick up her laundry on Monday. She and the Crosiers talked about the Westwood shooting. Clara told them she was glad she'd not been in Parkdale that Saturday, and they talked about Percy Clark's birth and funeral coinciding with two famous Parkdale shootings.

In response to Murdoch's questions, she testified that she'd never "walked out" with Frank Westwood and that she certainly didn't know Libby Black.

After two hours of testimony, Clara concluded: "The confession I made was all false, and I only told it to get out of the scrape I was in."

Murdoch handed Clara over to Dewart for cross-examination.

Dewart began by contrasting Clara's calm, articulate testimony of the past two hours, when her life was at stake, with her account of having been so frightened by the police that she made a false confession. Clara responded: "I ain't what you would call excitable," but the police had "badgered her so," that she got confused.

When asked about the many coworkers who'd testified as to her violent threats, she said that Vise was lying; of the others, only "Dorenwend, Gus Clark and his sister Carrie" were likely to call her a murderer.

When asked about her clothing, she said they'd been left behind by a man who'd boarded in the same house as her.

When asked about her marriage, she said she'd been married ten years ago in Chicago and lived with her husband for about a year.

When asked about her conversation with Flora, she argued that she'd said "alleged confession."

When Dewart tried to ask her about her original guilty plea, Johnston stopped that line of questioning. He said the magistrate had been wrong to ask her to plead on a capital crime. Boyd sustained this motion.

According to some newspaper accounts, Dewart led a remarkably weak cross-examination of a tale full of holes, but other reporters didn't agree. The *Mail and Empire* wrote: "From 4.10 to 5.25, Crown Attorney Dewart cross-examined her in a manner that showed his complete knowledge of the case, and that he'd noted the vulnerable points in her argument." Afterwards, "he was deservedly congratulated by many of those present in the court." In contrast, *The Star,* which was hostile to Clara, said that "the woman showed surprising cunning in getting away from Dewart's questions" and that he failed to "catch her." It reported that the detectives were disgruntled that Osler hadn't been there to handle the cross-examination. *The Globe,* by then very much in Clara's corner, said "her feckless demeanour on the stand," as she "told a story ... of alleged official tyranny, browbeating and cajoling, the like of which has seldom if ever been heard in a Canadian courtroom before," could not fail to impress: "Whatever value the jury may attach to her testimony, all who saw the girl stand in that witness box for three hours answering her own counsel or fencing with the Crown could not but admire her wonderful nerve and the indomitable will power that could sustain her in such a terrible ordeal."

Clara stood in the witness box for three and a half hours, a longer run time than *The Black Crook* and equally as spectacular. Reporters still assumed she was doomed, but she'd given them what they needed: a heroine with a dramatic monologue to enthral readers and sell out the special edition. And maybe, just maybe, she'd saved her own life.

THIRTEEN

TWELVE
HUNGRY MEN

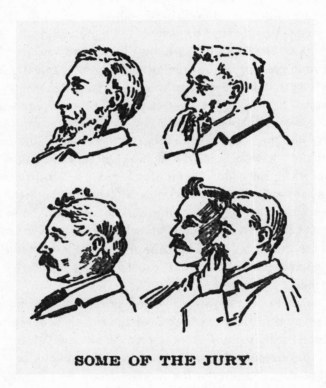

SOME OF THE JURY.

Newspaper illustrators scrutinized the jurors' reactions

The next day, Saturday, May 4, *The World* published excerpts from the letters to discredit Clara as a Good Negro Citizen and re-establish her as a Monster. Hector Charlesworth thundered that when "standing in a masculine attitude, with arms akimbo after the manner of her race ... she swore that she didn't know Frank Westwood, that he never spoke to her nor she to him, she alienated her sympathizers without convincing any one that she didn't tell the truth when she admitted that her hands are stained with the blood of the murdered boy."

When the trial recommenced Saturday morning, E.F.B. Johnston complained that *The World*'s malicious coverage was prejudicial and that the paper should be charged with contempt. Chancellor Boyd pointed out that the jury was sequestered and couldn't read the papers. Besides, he added, it was up to the attorney general (Johnston had resigned to resume his lucrative legal practice) to prosecute the publisher. The jury didn't hear this motion. They were excluded because the letters involved the reputation of two "ladies." Instead, they were watching a ballistic expert shoot bullets into sides of beef – a rare moment outside the stifling courtroom. But they returned to the court and heard *Telegram* reporters cast doubt on Clara's confession. The jurors, suffering from gastrointestinal distress from the city's water and sleepless nights in a cheap hotel, just wanted to go home.

With the time that remained, Clara's defence team focused on holes in the "alleged" confession and Clara's alibi. Charles Clark and George Barnett of *The Telegram* testified that the shoreline near the Old Fort had been under water and could not have been traversed on October 6. The deputy harbour master also testified. He revealed daily measurements taken on October 6, November 21 and 26 (when police attempted the route), and November 30 and December 3 (when *Telegram* reporters tried, the second time accompanied by Sergeant Reburn). The depth of Lake Ontario adjacent to the walls of the Fort had ranged from four inches to ten. The Crown claimed the records were not accurate and that someone who'd just shot a man wouldn't be stopped by having to wade through a few inches of cold water. Blackie Johnston asked *The Telegram* reporters whether they'd spoken to Reburn about Clara possibly going inland at the Exhibition Grounds, thus avoiding the water. The reporters said Reburn had insisted on that weak point of her confession: that she had returned to her lodgings via the waterfront, instead of using King Street.

The defence called only three character witnesses, but they were well selected. Catherine and Ida Clark testified that Clara had been "truthful and industrious" during her time as their tenant. They cast doubt on Christian Dorenwend's characterization of Clara as a slanderous troublemaker. Catherine Clark also testified that Clara never spoke of Frank. Reverend Ingles said Clara was a regular attendant at St. Marks, the Parkdale Anglican church, and that her reputation for "steadiness, truth and industry were good." Hartley Dewart limited his cross-examination to gaining an admission from Ingles that if he found out Clara was the author of the malicious anonymous letters he might change his opinion.

Then came the most important element of the defence: Clara's alibi. Three residents from the Dorsey boarding house testified that Clara had returned to her room at 11:00 p.m., and three employees of the Toronto Opera House testified to having seen her at the Saturday, October 6, evening performance of *The Black Crook*.

All six newspapers attempted to re-create Chloe Dorsey's testimony, and many shaped it into a racist narrative, complete with minstrel show enunciation. Chloe Dorsey, who had considerable experience with courts, was done with the forces of the law and didn't try to hide her contempt. Like Charley Slemin's cross-examination and Clara's testimony, it was great theatre.

According to *The Star:* "Mrs. Dorsey, a very stout and very good-natured old coloured lady, was a splendid alibi witness ... After a few remarks about the awful hereafter that would await her if she failed to tell the truth, she proceeded to talk about the events of Saturday, Oct. 6. Clara had a new coat that night and went out after dinner, saying she was going to the theatre. She came back about 11, said good night and went up to her bedroom."

Dorsey confirmed that she sat in the hallway every night to keep an eye on who was entering and exiting the restaurant and the lodgings upstairs. She made sure the front door was locked just after 11:00 p.m., as Clara knew. The day after Clara's arrest, the police came to ask her questions. They were "awful impertinent," accusing her of brewing moonshine to put her on the back foot and threatening to arrest her if she didn't give them the answers they desired. She told the court they'd opened a black bottle to see if it was illegal homebrew, only to find that it contained coal oil. She laughed heartily and looked up at the judge to share her joke. The chancellor wasn't amused. Dorsey concluded by saying that Clara was the most industrious and hardest-working lodger she'd ever seen. She wasn't guilty of murder, in her opinion.

Dewart took Dorsey through an extensive cross-examination. According to *The Telegram,* he asked, "Is Clara hot-tempered?"

"No more than you."

"Did you ever see me hot?"

"You're getting hot now."

Dewart, who felt he was losing this exchange, attempted to gain control. "Listen, Mrs. Crosier ..."

"Mrs. Crosier?" cried Mrs. Dorsey. "Don't call me that name!"

However, Dorsey herself confused the names of Frank Westwood and Gus Clark. She also admitted that the restaurant remained open after midnight some Saturday nights and that she could not remember details of several other nights.

Dorsey finished her testimony and went home, only to be summoned back to court. Chancellor Boyd asked her to read a paragraph from the *Toronto News*. The judge might have been checking her eyesight, but he also cast aspersions on her literacy. Dorsey put on her reading glasses and read the liver pill advertisement aloud. "We'll pass you as a good reader," the chancellor condescendingly said. Dorsey retorted "with an indignant air: 'You think I can't read, do you?'" Then she "marched out of the court."

Mamie Dorsey, Chloe Dorsey's twenty-four-year-old daughter, and Clara's friend and fellow boarder Eliza Reed, who worked at the restaurant that night, confirmed that Clara had returned just after 11:00 p.m. Even if Clara had caught a streetcar immediately after shooting Frank, she could not have returned any earlier than 11:30 p.m.

Of the three Opera House witnesses, the treasurer, William Graham, was the most impressive. He swore that the thirty-five-cent balcony tickets he sold Clara were only available on a Saturday night and that he'd seen her in the theatre and on the street on the night in question. She didn't appear to be with anyone. William Meldrum, an usher, stated that Clara had been there one night that week. He believed it to be Saturday. James McLaughlin, the constable who kept order in the theatre, said Clara usually attended on Saturday nights.

Finally, Austin, Lena, and Emma Card – three witnesses who'd been discredited at the inquest – testified once again about the strange whistling man.

After lunch, the Crown recalled several people to refute the defence's witnesses. Dr. Adam Lynd performed his last bit part in this drama by refuting the Cards' testimony. The four detectives – Stark, Reburn, Slemin, and Porter – vehemently denied all aspects of Clara's version of events. Slemin testified that when he'd called on Chloe Dorsey on November 21, she told him she didn't know when Clara had come in and that the restaurant regularly stayed open to midnight or half past on Saturday nights.

At 4:00 p.m. the chancellor turned to the jurors and asked whether they wanted to adjourn until Monday to hear closing arguments. After a brief discussion, the jury foreman said they wanted to "sit it out."

In his closing argument for the defence, Johnston relied on his considerable oratorical skills to raise sympathy for the accused and cast doubt on the Crown. He opened by stressing the severity of the sentence in a capital case: "The crime is murder or nothing. Either the accused is foully wronged or is guilty of one of the foulest murders ever committed in the country. Either this woman must hang or walk out a free woman. There is no midway. You must either allow the accused to return to society and earn an honest livelihood, as even her enemies agree she did, or she must be hanged."

Clara's respectability as an industrious and honest worker was being brought up once again as evidence that she wasn't a murderer. Johnston appealed to the farmers and small businessmen on the jury to consider the "unlimited funds" that allowed the Crown to retain "one of Canada's most brilliant criminal lawyers." Although B.B. Osler had to leave the case, he'd left it in the capable hands of a deputy attorney general, a Crown attorney, and the full Toronto Police Department. And "against all that array, a woman without a dollar." He and Murdoch, he emphasized, had "taken her case without fee or expectation of reward" because they believed in their client's innocence. But they were fighting "against terrible odds."

Johnston contrasted Clara, the Good Negro Citizen, with Gus Clark and Libby Black, both witnesses for the Crown: "And what is the character of those giving evidence against the prisoner? Gaol birds. The Crown has had to scour the moral sewers of this country to get its evidence." He contended that "if the evidence of gaol birds and detectives were removed, then the accused would be immediately acquitted." Johnston conflated the police with criminals, claiming that "detectives are living day and night with criminals and the very lowest classes, and in consequence they see sin where there is no sin."

Johnston made much of Clark's and Black's criminal convictions. Not only was "Libby Black now on her third sentence for drunkenness, to which should be added perjury," but Clark was "currently in prison for robbing his own mother, and that mother has come forward to say a kind word for the accused." Against these villains were the words of Frank Westwood, the victim of the crime, and his respectable family: "Young Westwood was at the point of death and he didn't recognize the accused as the one who shot him. Was it possible if there was any ill-feeling between young Westwood and the prisoner because of previous improper relations, the victim would not have recognized the identity of his murderer? No matter how Clara Ford was dressed, it was impossible to mistake her as a white man."

Furthermore, "the boy's own father has gone into the box and denied the statements of the witness [Libby Black] with regard to appearance of his son." Would Benjamin Westwood have done that if he suspected Frank and Clara had been lovers?

As for the letters written five years ago: "Clara was a woman of 28 and Frank a child of 13; what could they have had in common?" Was the evidence really "proof of a guilty connection? Was it even proof that she'd known him personally? The Westwoods lived in a big house and were well known throughout Parkdale." Indeed, the Crown's insistence that there was "an intimacy between the prisoner and the deceased" had cruelly "smirched the fair name of that unfortunate young man." What an ironic twist: the Crown had murdered the only thing the Westwoods had left of their son, his good reputation.

Johnston dealt quickly with the other evidence put forward by the Crown. He explained away Clara's possession of men's clothes and a revolver as the actions of a women who feared being attacked. The marks on the bullets amounted to nothing: it could have been one of a thousand guns in circulation in Toronto. The Crosiers' testimony had many small inconsistencies, suggesting that they might have been confused as to which night Clara visited.

Having enlisted the murder victim as an ally, the bulk of Johnston's rhetoric was dedicated to making the detectives out as villains. He made a clever choice: he ignored Charley Slemin, the small fry, who'd suborned perjury from Libby Black, and focused on Henry Reburn. If he could make the jury believe that the sergeant to whom Clara had confessed was a bully without a trace of chivalry, then the strongest element of the Crown's case, the confession, might fall apart. Johnston began this part of his summation by once again drafting Frank onto Team Clara. He asked the jury whether they'd "not believe the statement of a dying man before that of the officers, who were in the habit of going out and into the witness box as frequently as members of the jury were in the habit of going out and into their dining rooms."

Having been betrayed by the criminal Gus Clark, Clara was then bullied by the police, "kept in an office from 4 to 11.30, surrounded by detectives, without friend or advisor – with Reburn, as she'd so tersely put it, digging at her for seven long hours ... Was it any wonder that she, woman-like, would say anything to get out of the clutches of those vultures?"

According to Johnston, Inspector William Stark wasn't so much to blame, and Slemin and Porter were reasonably fair, but Reburn was another story. "Because he had a woman to deal with he thought he could tire her out, and make a reputation on her conviction. [Clara] was taken by the throat and the statement choked out of her by a man who was skilled, experienced, relentless, knowing that his whole reputation was at stake, subjecting her to brutal and merciless treatment. It made him ashamed to be a man, to belong to the same race of beings."

Clara had previously been the target of dehumanizing metaphors, now it was Reburn's turn. Johnston likened him to a vulture and even a traitor to his race, and he made another clever reversal. Clara's testimony, he argued, showed her to be an intelligent and composed woman, not an "ignorant girl" who could be tricked into a confession. Johnston used Clara's *sang-froid* as proof of her innocence:

> Clara Ford is no fool. If she was guilty, would she have made ... an alleged confession at all? The fact that she was guilty would have been uppermost in her thoughts, and knowing her cleverness, would she have admitted anything that implicated her in the slightest possible degree? Had she been a simple or foolish woman, she might, but being the woman she is, her lips would have been sealed. The statement she made [to Mary Crosier], that if she was up in Parkdale she might have been suspected, was the frankness of innocence, not a badge of guilt.

Johnston reminded the jury that it would be part of legal history, the first jury to hear a woman testify on her own behalf: "The act of this prisoner, in taking her life in her hands and entering the witness box, which she did with the charm and confidence of innocence, to admit that she made the confession, was the boldest, the noblest, the most heroic act ever witnessed in a criminal trial in this country. If Clara Ford shot Frank Westwood would she dare to go into the witness box and tell the story she did?"

Johnston ended with a final rhetorical flourish, telling the jurors they could take a stand against police brutality by finding Clara not guilty, that they could make a "fervent appeal for his client's life as a protest against the autocratic and Czar-like actions of the detectives in the cells." He concluded: "Give me her life. Take it away from the hangman and give it to me." What Johnston would want to do with a Black person's life a generation after the abolition of slavery is another question entirely.

Hartley Dewart knew he couldn't top Johnston's oratorical bombast, so he laid out the Crown's case in "a calm, deliberate, yet effective manner," as his hero, B.B. Osler, would have done. Dewart began by criticizing Johnston for his "grave and serious aspersions on the detectives," who'd treated Clara with "utmost fairness." Was Johnston saying that "the detectives perjured themselves?" Each of the men called to the stand "had been faithful servants of the city and guardians of the life and property of the citizens for years, performing many severe duties in the most faithful and conscientious manner." The detectives had been anxious to give "the prisoner every possible opportunity to clear herself of even the suspicion of being associated with this foul crime, and so had sent for persons who the accused herself stated could show that she was elsewhere than at Westwood's on the night of the murder." Had these alibi witnesses corroborated Clara's story, "she would at once have been released."

Dewart told the jury that the confession must be treated as true. Yes, Clara was clever, so clever in fact that she'd tried to manufacture an alibi before committing the crime. Once that "prop was knocked away, what was more natural than in sheer desperation to give in and admit 'Yes, I shot Frank Westwood'?"

Dewart also hinted that Clara had been coached by Johnston and that her performance on the stand was both unnatural and unwomanly: "I admit I was unable to cope with the ability of Clara Ford on the witness box ... Did you not note the legal mind? Did you not observe its counterpart in the address to the jury by the learned counsel for the prisoner?"

Then Dewart dug into his bag of racist tropes to remind the jury that Clara wasn't like them:

Now as to the demeanour of the woman in the box, I ask you whether it was the demeanour of a woman conscious of her innocence? Was it not rather the demeanour of a woman as could write such a letter as that she admitted having penned, a woman whose feelings of moral right and wrong had become so blunted that she valued neither the life of him who she slew, nor her own? Was it not the courage that comes from the spirit of bravado?

Has she not herself spoken of a spirit of devilment? You may have admiration for a woman who gives her evidence in the manner that Clara Ford did, but it is the admiration that you have for the Mexican bandit who, careless of his own life, goes to any length, or of the Indian stoic who, knowing no fear, would go so far as to shoot down a man, though he knows he might pay the penalty the next moment.

In the witness box the previous day, Dewart continued, "she had flatly contradicted 13 witnesses, at least nine of whom must be considered impartial and many manifestly friendly to the accused." In particular, there was the contradiction between her testimony and Flora McKay's: "Is there any reason why the putative child of the prisoner should tell a story so strongly against her mother if it is not true?" Flora's version of events had been confirmed by Mrs. Phyall. It wasn't simply Clara's word against sworn upholders of the law; it was Clara's word against that of her own daughter, who had no reason to want to see her mother falsely accused.

He concluded by arguing that the other witnesses for the defence could be easily dismissed. Of the three who saw Clara at the theatre, two said she'd been alone and were uncertain of the date, and none remembered Flora. Dewart reminded the jury of Chloe Dorsey's unreliable memory and the mixed figures in the logbooks of the deputy harbourmaster. Finally, given that David

Low and Gus Clark had alibis, there was no other reasonable suspect. Clara was guilty. The jury had no choice but to convict.

With that, the court adjourned for dinner, and the judge prepared his instructions for the jury. While waiting for the courtroom to once again be brought to order, *The Globe* reporter glanced around the room:

> The judicially stern yet kindly face of The Chancellor on the bench arranging his notes ... The twelve pale and tired-looking jurors, who [would] decide life or death ... The serried mass of spectators, silent, eager, attentive, following every word ... And lastly, the prisoner herself, the mulatto girl whose life hung in the balance, whose fate depended on the decision of that dozen of men before her. For the first time ... she showed some emotion, but even now it was scarcely perceptible; the mouth was slightly drawn and the eyelids drooped, as if in the very weariness of spirit. But beyond this, the prisoner at the bar was apparently, the least concerned of any in that packed courtroom.

As *The Globe* would understate in its coverage of Chancellor Boyd's summation, the judge "charged adversely" to the jury. It's possible that Boyd felt he needed to present the Crown's case, since Osler was absent and Dewart was, in the chancellor's opinion, not up to the task. There can be no other explanation for the next thirty-five minutes.

Boyd began by reminding the jury that they "must not be actuated by sympathy or compassion." Rather, they must answer the question: "Has the crime been brought home to the prisoner?"

He then turned to the reputation of the police, praising them in the back-handed manner of the privileged: "A good deal has been said about detectives and police officers. If we had no crime in this country, we would not need these officials, but so long as we have crime, we must have detectives." Without detectives, there would be "no security of life or property or stability of the social fabric."

While "both the deceased and the prisoner have good characters so far as we have heard ... There is the writing of the letters." According to Boyd, the letters destroyed the character of Clara Ford, the Angry Black Woman, but not the alleged source of the gossip, Frank the Respectable White Boy. The prisoner said she didn't know young Westwood, but "there is evidence that she did know him. There is evidence that she spoke to him; and there is testimony that she told Mrs. Crosier she knew him since he was so high." The Crown hadn't mentioned this testimony, but the judge felt it was incumbent upon him to remind jurors of this fact.

Boyd continued by reminding the jury that Frank Westwood had said in his antemortem statement that it was "a man who shot him, a man dressed in dark clothes and a fedora hat, medium height and middle-aged, wearing a dark moustache. He said, too, that he wasn't in any girl scrape. They must judge if this statement cleared Clara Ford or not." Boyd pointed out, however, that in her confession, Clara had said she'd been wearing men's clothes. In addition, the shooting happened in an instant, it was dark, and the light in the hall may not have illuminated the shooter's face. The Crown hadn't argued this last point, but the judge was there to help the jury make the correct conclusion.

In the most dismissive manner possible, Boyd brought back the allegation of sexual assault as a motive: "The confession said that Frank had insulted her. A good many young men are very good at home and quite different away. It may be that Westwood didn't remember the assault, or didn't place much importance on the fact, and consequently didn't associate her with the tragedy. Or he might have suspected it was her and didn't wish to grieve his parents by associating her name with the tragedy."

According to the judge, assault against Black women was so commonplace as to be forgettable, and certainly not noteworthy.

The Crown hadn't presented these scenarios (Frank forgetting or dismissing the assault or, conversely, shielding Clara because he felt guilt). Perhaps the judge felt he was helping to clean up after the Crown left the party.

Boyd reiterated the Crown's point that Frank's antemortem statement cleared Gus Clark. There were no other suspects, besides Clara, and Boyd characterized her alleged confession as "singular," as was the fact that she entered the box to explain it away: "A great deal has been said about the bravery of the prisoner in going into the witness box, but you are not to pay any attention to that. Remember that a man or a woman will do anything to save his or her life."

To illustrate this point, Boyd brought up the old saying: "'Skin for skin, yes, all a man has he will give for life.'" The chancellor didn't mention that he was citing Satan in the Book of Job to back up his arguments.

"What value," Boyd continued rhetorically, "under these circumstances could [the jury] place on her testimony?" The jury was instructed not to "sweep away all the other evidence without due consideration. The detectives were men with long experience in the force. Is this prisoner a woman to be awed by the questioning, or is she, on the other hand, not a woman to make up a story of this kind?" Boyd implied that the answer didn't need to be stated.

Then Boyd wheeled out his big cannons: "I am bound to tell you that if those officers ... treated that woman as she swears they did ... they deserve to be behind prison bars. But these men have been four, eight, ten and twenty years upon the force, have hitherto borne unblemished characters, and it is a grave thing to incriminate them based on the unsupported testimony of one who stands charged as the prisoner does." Acquitting Clara would mean convicting the detectives, and if the police were in jail, then who would maintain social order?

Boyd dismissed "the contention that the accused would not attempt to pass by the water front." If she'd committed the crime, she wouldn't hesitate to walk through a foot of cold water in October. He concluded by suggesting, in regard to his deferred judgment, "If they found the prisoner guilty, it was advisable they should state whether they would have been disposed to find her guilty if the evidence of her confession had not been admitted."

The jury filed out of the courtroom at 8:35 p.m. to the sound of shocked silence. Johnston slowly stood and respectfully asked the judge whether he might want to recall the jury to define reasonable doubt and remind them of the defence's version of events? These were, of course, legal requirements in summing up a case. The chancellor grimaced and asked the bailiff to bring the jury back. Then he read excerpts from the testimony of Eliza Reed, who'd said Clara had returned to their home at approximately the same time as the shooting, and William Graham, who'd said he'd sold Clara theatre tickets and saw her in the theatre and on the street that night. Boyd explained that the jury must weigh the evidence. If it was evenly balanced, the prisoner should have the benefit of the doubt. He glanced at Johnston for approval then sent the jury out again to deliberate at 8:55 p.m.

The Globe, once again, said it best: "The audience settled down for a long wait, the general impression being that the Judge's charge had been so strongly against the prisoner that it would either result in a prompt conviction or a long fight by those favorable to her." As they waited, "little groups all over the courtroom laughed and chatted, as though it was between the acts of a comedy." But "sometimes one member of the group would glance at the prisoner, note her hopeless expression, and the little group would become quiet."

The Telegram added that Johnston "retired from the courtroom while Mr. Murdoch sat idly playing with a pencil. Benjamin Westwood sat with folded arms and head slightly bowed, lost to the sights and sounds around him.... The hands of the old clock on the west wall of the dingy old courtroom went slowly around on their accustomed journey [while] the chimes from [St. James] cathedral pealed ... a quarter past nine, half past nine, a quarter to ten."

The intermission was surprisingly short. After exactly one hour and three minutes (the *Mail and Empire* reporter loved his watch), a "rap, rap" from the jury room signalled its return. The constable summoned his lordship to resume his place on the bench. The cathedral clock pealed out that it was 10:00 p.m. There was an "ominous hush of those who felt the woman was doomed." The court clerk asked the jury foreman, Joseph White, a wagon maker from Markham:

"Gentlemen of the jury, have you reached your verdict?"
"We have," said the foreman, rising to his feet.
"How say you of the prisoner at the bar? Is she guilty or not guilty?"
"Not guilty," came the prompt reply.

Spectators gasped, and those at the back of the court began to cheer. Soon, everyone joined in. Benjamin Westwood sighed and put his face in his hands. Chancellor Boyd sat quietly writing to the sound of foot stomping and hand clapping. After several minutes, the court clerk rose: "Gentlemen of the jury, hearken to your verdict as the court records it. You say the prisoner at the bar is not guilty and that is the verdict of you all?" Several jurors nodded, rousing another cheer from the back of the court.

As for Clara, *The Globe* reported: "As those words which gave her back her life and liberty fell upon the prisoner's ear she sat motionless, as if unable to comprehend her good fortune, and then sank back into the corner of the dock with a deep sigh, and as the plaudits of the crowd burst forward a moment later, she glanced round with a pleased and gratified smile."

The cheers subsided, and the Chancellor commanded, "Clara Ford, stand up." Clara stood, and Boyd read from the statement he had hastily composed: "The jury has acquitted you of the crime with which you were charged. I am not surprised at the result, and for your sake I am glad. I am not sorry at the verdict, because it has cleared your character and also the character of that poor young fellow who is dead. Let me say one word more: be kind to the little girl, Florence McKay, who has shown her love for you, though she was compelled to testify against you. I ask you to be kind to her, treat her gently and lovingly. You are free."

Boyd got the last word. The case was about Frank's reputation, not Clara's life, and my goodness, wasn't she a bad mother! Clara met the eyes of the judge who'd tried to condemn her to hang an hour earlier and gave him a little bow and a smile. She said in the "clear and ringing tones" she'd used throughout the trial, "Thank you, sir." A lifetime of forced deference lay behind three simple words.

From that moment, all "order and decorum," all Toronto-ness, was thrown to the winds. The constable's shouts went unheeded as the spectators rushed the dock to shake hands with the liberated woman. Among the first to congratulate her were her counsels, William Murdoch and Blackie Johnston. Then Eliza Reed pushed her way through the crowd, threw her arms around Clara's neck, and kissed her. With a hand at Clara's back, Eliza ushered her outdoors. As she exited the courtroom, "a well known bookmaker said to his companion, 'I touched her dress as she passed me; for luck, you know.'" Clara, face radiant, used both hands to greet her well-wishers.

An estimated two hundred "men and boys" accompanied her west to York Street, along the same four blocks on Adelaide Street she'd traversed five months before. At that time, her suit of men's clothes was in an evidentiary bundle, her revolver was in Slemin's pocket, and her heart was in her throat. Now, she was half carried by the crowd as it moved toward the Dorseys' restaurant and Clara's home. Just before Yonge, the crowd came across a newsboy selling a special edition of *The Star*. Someone handed

Clara a copy, and she read "Set Free!" by the electric light. If I could stop this narrative to take a photograph of Clara, it would be in that moment.

York Street was blocked to traffic by the jubilant crowd. Charles Clark, *The Telegram* reporter, was there: "Hundreds of people filled the street from kerb to kerb and crowded into the restaurant to catch a glimpse of Clara Ford. Vainly a couple of big policemen ordered and threatened ... It must have been fully fifteen minutes before [Chloe Dorsey] got the crowd out and bolted the door ... *The Telegram* reporter and his friend were admitted through to the back room where the liberated woman was holding quite a levee."

"What are you planning to do now?" Clark asked Clara.

"Well, I don't intend to starve. I'm not that kind of woman. I'd shovel coal first."

Chloe Dorsey patted her on the shoulder: "The good Lord was in it. I prayed to Him and He helped Clara."

Dorsey and her son John tried to fit as many customers as they could into their little restaurant. Among them were Catherine Clark "and her daughters." Three others who dropped by were the jury foreman, Joseph White, and two other out-of-town jurors, who were enjoying their last night in the big smoke. Clara gamely shook hands with all who entered, and "many curious eyes ... peered in through the big windows at the front, in spite of the endeavours of the police to keep the sidewalk clear of the curious crowd."

Clara made a speech thanking the "boys of Toronto," and much merriment was had, until Chloe Dorsey decided it was closing time. Just after midnight, she threw the well-wishers out and locked the front door. Clara, her lodger, obediently went upstairs to bed.

FOURTEEN

WHAT
CLARA DID
NEXT

Walter Smart, Stella Wiley, and George Williams
in John Isham's *Octoroons,* circa 1898

On the night of her acquittal, Clara slept in her own bed, a free woman. She woke up the next morning, still free, but out of money, unemployed, and in debt. A defence fund set up by Queen Street barber G.W. Smith, a Black friend of the Dorseys, had raised only thirteen dollars.

All Sunday, well-wishers, gawkers, and journalists thronged the Dorseys' restaurant. Clara drank coffee and received visitors, like a wealthy lady holding an "at home" in her parlour. She told the *Mail and Empire* that "the mental strain had been terrible, but she never lost heart, and felt sure she would be acquitted." As to the next step, "she has been offered several situations." She told the *Toronto News* that her philosophy from the time of her arrest had been that worrying would do her no good, so she'd remained calm. She was grateful to her legal counsel and the newspapers and members of the public who supported her. She'd been overwhelmed by visitors in the past twelve hours and hadn't had time to map out her future, but she'd "been offered work by several people in my trade and some gentlemen from the Musée have made me offers to go there."

As has been the case since she'd been twelve, Clara needed to find work to survive.

Sam S. Young, proprietor of the Musée Theatre, had visited Clara bright and early on Sunday morning. In March, he'd "exhibited" John Walker, a sixteen-year-old petty criminal acquitted of involvement in the double murder of a farming couple outside

Toronto. *The Star* saw nothing wrong with this tasteless tableau: "Walker is an entertaining youth and will no doubt draw crowds who will be anxious to see the lad who escaped two charges of murder." Six weeks after this stunt, Young approached Clara to see if she was interested in being exhibited in men's clothes, holding a revolver.

When Clara mentioned this opportunity to the *Toronto News* reporter, Chloe Dorsey interrupted. "I don't approve of that. She oughtn't to go and exhibit herself nowise. It's unchristianlike and not in keeping with the scriptures."

Dorsey was still angry at the judge's implication that she was illiterate: "Just imagine, me who lived here when this town was called Muddy York and there were no sidewalks or streetcar tracks or anything of the kind. Asking me if I could read! ... Me, who taught school here for eight years! How ridiculous! [The Chancellor] will come to some ignominious end! I predict it."

Flora McKay also visited her mother that afternoon, but there was a veil of silence drawn over what was surely a fraught reunion.

The backlash against the verdict began on Monday. Two front-page editorials in *The Star* criticized the unseemly conduct of "at least some of the jurors Saturday night in rushing to the reception held by the woman who they had just acquitted of murder." In the first editorial, the paper condemned their behaviour as the most "flagrant violation of judicial propriety and public decency [that] was ever perpetrated in this province." In the second editorial, it claimed that Clara's defence lawyers had unfairly criticized the police. Like so many at the time, the paper phrased its support for the police in an equivocal manner: "It is the fashion to berate detectives and policemen, and they are abused right and left, when they deserve it and when they do not, by people who apparently never reflected that for the wages paid it is scarcely possible to expect men of vast legal learning, consummate tact, and Chesterfieldian politeness ... Sometimes the police are overbearing and brutal, but not always, and the abuse which was showered on Reburn, Porter and Slemin for effect on the jury ... should not inflame the public mind as it has done with many people."

Unsurprisingly, *The World* wasn't happy with the verdict. It appealed to a higher authority: "This crime, which has created such widespread interest, will be forgotten in the lapse of years, but it will be bared again by the recording angel and justice such as only God can give will be meted out to the guilty and to the innocent."

The other newspapers hailed the verdict. The *Toronto News*, the purveyor of some of the most scurrilous rumours about Clara, declared in unusually modulated tones that the verdict "will meet with general approval": "No motive for the alleged crime ... was advanced; the attempt to connect the prisoner's pistol with the killing of young Westwood was brushed aside by the prosecution's own witness; and the evidence of Libby Black, instead of strengthening the chain of testimony against the accused, weakened it." The jury was justified in disregarding the confession, as "a friendless girl, who'd been subject to persecution all her life, was kept on the rack for hours in a private room with men whose business has rendered them incapable of dealing gently with those believed to be criminals; she was denied the privilege of consulting either with counsel or friends; and it's quite conceivable that in the distress of the moment she might have made statements, in order to secure temporary relief, for which there was no foundation whatever." The theatre employees' alibis seemed solid, and the repudiation of the confession under oath was convincing.

Accounts of the trial began to credit E.F.B. Johnston with saving Clara's life. *The Star,* writing about the "Aftermath of the Great Trial" on Monday, spoke of Johnston's "masterful effort" in his closing address. *The Globe,* at the end of 1895, spoke of Johnston's "bright career," ensured by the acquittals of Clara Ford and the Hyams brothers. Albert Hassard, in his 1926 book *Not Guilty and Other Trials,* said Johnston "won worldwide renown" because of his work in May 1895. And Stewart Wallace, in his

1931 book on famous Canadian murders, said it was Johnston's "cold and brilliant" defence that saved the day. In 1992, historian Carolyn Strange argued that "Johnston wrote a script" of "embattled virtue" around Clara, masterfully tackling Osler's seemingly "airtight case."

But it wasn't Johnston who shook the testimony of the most important witness against Clara – Sergeant Henry Reburn, the detective who'd elicited Clara's confession. If anything, it was that other denigrated woman, Libby Black, who struck the first blow against the police in the trial, albeit unintentionally. And it was Clara who provided a convincing enough counternarrative of deception and thinly veiled threats by the police to sway the jury. *The Globe*'s comment on the verdict was the simplest and the most accurate: "Between the detectives and the accused they accepted the word of the latter."

It wasn't some white man who saved Clara, it was Clara herself. But Clara can't be characterized as a feminist civil-rights leader. She didn't save others even as she saved herself. There was a short-lived "Clara effect" that took hold in Toronto over the next few years. Then, like a rubber band, society snapped back to its old constraints and injustices.

The Hyams twins trial that opened on Wednesday featured not only a rematch between the jousting foes Blackie Johnston and B.B. Osler but also greater vigilance by constables against overcrowding and unseemly courtroom displays. They'd learned their lesson after being berated for their poor control during the Ford trial. Dallas and Harry Hyams didn't testify, but in another legal precedent, Martha Hyams was allowed to testify against her estranged husband. The trial resulted in a hung jury. In the November Assizes, the case was retried, and the brothers were acquitted. There were rumours that an American "fixer" had visited and bribed the jurors' families. The Ontario justice system, which considered itself superior to its American counterpart, was showing itself to be surprisingly weak and corruptible.

A month after Clara's trial, in June 1895, a police detective named Harrison was sued for three thousand dollars by Mrs. Archie McWilliams, a resident of the Ward. According to the plaintiff, Harrison had a warrant to search the home of a woman who was lodging with her. He searched the whole house and then grossly insulted, threatened, and assaulted (that is, raped) her. The verdict was not recorded, but the reputation of the police had hit a low point.

At the next Assizes, in November 1895, Clara's case dominated the defence in an insurance fraud case. James McLaughlin, the constable at the Toronto Opera House who had helped establish an alibi for Clara, testified as to a damning conversation he'd had with the chief witness for the Crown, "the Jew" Rosenthal. Hartley Dewart asked McLaughlin if he made a business of supplying evidence for the defence. Rosenthal himself retracted his testimony on the stand, saying that he'd been bullied by the police into providing false evidence: "I knew if I was kept in the police cells, no one would look after [my wife and children] and a number of detectives got round me and made me admit things that aren't right ... It is Clara Ford all over again."

In 1899, Chancellor Boyd allowed another confession to be entered into evidence, but doubted it would help the Crown: "Clara Ford made confessions galore and contradicted them under oath. Her contradictions prevailed. She was acquitted and her jury held an 'at home' at her house." The "Clara effect" caused some soul searching in the Ontario justice system. But soon enough, old ways prevailed.

Two years after Clara's trial, on February 7, 1897, a symbolic purification ceremony took place. The central police station planned to auction unclaimed items with the profits going to its benevolent fund. Some items had been held for three or four years, "adding to the odors for which the Police Court is justly famous." When the auctioneer didn't show up because of snowy weather, Inspector Stark took over. Stark was a "temperance man," but there "were three or four bottles of champagne, two of whiskey and some port wine" that had been confiscated – no one quite knew when. Stark smelled the bottle mouths "and pronounced the contents to be excellent with the air of an expert." Constables were posted at each entrance to ensure that Inspector Archibald, the head of police, didn't raid the auction as an illegal liquor sale.

They auctioned revolvers of all sizes and patterns. Bids started at twenty cents. Clara Ford's gun was almost certainly one of them. Inspector Stark, in auctioneer mode, said that "no one need go home without one." William Murdoch, that faithful attendant of Magistrates' Court, walked in late as a brown paper parcel was being auctioned off. He purchased it and later discovered it contained "ladies' apparel." One of the final items, "a black leather valise, which once belonged to Clara Ford, fetched 55 cents." This is the last trace of Clara in Toronto.

By then, Clara was long gone. She'd received only one work offer on her first day of freedom: exhibiting herself like a zoo animal at the Musée. She declined, but after failing to find tailoring work, and with her defence fund showing no sign of meeting her legal fees, she changed her mind. But the police had their petty revenge. Inspector Stark refused to release Clara's suit, so the offer went away.

Clara made another, more successful, attempt to replenish her defence fund through a public lecture at the Temperance Hall on May 21, three weeks after her acquittal. According to *The Telegram*, the event was a sold-out success: "All the belles and beaux of York Street were there." Clara sat at a table on a raised dais, "in black with white cuffs and her air of continual self-possession." Flora sat next to her but did not speak.

The night commenced with a musical program, and Clara didn't ascend the lectern until 9:00 p.m. She spoke for forty-five minutes, and according to *The Telegram,* "displayed ability that, with a little training, might be turned to very good account on the [stage]." The *Winnipeg Free Press* reported that she did not mention the Westwood trial, other than commencing by advising "the audience never to make confessions," which elicited laughter from the crowd. Instead, "She spoke of the pluck and perseverance necessary for a woman to make her way in the world," including her trip to Portage La Prairie on false representations and her return to Chicago penniless on a freight train. The trip lasted nineteen days, during which she had no food. She spoke highly of her treatment in Don Jail, thanked the audience for attending, and "paid tribute to *The Telegram* for its impartial course."

According to Hector Charlesworth, E.F.B. Johnston then sent for Clara and "told her that but for him she would be facing the gallows; and that if there were any remnants of decency left in her she would immediately leave Canada." Clara might have been run out of town by her lawyer. Or perhaps she simply, once again, went west to seek her fortune.

During Clara's arrest and trial, Sam T. Jack had also had a trying few months. In April 1895, his theatre manager, John Isham, had defected to form his own Black-owned company. He took more than half the players with him, including the Mallory Brothers and Madame Flowers. Isham announced that he would call his break-away troupe the "Creole Opera Company," but Jack threatened to sue. In May, Isham snarked to the newspapers that "due to inferior companies under the title Creole, I have decided to call my company The Royal Octoroons."

Jack had only two months to regroup before the new season started in late August. In typical fashion, he decided to double down. In July, he announced to the *Chicago Tribune* that he was going to put not one but three travelling shows on tour. Added to *The Creole Show* would be *Adamless Eden,* which would (if possible) have even more beautiful girls on stage, and there would be an action-adventure called *The Bull Fighter.* For all of this, Jack would need new performers, lots of them and quickly. Advertisements appeared: "Young, well-dressed, live, energetic up-to-date women: $10 a day to hustlers." On August 24, the new season of *The Creole Show* premiered in Chicago, "including Florence Hines ... at the newly remodelled Sam T. Jack Theatre." In the show's chorus, which featured "an amusing cakewalk and dancing contest," was Clara Ford.

Once again, Clara had moved south of the border to earn more money. Ten dollars a day was a strong lure to a woman who rarely earned seven dollars a week, and Clara wasn't getting tailoring jobs in Toronto. Contrary to Charlesworth's calumny, there is no evidence that Clara talked about the Westwood murder or even that Sam T. Jack capitalized on her notoriety. She wasn't a star player, merely another handsome face and pair of good legs in the chorus. However, Clara's acquittal had garnered international attention, and her presence in the company didn't go unnoticed. In September, the *Buffalo Evening News* sarcastically reported: "Clara Ford, the heroine of a recent Toronto murder trial, is now exhibiting herself in a variety show in Buffalo. Slowly but surely the stage is being elevated." Clara's good voice, attractive features, and ability to perform allowed her to take up a new trade.

Clara Ford disappears soon afterwards from newspapers and census and directory records. She and Flora likely changed their names. The last newspaper mention of Flora is immediately after the trial, when she was still living at Agnes McIntyre's shelter for "erring girls" on Agnes Street: "She is a quiet, tractable child, and only requires such care as Miss McIntyre's to turn out a bright young woman."

As for Clara, there is a small item in the November 12, 1896, issue of the *Massillon Independent*. In this town south of Cleveland, under "Local Happenings," a wedding was announced:

Coloured society circles – and white circles too, for that matter, will be interested in the culminating event in the remarkable career of Mr. Charles Jeremiah Crawford, the eminent cake walker, which occurred on Friday last. On this occasion Mr. Crawford was married to Miss Clara Ford, a beautiful mulatto, the marriage taking place at Mr. Crawford's present home, 116 Central Avenue, Cleveland. Miss Eva Bloodsaw was the bridesmaid and James Crawford the best man. A romantic and marvellous history is that of the bride, Miss Clara Ford, who is at present a member of the ballet in Sam T. Jack's Creole Company. Born and brought up alone on her father's plantation near New Orleans, she became her father's slave after the death of her mother, who didn't survive the birth. Her father was a native of England and her mother was a light coloured woman. She intends to remain with the company during the remainder of the season and return some time next spring to settle down.

Clara's final tall tale brought together themes central to her story. She'd reinvented herself once again, into an American, a Southerner. She gave herself the approved exoticism of a Creole heritage along with an English father, which might help explain her accent. Her story came from multiple nineteenth-century fictions that built up the trope of the Tragic Mulatto Girl, but this time the heroine had subverted the trope to give herself a happy ending.

Charles Jeremiah Crawford owned a tavern in Cleveland, and every summer he organized a cakewalk contest in Massillon. Clara didn't settle down with him at the end of the performing season in April 1897. Subsequent articles in the Massillon newspaper make it clear that Crawford was doing the cakewalk without her, and he remarried in 1906.

The very last sighting of Clara Ford was reported in *The Star* exactly three years after she was acquitted, in May 1898. "Clara Ford's Hard Luck" describes how the woman "who created so much excitement in a shooting case in Parkdale a few years ago" arrived in Oshawa, a town thirty miles east of Toronto. She didn't have money for a train ticket, so she asked the chief of police to provide her with funds to reach Brockville, 200 miles farther east. He compromised and gave her enough money to reach Belleville, which was 120 miles in the right direction.

Was Clara visiting one of her daughters? Was she looking for work in the small and almost entirely white town of Brockville? Sam T. Jack's touring season had ended in April. Did Clara rejoin the troupe in August under another name? What did Clara do next? With the intense media interest now gone, we'll never know. We're forced to say farewell to Clara at Oshawa Station, where she brazened her way onto another train, heading halfway to where she wanted to go.

CLARA,
ARMED

Anique Jordan's *arming by clara*, 2017

Just as John A. Macdonald dominated Canada's development as a nation in the late nineteenth century, William Lyon Mackenzie King set the tone for the next half century of its social and political evolution. Grandson of William Lyon Mackenzie, reformer and Toronto's first mayor, King was the longest-serving Canadian prime minister, leading a Liberal government from 1920 to 1930 and from 1935 to 1948.

In late 1897, King, then a twenty-three-year-old journalist, wrote a two-part feature on "The Foreigners of Toronto" for the *Mail and Empire*. "Of the 'great city' problems," he began, "there is none ... as complex as the difficulties that arise from the composite nature of their populations and the relations of these foreign elements to the social, industrial and civic life." While Canadian cities had escaped the worst depredations visited on US cities such as Chicago and New York, a sizeable "percentage of these foreigners have been anything but a desirable class, and have after their arrival taken up residence in the poorer sections of the city, thereby aiding in the development, if not the creation of dangerous slums."

Not all foreigners were born equal, of course. German immigrants, such as Christian Dorenwend's father, Hildebert, were judged "thrifty ... healthy and law abiding." Although Jews such as Samuel Barnett had an unfortunate tendency to "congregate in York Street and the south side of St. John's Ward ... in back lanes," at least they had a respect for education, and almost "no heavy drinking or crime."

King characterized French Canadians and Black people as foreigners, even though, by his own admission, almost all had been born in Canada. His perspective was that they hadn't assimilated into Toronto's civic culture: they were linguistically, in one case, and visibly, in the other, "different." He estimated the "coloured population" at eight hundred, a diminishing proportion of the city's population since the high-water mark in the 1840s. Although "concentrated in St. John's Ward," some had moved to suburbs "because of cheaper rents and better sanitary conditions." King reported that Black Torontonians "complain it is difficult for them to secure the positions for which they are desirous and capable of filling, and that they have been forced to leave" for the United States, "where their labour and ability seems to be more appreciated." Of those who remained, almost a third were without steady employment, and many others were trapped in a narrow employment ghetto. If they were men, they were working as "Pullman porters ... barbers, letter carriers, waiters and restaurant keepers." If they were women, they were working as domestic servants, laundresses, or seamstresses. Despite being discriminated against in the labour market, they were, according to King, "generally regarded as peaceable citizens." His conclusion: "A few become troublesome at times, but as a rule, the Negro is inclined to be friendly to his neighbours, and congenial to those he meets. They take earnestly to education and are fond of reading."

This is the voice of George Brown's *Globe*, of *The Telegram*, and of the Liberal Party. This is a portrait of Good Negro Citizens in their proper subservient place, a remnant of the time when Canada served as a temporary, contingent place of refuge. The dominant culture in Toronto was rarely overtly or violently racist toward its Black minority, despite John A. Macdonald's reminder that lynching might be necessary if the law did not control Black men. Instead, Toronto's racism in the late nineteenth century was shabbier, based in the assumed, self-satisfied superiority of the white

British Protestant majority. There was economic mobility for a few exemplars and limitations for the rest. For Black women such as Clara Ford, racism meant constant visibility, limited economic opportunity, a miasma of everyday harassment and violence, discrimination by police and courts, and the assumption of sexual availability.

By the late 1890s, when Clara Ford left Toronto, the social cleansing of the Ward, and York Street in particular, was well underway. There was a panic about the fire and health risks of houses "in hailing distance" of the new city hall, erected on top of Clara's childhood home on Queen Street West. After ten years of construction, the massive gothic revival building opened in 1899. The wooden houses in the area were not maintained. Speculators were simply waiting for the right time to demolish them to capitalize on the land value underneath. The Louisa Street School and the House of Industry made way for Eaton's warehouses and the Toronto General Hospital. York Street, in the shadow of the Osgoode Hall law courts, became too valuable for working-class Black people such as Chloe Dorsey to live there. After sixty years, she and her family moved to Seaton Village, and her legacy was erased from Toronto the Good.

Parkdale, too, was losing its lustre as the Flowery Suburb. By the early twentieth century, Rosedale was the firm favourite of rich families such as the Westwoods, who wanted to be well away from mixed land use and social diversity. More of Parkdale's larger houses had been converted to rooming houses, although Lakeside Hall remained a single-family dwelling until it was demolished for the Gardiner Expressway in the 1950s. By then, South Parkdale was considered a polyglot slum. The grand houses on Jameson Avenue had been torn down for apartment buildings.

One by one, the key people in Clara's life and trial began to exit the stage. William Murdoch was the first actor to take his bow, and in a most spectacular manner. On Dominion Day, 1897, not long after he'd mistakenly bought some ladies' undergarments at the police auction, he went lawn bowling and then to a bar with a friend. Suitably fortified, the two men began fencing with their umbrellas, and Murdoch stumbled. The point of his friend's umbrella entered four inches into his eye. Murdoch refused to go to hospital, but once home, he began to vomit blood. By the time an ambulance was called, it was too late.

If Libby Black is the same person as Lizzie Smith, she, too, met with a newsworthy end, dying after a hit-and-run by a female cyclist at the corner of Carlton and Sherbourne. At the inquest, held in June 1899, the medical examiner said she had advanced heart disease but that her death had been accelerated by an unknown yet pernicious menace in bloomers.

Gus Clark continued his slow slide into the abyss. Released from his six-month sentence for stealing from his mother, he was found sleeping in a shed in the rear of Spencer Street in Parkdale and was picked up for vagrancy in mid-June 1895. By July, he'd been sentenced to a year in Central Prison for burglary. In January 1897, a "George" Clark was in hospital. After a drunken bender at his mother's tavern, he'd swallowed a dose of strychnine. Later that year, Clark again stole from the tavern and received an eighteen-month prison sentence. In 1901, he was once again in Central Prison; shortly thereafter, he disappeared.

Christian Dorenwend and his wife, Carrie, also fade from the historical record around this time, after the vibrator emporium failed.

Clark's mother, Catherine, had a happier fate. She continued to live with her younger children in the CPR hotel on Yonge Street, not far from the current Toronto Reference Library, where much of the research for this book was undertaken. As part of a crackdown on health and morality infractions, she was given two months to sell her licence in April 1906, and she immediately transferred ownership of the tavern to her son Cass. She died above the tavern in 1910, aged sixty.

Chloe Dorsey lived ten more years after the trial. She died of dementia in 1906, at the age of seventy-six. Mary Crosier also lived a long life: she died at the age of eighty-seven in 1931. Charles Ingles continued as St. Mark's pastor until shortly before his death in 1930, at the age of seventy-four.

Frank Westwood's postmortem indicated that he'd been strong and healthy up to the point of being shot, and his family were long-lived advertisements for temperance. The Westwoods continued to live in Rosedale. Benjamin Westwood died two months before his ninetieth birthday, in 1935. Clara Westwood died two years later, at the age of eighty-eight. Bert Westwood, a successful businessman and active member of his country club, lived to be ninety-three, and Emily Westwood Kennedy also made it to the age of ninety-three, dying in 1975. William Westwood is more of a mystery. After marrying in 1912, he and his wife, Georgina, moved to St. Petersburg, Florida, where he appears to have become estranged from his family. His date of death is unknown.

Henry Reburn, E.F.B. Johnston, and Hartley Dewart were all remembered for the Clara Ford case when they died, all between 1919 and 1922. When Reburn retired, he'd reached the rank of inspector, and he'd served more than forty years on the force, all without one disciplinary action. Clara Ford was probably his most famous arrest, but the jury's decision didn't appear to harm his career. Dewart later found himself on the other side in a trial about "wounded womanhood" when he defended Carrie Davies, a domestic servant who'd killed her employer, the industrial heir Charles Massey, when he tried to sexually assault her in 1915. Charley Slemin eventually became a police chief in Brantford, but not before he crossed paths with E.F.B. Johnston in another racially charged case.

Of the 118 documented cases of rape prosecuted in Toronto and York County in the fifty years between 1880 and 1930, only one matched the scenario described by John A. Macdonald as "frequent" – that of a Black man accused of raping a white woman. This was the case of David Hawes, a porter for Canadian Pacific Rail, who was accused in July 1901 of luring a seventeen-year-old servant named Louise Lebar into a deserted car at Union Station and assaulting her. Despite the presence of signifiers that would have doomed other contemporary rape complaints (no cries for help, no signs of struggle, the complainant had been seen chatting in a friendly manner with the defendant before the crime), Hawes was convicted and sentenced to ten years at Kingston Penitentiary in November 1901. The judge lamented that the death penalty was no longer mandatory in cases of rape, and the *Toronto News* sneered that Hawes was lucky to live in Canada, where lynchings didn't occur. Toronto's racial tolerance was once again trumpeted by setting a low bar for itself. Detective Slemin prepared the case, and this time, Johnston's legal abilities couldn't help the defendant.

Less than a year later, there was another rape case in the Toronto court, one barely mentioned in the papers. In August 1902, Arthur Simonski, the twenty-five-year-old son of a middle-class Jewish family, was accused of "a serious crime" by a fifteen-year-old "mulatto girl" named Annie Mitchell, who claimed "to be the daughter of Clara Ford." Mitchell, a resident of the Girls' Home in 1901, was working as a servant for Simonski's parents at the time. In October, Simonski was found guilty of rape (a term used in the Hawes case but replaced with the euphemism "serious crime" in Simonski's case) and sentenced to nine months in Central Prison. Six weeks later, he was pardoned and released. Mitchell gave birth to a son named George in March 1903; no father is named on the birth certificate. By 1909, Arthur Simonski was a successful merchant on College Street, and Annie and her son, like her sister and mother, had disappeared from the historical record.

By 1908, when *The Star* ran a feature on the Westwood murder, newspapers had begun to transform Clara Ford from a person into a legend, and her story has continued to attract attention. In the

1920s, the two baroque racists George Denison and Hector Charlesworth reflected on their small parts in the case. In *Recollections of a Police Magistrate,* Denison recounts (complete with "minstrel show" spelling and grammar) tales of "the negro element ... formerly very large [although] most seem to have drifted southward ... [They were] a source of amusement in court because of their many peculiarities." Clara appears in the book as an exemplar of Negro Lawlessness. Denison recollects that when the Westwood investigation came before him in November 1894, "Clara said she didn't mind [Frank's] insult at the time because young people were always teasing her about her colour." In Denison's rendering, the newspapers had said terrible things about the police during the trial, and so she was acquitted.

Hector Charlesworth's memoir was both more detailed and less accurate, yet it became the go-to source for the story of the murder and trial. There are at least a dozen falsehoods in his three-page treatment of the case, which goes like this. Clara, frustrated in her sexual desire for Frank (1), procured a set of men's clothes to shoot him (2). On his deathbed, Frank described a "slender young man" as the suspect (3), and the shooting was heard by some schooners on the bay (4). When Charlesworth wrote Arthur Conan Doyle, the murder had been a mystery for "some months" (5) (instead of one week). Fortunately, Clara "boasted to a pickpocket friend of hers," Gus Clark (6 and 7), who then reported it to the police (8). When arrested, Clara "falsely traduced the victim" by claiming sexual assault. She would have been convicted if B.B. Osler's wife hadn't died just before he made his final address to the jury (9). Following the acquittal, Charlesworth saw Clara "proceed in a carriage through the streets followed by a cheering throng [(10)], and in gratitude, she asked the jurors to supper at the negro restaurant where she had boarded" (11). Then Clara travelled though the western states bragging about killing a man (12).

These lies have been repeated for 125 years.

The third account written in the mid-1920s was by Albert Hassard, as part of a series on famous Canadian trials. Hassard points out (several times) that Clara was "not of our race" and contends that she was treated carefully because of it. He admires Dewart's summing up, calling him "dispassionate and poetic, scholarly and dignified." The chapter has a scent of nostalgia for a world being disrupted by women such as Clara, who were "brazen [in] commencing to appropriate to themselves the garments of the male sex." Hassard's verdict on the trial has a simple and not inaccurate moral: "The actor left surviving tells the tale." This was less true for Clara than it was for Denison and Charlesworth, who continued their racist and corrupt lives in Toronto long after Clara was forced out. In 1931, Stewart Wallace published a similar account. In Hassard's and Wallace's accounts, Clara is once again a Monster who disrupts Toronto's pristine Eden of civility and charm.

In the 1940s, there were two accounts of the trial by lawyers who focused on Clara's interactions with the police and concluded, as the jury appears to have done, that her confession should have been set aside. Edwin C. Guillet's self-published nineteen-page folio *The Shooting of Frank Westwood* repeats Charlesworth's canard that "Clara was infatuated with Frank and he spurned her." But Guillet also points out that Clara may have needed to carry a revolver to protect herself in an unsafe part of the city, by which he means the Ward, not Parkdale. Guillet concludes that even if she shot Frank, the killing may have been closer to manslaughter than murder. Thus, "to have hanged Clara Ford would have been a greater miscarriage of justice than her acquittal; and it certainly seems that, however guilty she was, her confession was extorted from her by high-pressure methods." Similarly, a legal pundit named J.V. McAree argued in the *Globe and Mail* that perhaps confessions should be barred from testimony, given the propensity for police, at least in the United States, to torture them out of prisoners. He used the Clara Ford case as an example of juries being hesitant about "alleged confessions" that may have been forced.

A 1971 book about by Irish author Peter Costello on Arthur Conan Doyle as a "detective" and "investigator" contends that Clara, infatuated with Frank, "out of jealousy ... shot him." Costello then repeats the Charlesworth lie that she "boasted [of the murder] to a pickpocket, who turned her in." He goes off the deep end when he contends that Clara may have been inspired by Irene Adler's cross-dressing, continuing that "a murder in travesty [that is, cross-dressing] became a travesty in justice." He concludes: "As a man of chivalry, [Conan Doyle] would have hated Frank Westwood for insulting a black woman, but the murder appears to have arisen from a personal obsession of a sexual nature, too obscene for the kind of popular fiction [he] was obliged to write."

Charlesworth's lies continue to dominate a 1996 version of the case by *Toronto Star* columnist Frank Jones (who also wrote about the case in 1989). Jones repeats the falsehoods that Clara was turned in by a pickpocket friend and that she toured the United States after the trial bragging about the murder. Jones compares Clara's trial with that of O.J. Simpson and ends by wondering whether Simpson would brag about killing his wife and her friend (Simpson did; Clara didn't). According to a 2011 online account by local historian and genealogist Bill Gladstone, who draws his recital of the case from *The World*, Clara was a straight-shooting, hard-drinking mama who lived at "Mamie Dorsay's," which sounds like a Wild West saloon. The "Toronto Then and Now" website, run by Richard Fiennes-Clinton, has a wonderfully illustrated but woefully inaccurate 2015 account that describes Gus Clark as a stone hooker and contends that Flora McKay was eight years old at the time of the murder. Once again, Chloe Dorsey is confused with her daughter Mamie; contemporary newspaper nonsense such as "she had been charged for impersonating a choir boy, a police constable, and a male professor" is repeated seriously; and there is the Jezebel-tinged allegation that "Clara Ford invited members of the jury – the all-male jury – back to the boarding house where she was staying, for 'dinner and entertainment.'"

A book about Clara's trial was published in 2005. Patrick Brode, a legal historian, provides a good overview of the judicial and media context in which Clara was acquitted. But once again Gus Clark is dismissed as a "peculiar" low-life friend of Clara's. By doing so, he not only ignores a fascinating suspect, but he also misreads Clara's character. The McKay-Ford household is described as living behind the Salvation Army mission, and the Clarks are erased from the story. Most serious, in terms of understanding the case, is the claim that Clara had been arrested by 9:00 p.m. and that she refused the legal counsel offered by Reburn the next day because of "pride." As for motive, Brode only offers this: whether it was "a clumsy attempt at rape or an adolescent comment on her mannish ways, it was enough to propel her (with the aid of a little whiskey) to carry out the deed on October 6."

There are few accounts of Clara's trial by women, and none (including this book) by Black women. A 1980 play *Clara* by francophone writer Marcelle McGibbon was performed in the former Adelaide Street courthouse, an appropriate setting if ever there was one. That play, essentially a performance of the transcript of the inquest and trial, leaves the viewer with questions rather than answers, including whether Frank slept with his sister-in-law, Maggie, leading to his older brother taking revenge, an unlikely theory that was dropped almost as soon as it was bruited in October 1894. Carolyn Strange wrote an article in 2003 comparing the cases of Clara Ford and Carrie Davies in relation to notions of judicial "chivalry" toward "wounded womanhood."

The most recent allusion to Clara Ford is by artist Anique Jordan. In 2017, as part of an exhibit focused on diversity in Toronto's "ethnoburbs," Jordan created a set of twelve-foot corrugated iron sculptures to depict Clara's various representations.

One of the figure's hands is relaxed, another clenched, as though around a gun. Jordan describes her work as an

> armed and armoured monument commemorating the life of Clara Ford and the lives of Black bodies, whose survival is often read as threatening or encoded in a grammar of militancy. *arming by clara* is inspired by the story of Clara Ford, a Black, Toronto-born person accused in 1895 of murdering a wealthy white man who assaulted her. Known for wearing men's clothing and carrying a loaded revolver, Clara appeared in court in a Victorian dress, ultimately leading to her acquittal as the jury imagined no woman, much less a Black one, could perform a crime as lethal as murder. Clara went on to join Sam T. Jacks Creoles, the first all-Black woman burlesque company in the United States. I am very interested in the links between her survival and my own haunting. Much of what haunts me is a response to the judicial system, incarceration, slavery, colonialism and the ways we experience and resist these violences in our daily lives and through intimate relationships. What haunts me is a fear of lost freedom.
>
> This is a monument to Black bodies, negated, some thrice or four times, which carry with them the subconscious awareness that stepping outside the threshold of "home" and maintaining and/or protecting freedom means arming oneself psychically, emotionally, physically, spiritually. It means we have to learn from what haunts us.
>
> Like the narratives embedded in the coloured figures, the things we hold onto that enable this survival are not accessible to everyone, nor are they commodifiable or even material; they are intimate moments: teachings from a parent, blood memory and the encoded lessons in cyphers, movements, gestures and rhythms. The head of the V, where viewers are invited to stand to complete the

formation, is a site of negotiation, of sovereign power and of witnessing, or releasing an armour, which is often and necessarily invisible.

This book is an attempt to extricate Clara's life from 125 years of societal coding intended to determine the "place" of a Black woman in the Canadian city. There is no way to know exactly what happened on or before October 6, 1894, between Frank Westwood and Clara Ford. Frank's description of his assailant – a medium-sized, relatively heavy-set, middle-aged and moustached man in a dark overcoat and fedora – is a poor fit with the two most likely suspects. There is no photograph or good description of Gus Clark, but he wasn't middle-aged, and he was clean-shaven. On the other hand, no man's overcoat or a false moustache were ever found in Clara's possession, and it's more likely that Clark rather than Clara fit the description of a white man wearing a dark overcoat.

Clark possibly shot Frank because Frank had prevented a boat-house burglary four weeks earlier. During that burglary, Clark threatened to shoot two stone hookers, and he almost certainly had a gun. Clark may have been inebriated the night Frank was shot, the same night of his brother's funeral, to which he was seemingly not invited. Perhaps he was in the mood to settle a score or prevent another arrest for burglary. Frank may have known details about Clark's break-in at the Parkdale Methodist Church, which occurred in late September 1894; thus, he mumbled "we were only fooling in the hall." I am unconvinced that "mum's the word" refers to a desire by Frank to not falsely accuse Clark.

Gus Clark had motive, opportunity, and means. If the police ever checked on his inexplicable alibi that he'd been asleep in his employer's home, instead of comforting his family after Percy's funeral or getting drunk, no explanation was ever provided in Toronto's seven newspapers. While none of Clark's multitudinous crimes appear to have involved violence against others, he certainly threatened violence (and attempted suicide a year later). It is hard not to conclude that Slemin and the rest of the Toronto Police gave the first, obvious, suspect every protection and that Benjamin Westwood was also anxious to deny any links between his son and Clark. All that Benjamin had left of his son was Frank's respectable reputation. Erasing Gus Clark as a suspect helped preserve that reputation.

Three staff people from the Opera House testified as to Clara's presence on Saturday night. It's possible she was there (with or without Flora) and left early (either to get Flora back to her employer or herself back to the Dorseys before 11:00 p.m.). That is the alibi supported by Chloe Dorsey, her daughter Mamie, and Eliza Reid. Clara's testimony at her trial may have been substantively correct – that she was innocent and railroaded by the police. There are certainly lies in her testimony (that she and Frank never spoke is a good example), but the most important elements might be true.

On the other hand, Clara provided a detailed and believable confession, albeit under duress. *The Telegram* was right: it made no sense for Clara to follow the dark and dangerous shoreline when she could have made a shortcut through the Exhibition Grounds or walked back along King Street after retrieving her skirt. It's possible the police got this detail wrong and decided that any attack on their version of her confession could not be tolerated. She could have hidden a pair of trousers and an overcoat before she visited the Crosiers and changed her clothes in a secluded spot near the Exhibition dock. It's also possible that Clara never changed into men's clothes, that Frank recognized her and protected her because of a guilty conscience or to protect his family's reputation, just as *The Globe* said soon after Clara's arrest.

I find the rest of Clara's confessed account of the night of October 6, 1894, eminently believable – that she visited the Crosiers in a clumsy attempt to manufacture an alibi and then walked to Parkdale along a route she knew well from her Sunday visits, that she entered the Westwood residence through a hole in the fence and then watched and waited for Frank and his mother to finish their conversation, that she rang the doorbell knowing that Frank would answer, that she shot him before he recognized her, and that she arrived back at the Dorseys before midnight. When the police visited Flora on November 20, it was simply to obtain Clara's address. Perhaps they intimidated her into providing an alibi for her mother, which she then immediately denied. But successfully bullying five members of the Crosier family into lying on the stand twice is less believable, especially given the amateur nature of Libby Black's suborned perjury. The Toronto police were simply not that good at railroading witnesses.

The Crosiers were consistent in their story – that Clara had arrived at their home in distress at around 8:00 p.m. on the night of the shooting and that she'd had her gun and mentioned going to Parkdale to fetch Flora (who was living downtown) before going to a show that had already started (as Mary Crosier pointed out). Harriet Phyall had no reason to lie that Flora had visited her on Saturday at 8:30 p.m. to say that Clara hadn't shown up for their scheduled date to see *The Black Crook*. The Dorseys' restaurant might well have been open until midnight on the Saturday Frank was shot, and Clara could have walked back from Parkdale in the hour after he was shot at 10:50 p.m.

Regardless of its truth, Clara's confession should never have been allowed in court. The police acted in a manner contrary to the contemporary rules for detaining and questioning suspects. I do not doubt that Reburn used a mixture of lying, cajoling, and bullying over at least six hours to get a confession, without allowing Clara to have a friend with her or seek legal counsel.

But I still find myself wondering why. I have not read a single account – other than *The Globe*'s on November 22, 1894, and Anique Jordan's 125 years later – that takes Clara's account of being sexually assaulted by Frank seriously. Clara repudiated her story afterwards. Many women repudiate their charges of sexual assault to this day, in the sound belief that they will never achieve justice through the law. I certainly believe that Frank could have tried to rape Clara, or that he actually raped her. It's extremely implausible that they were engaged in a consensual affair, just as it's plausible that Frank hated her enough to rape her.

I'll ask a slightly different question. If Clara was sexually assaulted by Frank in July or August of 1894, as she stated in her "alleged confession," why wait until October 6 to take her revenge?

Dozens of Clara's friends and acquaintances testified that she was quick to anger when harassed or assaulted. Punching a fellow streetcar passenger who made racial slurs, threatening intruders in her room at the Dorseys, going to the police when she wasn't paid by an employer ... all of these incidents were grossly exaggerated by the newspapers, but the stories, at their base, appear to be true. The Angry Black Woman is a trope, but Clara had plenty of legitimate reasons for occasional rage. However, there is little evidence to suggest that she was a careful plotter or a person who brooded for months before acting. When Clara got angry, people found out soon enough. The only temporally proximate motive for a violent reaction against Frank was the late August article in *The Telegram* intimating that she would be arrested for wearing men's clothes. This does not seem to me to be an adequate motive for murder, even if layered onto years of racial harassment by Frank and his family, up to and including the loss of her family's home in early 1892 and sexual assault in the summer of 1894.

The eight-to-twelve-week period between the alleged sexual assault and the murder does suggest the time it would take for a pregnancy to become apparent. If Clara got pregnant through being raped by Frank, it would take a massive cover-up to hide a miscarriage or a birth in the Don Jail (reporters visited in January and March 1895).

Let me suggest an alternative scenario: that Frank got Flora pregnant, either through "seduction" or rape, and that Clara, as an aggrieved parent, invoked "the unwritten law" and shot him in revenge. Flora's domicile and employment, between early 1893 and her starting work in Cabbagetown in late summer 1894, are unknown. However, Harriet Phyall said Flora worked for her family when they were caretakers of the Magann house, just to the west of Lakeside Hall on the Parkdale waterfront. It's possible Flora continued to work in Parkdale as a servant after Clara left the suburb in early 1893.

On Friday, October 5, both Clara and Flora agreed that Clara had visited Flora's workplace. They made plans to go to the theatre together the following night. There is no reason to doubt Flora and Clara on the fact of this meeting or to doubt Flora's account of waiting at the street corner from 7:30 to 8:15 p.m. the following night, after which she then walked to the Phyalls' boarding house, a story corroborated by Harriet Phyall.

What else did Clara and Flora discuss that Friday? Perhaps something that got Clara so upset she got a little drunk the next night, behaviour that, according to Mary Crosier and Samuel Barnett, was unusual; something that angered Clara so much that instead of meeting with her daughter, she decided to take her gun and confront Frank – Frank, who his peers said was prone to entanglements with girls, Frank, who answered the door on the night of his shooting without his mother or any other member of the household hearing the doorbell. Had Frank agreed to meet Clara that night at his home (after all, Clara and Frank, despite their different social standing, worked one block from one another in downtown Toronto and both were at work on Saturday) to discuss what newspapers at the time described as a common scenario, a betrayed young girl with an angry parent seeking redress? Did Clara write him a note that Saturday asking to meet him that night? Did Frank lie when he described his assailant?

Is it possible that Flora was pregnant? Early October, two or three months after an assault near the boathouse in July or August of 1894, is when fourteen-year-old Flora might have had to mention a sexual encounter to Clara, if she was showing signs of pregnancy. Two of Flora's employers said that Clara was anxious that Flora stay at home at night and be under constant supervision. Flora left the Phyalls after "some words" in December 1894. She was next mentioned as living in a home for "erring girls," the police having "hidden her" throughout winter and spring 1895.

It's impossible to track information on Clara's, Flora's, or Annie's birth, let alone a child born in the Burnside Lying-In Hospital (used by most indigent women unable to hire a midwife) in March or April 1895, which would have been nine months after an alleged boathouse incident in July or August 1894. Flora disappears from news, directory, and census records immediately after the trial. It's possible the fifteen-year-old girl abandoned a baby in an orphanage, if she got pregnant and carried to term. Miscarriage is also a possibility. Since she was under supervision, abortion or infanticide is less likely.

Seduction or rape was an all-too-common story for working-class girls and women, as it was for Flora's fifteen-year-old sister, Annie, a few years later. Flora's and Annie's births appear to have been the result of Clara being betrayed, if not raped, by white men who didn't provide any financial support for their children. In fact, there are three generations of bad fathers – men who appear to have done little other than contribute their sperm – in the McKay-Ford-Mitchell family. If Clara benefitted from chivalry during her trial, she certainly felt its obverse: constant and crushing betrayal by men in her life. "Just fooling around in the hall [or the boat-house]," that phrase that Frank muttered on his deathbed, generally had no lasting consequences for respectable white boys. For girls such as Sadie Lavelle, it was frequently a death sentence. Perhaps it carried a death sentence for Frank as well.

We know about Clara's life because of the murder of Frank Westwood. The corollary is also true: what we know about Clara has been shaped by the fact that we know her as a putative murderer. Any information we have about Clara is coloured by the hypocrisies and prejudices, the things said and, more importantly, never brought out into the open, at least in the nineteenth century. The media of the time rarely looked beyond a handy set of tropes to judge her. Even today, most people who write about Clara Ford assume she wasn't her mother's biological daughter, that she murdered Frank Westwood because of jealousy or some irrational overreaction to a newspaper article, and that she used her mighty Black sexual charisma to seduce jury members – or to make them feel sorry for a Tragic Mulatto Girl. While we can now talk openly about Flora being Clara's daughter, no one mentions Annie or her fate.

Hector Charlesworth said – and many contemporary writers repeat – that after the murder, and then after the trial, Clara went around shamelessly bragging that she murdered Frank Westwood. I hope it's clear by now that this is untrue. Another Charlesworth lie – that she was betrayed by a pickpocket whom she told about the murder – covered up the much more complex and fascinating story of Gus Clark, an alcoholic, middle-class failure jealous of Clara's close relationship with his mother and justifiably fearful of being arrested for the murder.

Clara Ford has been described as a delusional or, at best, as an eccentric puppet at the trial, expertly handled by a brilliant lawyer. But, except for the period immediately after her arrest, Clara controlled her own destiny and wrote her own narrative, to the extent that she could under desperate circumstances. She was eminently sane.

The Clara who emerges from the historical record is an intelligent, funny, talented, strong survivor. She told tall tales about herself for three reasons: to amuse her friends and people she wished to impress, to deflect intrusive questions, and to save her own life. She reacted strongly to the everyday violence she was subjected to, in a way that was considered unacceptable for a Black woman of her time and is scarcely more acceptable today. She might have murdered a privileged young man who probably would have lived a long and prosperous life and who might, like many other men then and now, have been a rapist.

As for Clara's times, while the past may be a distant country, in some respects it's only a short stroll away. Nineteenth-century Toronto saw itself as a homogenous and unified city, with a distinct persona: Toronto the Good. Members of the city's elite were certain that Toronto was at the vanguard of a new Canadian identity, one that erased the land rights and even the existence of Indigenous peoples and reviled Black people when they weren't being used to demonstrate the moral superiority of Canada. The most powerful white men were unabashedly colonialist, racist, and sexist. Institutions – the media, schools, welfare agencies, the police, the law, and the courts – were dedicated to perpetuating an unjust economic and social order and purifying Toronto's working-class majority into Good Citizens. The elite shaped the lives of low-income and racialized women and men through moral crusades and vicious policing to check the supposedly chronic bad behaviour of the underclass: substance use, sex work, and sleeping and loitering in public spaces. Everyday violence was ignored and erased, and it was nearly impossible to get justice for rape or racial harassment. Cultural diversity was feared. Economic inequality was stark, and female heads of households found it almost impossible to survive on wages that forced a choice between paying the rent and feeding their families. They were shamed if they sought succour from an overburdened and inadequate welfare system. Much has changed in 125 years. Too much has not.

Twenty years ago, Clara's words leaped out from old newspaper clippings and captured my imagination. I fell a little in love with her then. I felt the need to explore her world, to the extent that I could from the distances of time and social inequality. Clara Ford demands to be heard. For a short period in late 1894 and early 1895, she shocked a city and exposed injustice. Then she went off to continue her life. Clara leaves us behind as the curtain falls, to work out what we think happened, and why it still matters.

ACKNOWLEDGMENTS

What gives me the right to tell Clara Ford's story? Honestly? Nothing. I am a white, cisgendered, heterosexual woman whose only qualification is the privilege of time to research and write.

When I was young, my maternal grandmother used to tell me stories of her maternal grandfather, who escaped from being a child soldier during the Crimean War. There is so much I do not know about Clara's life after her trial, but I highly suspect that she didn't get a chance to tell her grandchildren her stories. This, I think, is the greatest privilege I have: an existential security born of knowing where I come from and being able to hand down stories from my ancestors. Clara had a different ancestry from me, one that constrained her life choices. (My grandmother, born the year of Clara's trial, worked as a tailor. Unlike Clara, she eventually borrowed money to buy her own house and clothing store, which remains in Cornwall, Ontario, to this day.) I acknowledge that I may have gotten quite a bit wrong about Clara, ranging from pronouns to motivations.

I first read historical newspaper articles about Clara in 2001 while I was researching social conditions, neighbourhood transitions, and housing policy in relation to my PhD thesis research on Parkdale, Toronto. My wonderful supervisor, Richard Harris, gave me the confidence twenty years ago to write history the way I wanted to read it. I waited two decades for someone else to tell Clara's story right. Then I decided to leave academe. Thank you to the University of Melbourne's Faculty of Architecture, Building and Planning for a year's research leave at the end of my time there in 2018–19. They knew the scholarly publications that would result (and did), but I also told them from the first that the "Clara book" took precedence.

Writing about Clara Ford's life would have been impossible if not for several people. Marc Côté and John Pugsley were the original sounding boards for my rehashing of what I remembered from the newspapers, and they hosted me in Toronto for several weeks while I tracked down the originals. My brother Stephen Whitzman let me borrow his Toronto Public Library card and was my go-to for legal questions. I want to thank the Toronto Reference Library and its magnificent staff: their access to digitized *Globe* and *Star* articles, obscure local history books, and street directories were invaluable, as much of my research was done while I lived in Australia. When I returned to Toronto and sat day after day reading old newspapers on microfiche, they took good care of me. FamilySearch is an easy-to-use and free genealogical research tool, much better than better-known commercial alternatives. Toronto City Archives did their usual fantastic job in allowing me easy access to assessment records, at least until COVID-19 shut everything down.

The University of Ottawa – and in particular Professor Marie-Josée Massicotte, the director of the Institute for Feminist and Gender Studies – offered a welcoming landing pad as I transitioned from academic to policy research and from Australia to Canada. I've been incredibly fortunate over the past two years to work with the greatest group of supportive and powerful feminist housing-policy researchers and advocates I could imagine: Janice Abbott, Khulud Baig, Michele Biss, Marie-Eve Desroches, Leilani Farha, Alexandra Flynn, Penny Gurstein, Kaite Burkholder Harris, Hajar Masoud, Alex Nelson, Emily Paradis, Margaret Pfoh, Sahar Raza, Leila Sarangi, and Kaitlin Schwan. The UBC Housing Research Collaborative gang, including Craig E. Jones, Andrés Penaloza, Katrina Tarnawsky, and Mikayla Tinsley, have been tremendous fun to plot with in my day job. I am thankful to Zoom technology for allowing me to telecommute to Vancouver. I am grateful to the Canada Mortgage and Housing Corporation for funding my housing research.

Thank you to Melissa Pitts and James McNevin from UBC Press/On Point Press, who enthused about this manuscript, so different from my thesis-into-book about Parkdale they published thirteen years ago. Lesley Erickson provided me with excellent editing advice as I painfully learned the difference between academic and popular history prose. My thanks also go to the team at On Point Press – Katrina Petrik, Carmen Tiampo, Laraine Coates, and Kerry Kilmartin – for their speedy and responsive work in producing and marketing the book.

The last two years have been trying. My husband, David, and I returned to Canada and moved to a city we barely knew to take care of my mother in her final illness. My mother's final year was made infinitely more difficult because of a worldwide pandemic layered on top of society's contempt for frail old people. I want to thank those long-time friends and family who helped me feel supported and loved: sister (in-law) Jane Hunt and cousins Paula and Manny Agulnik in Ottawa; Cynthia Davis and cousins Jeffrey Kastner, Karen Ocana, and Nancy Breitman in Montreal; Andrea Cook in Stratford (and Melbourne, Australia); and Jennifer Ramsay and Lin McInnis in Toronto. Mary Fairhurst Breen's year in Ottawa allowed for the reconnection of an old friendship, and her reinvention as a successful author provided inspiration. My Hintonburg Read Whatever Book Club buddies (particularly Kayleigh Chaston-Vickers, Jo-Anne Guimond, and In-Leng Ng) and my Or Haneshamah circle (particularly Rabbi Liz Bolton, Elijah Klassen, Jean Hansen, and Diana Ralph) provided social warmth in our new city. My Melbourne friends (especially Shakira Hussein and Sol Salbe) didn't let distance get in the way of a good friendship.

Above all and always, my love and gratitude go to my family. My husband, David Hunt, has always been my biggest supporter as well as a fellow travelling companion in the Wandering Jew reinvention of our thirty-six years together. Simon Hunt and Sydney Schneider and Molly Hunt and Lewis Wiegand are amazing adults. I've learned so much from my children. Basically, I am grateful to everyone who has let me blather on about this book over the years.

NOTES AND
FURTHER READING

I am used to writing academic books and articles where I can give introductory credit to the authors who inspired me. I acknowledge that I am awkwardly perched on the shoulders of giants in telling Clara's story. Darlene Hine, in a metaphor I use, has spent a lifetime introducing previously forgotten Black actors onto "history's centre stage, until recently a small proscenium occupied by privileged white men": see *Hine Sight: Black Women and the Reconstruction of American History* (Bloomington: Indiana University Press, 2004), xxiii. In Canada, Mariana Valverde has written about the white Protestant social reformers who linked sexual health, racial purity, and the eradication of slums to regulate the lives of people living in the rapidly growing cities of English Canada: see *The Age of Light, Soap and Water: Moral Reform in English Canada, 1885–1925* (Toronto: McClelland and Stewart, 1991). Carolyn Strange has described the moral panic that accompanied the rapid entry into the workforce of young women, who were perceived to be a threat to social norms: see *Toronto's Girl Problem: The Perils and Pleasures of the City, 1880–1930* (Toronto: University of Toronto Press, 1995). Constance Backhouse and Barrington Walker have focused on the justice system to gain insight into both the lives and the systemic oppression faced by women and Black people in Canada, respectively: see Backhouse, *Petticoats and Prejudice: Women and Law in Nineteenth-Century Canada* (Toronto: Women's Press, 1991) and Walker, *Race on Trial: Black Defendants in Ontario's Criminal Courts, 1858–1958* (Toronto: University of Toronto Press, 2010). Robyn Maynard has traced the links between two centuries of Black slavery in Canada and current institutional discrimination in schools, employment, policing, and prison systems: see *Policing Black Lives: State Violence in Canada from Slavery to the Present* (Winnipeg: Fernwood, 2017). And Saidiya Hartman, with poetic empathy, uses newspaper accounts and trial records to describe the intimate lives of working-class Black women at the turn of the twentieth century: see *Wayward Lives, Beautiful Experiments: Intimate Histories of Social Upheaval* (New York: Norton, 2019). I owe all of these authors a debt of gratitude: my excitement about their work helped shape this book.

The stories of Black Canadians are being retrieved from obscurity. Mary Ann Shadd Cary moved with her family from the United States to Canada West, as Ontario was known before Confederation, in 1853. She became Canada's first female editor when she published the *Provincial Freeman* and tried to convince other African Americans to immigrate to Canada. Later, she had much to say about Canada's broken promises to Black migrants. See J. Rhodes, *Mary Ann Shadd Cary: The Black Press and Protest in the Nineteenth Century* (Bloomington: Indiana University Press, 1994). William Hubbard, whose father was also a refugee from the United States, was elected as a Toronto alderman in 1894 and became Toronto's first – and only, to date – Black deputy mayor. See Hubbard, *Against All Odds: The Story of William Peyton Hubbard, Black Leader and Municipal Reformer* (Toronto: Dundurn, 1987). Anderson Ruffin Abbott was the first Black Canadian to be licensed as a doctor, in 1861. He became a surgeon in the army of the northern United States during the Civil War and received a shawl from Mary Todd Lincoln in gratitude for his medical assistance the night Abraham Lincoln was assassinated. See Daylce Newby, *Anderson Ruffin Abbott: First Afro-Canadian Doctor* (Markham: Associated Medical Services/Fitzhenry and Whiteside, 1998). Thornton and Lucie Blackburn, who escaped slavery in the 1830s and won a legal battle over extradition to the United States, went on to found Toronto's first taxi company, whose red and yellow livery colours have been adopted by the Toronto Transit Commission. See Karolyn Smardz Frost, *I've Got a Home in Glory Land* (New York: Farrar, Straus and Giroux, 2007). My best hope for this book is that it will inspire people to dig up more hidden and warped histories for re-examination.

Previous works on Clara Ford and her trial include Patrick Brode, *Death in the Queen City: Clara Ford on Trial* (Toronto: Natural Heritage Books, 2005); Carolyn Strange, "Wounded Womanhood and Dead Men: Chivalry and the Trials of Clara Ford and Carrie Davies," in *Gender Conflicts: New Essays in Women's History,* edited by Franca Iacovetta and Mariana Valverde (Toronto: University of Toronto Press, 1992), 149–88; chapters in Albert Hassard, *Not Guilty and Other Trials* (Toronto: Lee Collins, 1926); George T. Denison, *Recollections of a Police Magistrate* (Toronto: Musson, 1926); Hector Charlesworth, *Candid Chronicles: Leaves from the Note Books of a Canadian Journalist* (Toronto: Macmillan, 1925), and W. Stewart Wallace, *Murders and Mysteries: A Canadian Series* (Toronto: Macmillan, 1931).

NAMES, IDENTIFIERS, AND PRONOUNS

Nineteenth-century journalists played fast and loose with people's names (as they did with facts more generally). In the case of surnames, I use the spelling found on official documents. Gus Clark's surname is usually spelled "Clarke" in newspapers, but the death certificates of his father and brother do not have an "e." Dorsey is often spelled "Dorsay" in newspapers, but Chloe Dorsey's marriage and burial certificates use the more common spelling. The same goes for Murdoch (Murdock), Ingles (Inglis), Crosier (Crozier), Phyall (Phyle), and so on.

In the case of first names, I use the most common term used by newspapers quoting friends and family. C.H. Westwood is known variously as "Charles," "Herbert," and "C.H." in newspapers and census documents, but "Bert" seems to be the most common variant used by his brother Willie and by Gus Clark. The Clarks gave their children elaborate names such as Augustus, Carlotta, and Percival. In both censuses and newspaper reports, they are usually abbreviated to "Gus," "Carrie," and "Percy." Flora McKay is referred to in the 1881 and 1891 census as "Florence," but she is "Flora" when newspapers quote friends of the family, with the occasional "Florrie" from Clara.

Clara and Flora were both referred to as "mulatto" by newspapers, a nineteenth-century term denoting mixed race (a combination of African and European ancestry). Clara wasn't identified as "negro" or "African" in the 1871 census (the one census record for her), and the same is true of Flora in the 1881 census and Flora and Annie in the 1891 census. (Annie, however, is identified as Black in the 1901 census.) It was only when they came into conflict with the law that they got labelled. I refer to them as Black, the most common current self-identifier in Canada for those with African or mixed African European origin. As to why I capitalize "Black" and not white ... Gabrielle Foreman (see the notes below) quotes a 1906 speech, "Who Are We?" from US journalist T. Thomas Fortune: "All the white newspapers of this country regard you as 'negroes' and write Negro with a little 'n' ... I AM A PROPER NOUN, NOT A COMMON NOUN."

I have simplified the names of contemporary newspapers, for example, from *Evening Star* to *Star*.

Finally, and as discussed in Chapter 6, it's impossible to know what Clara's views were on her sexual and gender identity. Nineteenth-century English-speaking society simply didn't have terms to express transgender identity. Clara referred to herself as female (including in her explanations of why she sometimes dressed – and possibly lived – as a male), so I use female pronouns. Similarly, Clara never publicly expressed desire for women, so I am being cautious in not referring to her as a lesbian, although she was certainly subject to homophobia, and she preferred the company of women.

EPIGRAPH AND A NOTE ON SPEECH ACCURACY

I originally included as an epigraph to this book the first lines of what I thought was Sojourner Truth's "Ain't I a Woman?" speech at the 1851 Akron Women's Rights Conference. To me, "Well, children, where there is so much racket, there must be something out of kilter" described the racket surrounding Clara and how it disclosed a society out of kilter.

Then, when I looked up the speech, I learned that in 1863, a white abolitionist named Frances Dana Barker Gage had not only changed the words of Sojourner Truth's speech but also used a fake "Southern Black slave" dialect, which bore no resemblance to Truth's Pennsylvania Dutch accent. The original speech, printed several weeks after its delivery by Truth's friend the Reverend Marius Robinson in the *Anti-slavery Bugle,* has some themes in common. But it's a very different wonderful speech. I highly recommend Leslie Podell's website (https://www.thesojournertruth project.com/), which is based on Professor Nell Irvin Painter's research and includes audio recordings that try to give a sense of how the speech was delivered. This serves as a reminder that all quotes from contemporary newspapers, including Clara's testimony, must be taken with caution. I am referring not only to untruths but to accents. I do not know whether Clara used terms such as "ain't" and "then he says" or whether journalists were substituting "minstrel dialect."

OVERTURE: CAKEWALK

4 **The curtain rises**: Sam T. Jack's Creole Company's week-long engagement at the Academy of Music was advertised in *The Star,* April 13, 1894, along with competing attractions.

4 **Florence Hines is dressed as a man**: Hugh Ryan, "This Black Drag King Was Once Known as the Greatest Male Impersonator of All Time," *Them,* June 1, 2018, https://www.them.us/story/themstory-florence-hines.

4 **"Lovely woman was made to be loved"**: ibid.

5 **hunter green Eton jacket**: Crosier's comment on the jacket (October 6), *Globe,* November 28, 1894; Flora's grey tam-o'-shanter and being lighter-skinned (could almost "pass for white"), *World,* November 29, 1894.

5 **Jessie McKay ...died a month ago**: death, March 26, 1894, "Canada, Ontario, Toronto Trust Cemeteries, 1826–1989," obtained from *FamilySearch*, February 19, 2021.

5 **first woman ... testify on her own behalf**: Albert Richard Hassard, *Not Guilty and Other Trials* (Toronto: Lee Collins, 1926), 18. For background on changes to Canada Evidence Act of 1893, see Ed Ratushny, "Is There a Right against Self-Incrimination in Canada?," *McGill Law Journal* 19, 1 (1969): 1–77.

5 **first person described ... as "homosexual"**: *World*, November 22, 1894. In *One Hundred Years of Homosexuality: And Other Essays on Greek Love* (London: Routledge, 1990), 15, David M. Halperin claims the English word "homosexual" was first used in the 1892 translation of Krafft-Ebing's *Psychopathia Sexualis*. I searched the databases of several newspapers, including the *New York Times* and the *Chicago Tribune*, and found no earlier example.

6 **disappear into her room to read**: *Mail*, November 23, 1894.

6 **she and Flora would treat themselves to a show**: *Mail and Empire*, May 2, 1895.

6 **sang in a church choir**: *Telegram*, November 23, 1894.

6 **"excellent male impersonator"**: *Paterson Daily Caller*, November 23, 1891, quoted in Ryan, "This Black Drag King."

6 **"The utmost intimacy has existed"**: *Cincinnati Report*, quoted in Ryan, "This Black Drag King."

7 **He hired Black women and men to write**: On Sam T. Jack's Creole Burlesque Company and players, see Lynn Abbott and Doug Seroff, *Out of Sight: The Rise of African-American Popular Music* (Jackson: University Press of Mississippi, 2009); John Kenrick, "A History of the Musical: Minstrel Shows," "History of the Musical Stage, 1870s–1880s: Burlesques and Pantomimes," and "History of the Musical Stage – The 1890s: Early Black Musicals," Musicals101.com; and Marvin McAllister, *Whiting Up: Whiteface Minstrels and Stage Europeans in African American Performance* (Chapel Hill: University of North Carolina Press, 2011).

7 **the most famous performers of the cakewalk**: Abbott and Seroff, *Out of Sight*.

8 **film capture of the cakewalk**: American Mutoscope and Biograph Co., May 11, 1903, Library of Congress, H31674, https://www.youtube.com/watch?v=QifiyNm6jG4.

8 **"sentimentalized the nightmare life"**: Kenrick, "A History of the Musical."

8 **"a comedic tradition"**: McAllister, *Whiting Up*, 79.

8 **"black people imitating white people"**: ibid., 80.

ONE: THE MURDEREE

13 **The Murderee**: This term is taken from Martin Amis's *London Fields* (London: Jonathan Cape, 1989).

14 **under the weather**: *Star*, October 8, 1894.

14 **the forecast**: *Star*, October 6, 1894.

14 **warm tan overcoat**: *Globe,* October 13, 1894.

14 **Westwood and his Parkdale villa**: G. Mercer Adam, *Toronto, Old and New* (Toronto: Mail Printing Company, 1891), 170–71.

14 **failed to sell the property**: *Telegram,* October 10, 1894.

15 **founding member of the Maroons Canoe Club ... spotted swimming nude**: ibid.

15–16 **Benjamin's biography**: Benjamin's early life, business career, and becoming a lay preacher: Adam, *Toronto, Old and New,* 170–71. Marriage to Clara Bonnick: Benjamin Westwood and Clara Bownick, April 21, 1870, "Canada, Ontario Marriages, 1869–1927," obtained through *FamilySearch,* March 8, 2021, citing registration, Yorkville, York, Ontario, Canada, Archives of Ontario, Toronto; FHL microfilm 1,862,475. Bert's birthplace as United States: is from 1881 census; the Westwoods aren't in the Canadian census for 1871; the births of the other children is from the 1891 census.

16 **ALW fishing rods**: "We Used to Make Things in This Country #219: Allcock, Laight & Westwood Company Limited, Toronto, Ontario," *Progress is fine, but it's gone on for too long* (blog), November 30, 2015, http://progress-is-fine.blogspot.com/2015/11/we-used-to-make-things-in-this-country.html.

16 **Parkdale Methodist Church**: Margaret Laycock and Barbara Myrvold, *Parkdale in Pictures: Its Development to 1889* (Toronto: Toronto Public Library, 1981), 43.

16 **8:40 a.m. train**: ibid., 23.

16 **trim grid**: Adam, *Toronto, Old and New,* 44.

17 **"graced with stately dwellings"**: Albert Richard Hassard, *Not Guilty and Other Trials* (Toronto: Lee Collins, 1926), 6.

17 **"flowery suburb"**: Carolyn Whitzman, *Suburb, Slum, Urban Village: Neighbourhood Transition in a Toronto Suburb, 1875–2002* (Vancouver: UBC Press, 2008), 62.

17 **"ostracized the saloon keepers"**: ibid., 63.

18 **Ford-McKay household**: City of Toronto, assessment records, 1889–92.

18 **public shouting match**: *Star,* November 24, 1894.

18 **arrest of a male impersonator**: *Telegram,* August 27, 1894.

18–19 **Parkdale's population, industries, and institutions**: Laycock and Myrvold, *Parkdale in Pictures,* 11–13, 48–53.

20 **"displays of Toronto and Provincial manufacturers" and "New Fort"**: J.M.S. Careless, *Toronto to 1918: An Illustrated History* (Toronto: James Lorimer, 1984), 109–12, 31–33.

20 **"If ever the time came that either"**: D.C. Masters, *The Rise of Toronto, 1850–1890* (Toronto: University of Toronto Press, 1947), 189.

20 **Henry Smith's department store**: *Might's Directory,* 1894.

21 **a clerkship in a thriving business**: Michael Heller, "Work, Income and Stability: The Late Victorian and Edwardian London Male Clerk Revisited," *Business History* 50, 3 (2008): 253–71.

280 NOTES AND FURTHER READING

21 **"always well behaved"**: *Telegram,* October 8,1894.

21 **"a sturdy, fine-looking young fellow"**: *Telegram,* October 9,1894.

21 **"drank no strong liquors"**: *Empire,* October 9,1894.

21 **four "negro-owned" eating houses**: *Might's Directory,* 1894.

22 **the Ward, like Parkdale, was under threat**: Richard Dennis, "Private Landlords and Redevelopment: 'The Ward' in Toronto, 1890–1920," *Urban History Review* 24,1 (1995): 21–35.

22 **After work, Frank might have ...**: The description of the night of Frank's shooting comes from the testimony of Benjamin, Clara, and Willie Westwood; Edgar Lennox, Temple Cooper; Isaac Anderson; John Gray; Charles Slemin; Mary Mitchell; and Bessie Stephen at the inquest, as reported in newspapers.

23 **Liver pills, according to advertisements of the day**: *Star,* October 6,1894.

23 **She didn't hear the doorbell ring**: Clara Westwood's testimony at the inquest: *Globe,* October 24, 1894. Frank, in his antemortem statement, said the doorbell rang: *Globe,* October 30,1894.

TWO: THERE'S A GIRL IN IT

27 **Hector Charlesworth, a twenty-two-year-old journalist**: Hector Charlesworth, *Candid Chronicles: Leaves from the Note Book of a Canadian Journalist* (Toronto: MacMillan, 1925): "Under the circumstances," 14; "Terrified of negroes," 25; went to school with Bert, 88; and "fakes," 56.

28 **In 1894, there were seven daily newspapers**: Paul Rutherford, *A Victorian Authority: The Daily Press in Late Nineteenth-Century Canada* (Toronto: University of Toronto Press, 1982); Minko Sotiron, "Maclean, William Findlay," in *Dictionary of Canadian Biography,* vol. 15, University of Toronto/ Université Laval, 2003–, http://www.biographi.ca/en/bio/maclean_william_findlay_15E.html; Charlesworth, *Candid Chronicles*; and Philip Gordon Mackintosh, *Newspaper City: Toronto's Street Surfaces and the Liberal Press, 1860–1935* (Toronto: University of Toronto Press, 2017).

29 **Benjamin Westwood and temperance**: *Globe,* October 6,1893.

29 **"WL Mackenzie, first Mayor"**: *Globe,* May 10,1894.

30 **"family paper for those ...liberated"**: Rutherford, *A Victorian Authority,* 53.

31–32 **final days of Frank Westwood, including notices on fence**: *Globe,* October 8–11,1894.

32 **the bullet had entered an inch below his right ribs ...**: inquest testimony, *Globe,* November 13,1894.

32 **Benjamin's revolver**: *Globe,* October 24,1894.

32–33 **and he'd given his son Bert ...a .22 calibre**: *Globe,* October 30,1894.

33 **Both King and Queen Streets were served by streetcars**: Samuel Sheppard, streetcar conductor, inquest testimony, *Globe,* October 16,1894.

34 **"there must have been some deep-seated feeling of hatred"**: *Globe,* October 8,1894.

34 ".44 calibre bullet": *Empire*, October 8, 1894.
34 "Frank Westwood and his father had not been on good terms": *Empire*, October 11, 1894.
34 "a family affair": *World*, October 8, 1894.
34 "there is a woman somewhere in the case": *Star*, October 9, 1894.
34 "There's a girl in it": *Telegram*, October 8, 1894.
35 "You can't pump me": Slemin's testimony at the inquest, *Star*, October 30, 1894.
35 "withdrew, not wishing to be observed": *Empire*, October 12, 1894.
35 "Are the Relatives Keeping Something Back?": *Empire*, October 8, 1894.
35 "there might be a woman in the case": *World*, October 8, 1894.
35 "the father of a young lady who lives not far": *News*, October 8, 1894.
36 "another groundless story": *Star*, October 9, 1894.
36 Willie's denial: ibid.
36 "Edith told me to be sure": *News*, October 9, 1894.
36 "affectionate message from a young lady": *Mail*, October 10, 1894.
36 "accompanied by young ladies on his boat": *Mail*, October 8, 1894.
36 "a man who owns or rents his boathouse": C.S. Clark, *Of Toronto the Good* (Montreal: Toronto Publishing Company, 1898), 95.
36 Sadie Lavelle's death: *Globe*, September 1, 1891.
37 allegations that ... Frank ... seduced ... Maggie: *News*, October 8, 1894.
37 Bert and Maggie had been married: marriage, Charles H. Westwood and Maggie May Nafe, December 12, 1893, "Ontario Marriages, 1869–1927," obtained through *FamilySearch*, March 11, 2018, citing registration, Toronto, York, Ontario, Canada; Archives of Ontario, Toronto; FHL microfilm 1,870,704; and birth, John Henry Harry Neville Westwood, June 3, 1894, "Ontario Births, 1869–1912," obtained through *FamilySearch*, August 8, 2017, citing birth, Toronto, York, Ontario, Canada; Archives of Ontario, Toronto; FHL microfilm 1,846,244.
37 "In the event of the Crown's endeavouring": *World*, October 11, 1894.
37 Bert had a good alibi: Harvey German, inquest testimony, *Globe*, October 23, 1894.
38 births out of wedlock: Constance Backhouse, *Petticoats and Prejudice: Women and Law in Nineteenth-Century Canada* (Toronto: Women's Press/ Osgoode Society for Canadian Legal History, 1991), 41.
38 "personal depravity": ibid.
38 The notion of consent: ibid., 41–75
39 An 1862 article in the Upper Canada Law Journal ... The National Council of Women: ibid., 67.
39 "unwritten law": Lawrence Friedman and William Haveman, "The Rise and Fall of the Unwritten Law: Sex, Patriarchy, and Vigilante Justice in American Courts," *Buffalo Law Review* 61, 5 (2013): 997–1056.
39 Brigdin trial: *Globe*, October 4, 1856.

40 **Black man named William Custard raped**: Barrington Walker, *Race on Trial: Black Defendants in Ontario's Criminal Courts, 1858–1958* (Toronto: University of Toronto Press, 2010), 47–48.

40 **In 1897, Euphemia Rabbitt**: Backhouse, *Petticoats and Prejudice*, 101–7.

40 **Cora Wesley's inquest testimony**: *Globe*, October 13, 1894.

40–41 **Isaac Anderson and Ed Lennox's inquest testimony**: ibid.

41 **Maggie Westwood's inquest testimony**: *Mail*, November 6, 1894.

41 **"a servant girl"**: *Empire*, October 9, 1894.

41 **Reverend Scott's sermon**: *Globe*, October 13, 1894.

THREE: AMATEUR DETECTIVES

43 **The jury, who'd been sworn in**: *Globe*, October 13, 1894; *Might's Directory*, 1894; and, on Liberal alliances, see G. Mercer Adam, *Toronto, Old and New* (Toronto: Mail Printing Company, 1891).

43 **"in deep distress"**: *Globe*, October 13, 1894.

44 **Lakeside Hall would be for sale**: *Star*, October 23, 1894.

44 **"destructive rather than constructive"**: *Globe*, October 30, 1894.

44 **a five-hundred-dollar reward**: *Globe*, October 27, 1894.

44 **"murder in his eyes"**: *Globe*, October 8, 1894; and inquest version, *Globe*, October 16, 1894.

45 **Emma Card's testimony**: *Star*, October 10, 1894.

45 **Austin and Emma Card's inquest testimony**: *Globe*, October 13, 1894.

45–46 **testimony of O.B. Sheppard (stage manager, Grand Opera House), Samuel Sheppard (streetcar driver), and Dorr Keller**: *Globe*, October 16, 1894.

46 **Cora and Ellen Wesley's story**: *Star*, October 10, 1894.

46 **Stephen Leslie's testimony**: *Globe*, October 16, 1894.

46 **Robert Carswell's testimony**: *Globe*, October 23, 1894.

47 **Angered by the presence of the stone hookers**: *Globe*, October 16, 1894.

47 **Albert and William Peer testimony**: *Globe*, November 13, 1894.

47 **The duck hunters**: *Globe*, October 16, 1894, and November 6, 1894.

47–48 **Hornsby and the scraps of paper**: *Mail*, October 13, 1894; *News*, October 12, 1894; *Empire*, October 12, 1894; and inquest testimony, *Mail*, October 16, 1894.

48 **Arthur Conan Doyle**: Hector Charlesworth, *Candid Chronicles: Leaves from the Note Book of a Canadian Journalist* (Toronto: MacMillan, 1925), 90; *World*, October 29, 1894; and Peter Costello, *Conan Doyle, Detective: True Crimes Investigated by the Creator of Sherlock Holmes* (New York: Carroll and Graf, 1991).

49 **"Still Unsolved"**: *Mail*, October 11, 1894; "entirely at sea," *Star*, October 9, 1894; "baffled," *Globe*, November 9, 1894; "darker than ever," *Star*, October 30, 1894; "no light yet," *Globe*, October 13, 1894; "no clue," *Star*, November 6, 1894; and "still no clue," *World*, October 29, 1894.

49 **Benjamin Westwood turned on the police**: *Star*, October 9, 1894.

49 **"the southern part of the Flowery Suburb"**: *Telegram*, October 9, 1894.

49 **"the reticence of the police"**: *Telegram*, October 11, 1894.

49 **"The police have a theory"**: *Telegram*, October 30, 1894.

49 **"questions of ideology, political partisanship"**: Nicholas Rogers, "Serving Toronto the Good: The Development of the City's Police Force, 1834–84," in *Forging a Consensus: Historical Essays on Toronto*, ed. Victor Russell (Toronto: University of Toronto Press, 1984), 116.

50 **the origins of the force and relationship with the Orange Order**: J.M.S. Careless, *Toronto to 1918: An Illustrated History* (Toronto: James Lorimer, 1984); Gregory Kealey, "Orangemen and the Corporation," in Russell, *Forging a Consensus*, 41–86; and David Wilson, *The Orange Order in Canada* (Dublin: Four Courts Press, 2007); "the Belfast of Canada" from Wilson, 10

50 **"scheming brain and steady purpose"**: *Globe*, April 6, 1889.

51 **"the brutal treatment of prisoners"**: *Globe*, August 13, 1887.

51 **working-class constables and slightly higher-status detectives**: C.S. Clark, *Of Toronto the Good* (Montreal: Toronto Publishing Co., 1898), 64; heckler, 16; and brutishness, 17.

52 **most terrifying to working-class Black, Irish Catholic, and union members**: Kevin Plummer, "Historicist: Patriarch of the Police Court," *Torontoist*, February 26, 2011, https://torontoist.com/2011/02/historicist_paternal_patriarch_of_the_police_court/.

52 **"a legacy of antipathy"**: Norman Knowles, "Denison, George Taylor," in *Dictionary of Canadian Biography*, vol. 15, University of Toronto/Université Laval, 2003–, http://www.biographi.ca/en/bio/denison_george_taylor_1839_1925_15E.html.

53 **Denison was bored by the finer points**: George T. Denison, *Recollections of a Police Magistrate* (Toronto: Musson, 1926), 34.

53 **650,000 cases**: Ted Dunlop, "Toronto's First Street Kids and the Origins of the Child Welfare System in Canada, Part 1: The Early Years," *Scottish Journal of Residential Child Care* 16, 3 (2017): 1–44.

53 **250 cases in 180 minutes and "scatters legal intricacies"**: Constance Backhouse, *Petticoats and Prejudice: Women and Law in Nineteenth-Century Canada* (Toronto: Women's Press/Osgoode Society for Canadian Legal History, 1991), 238.

53 **The Priestman case was used as a cautionary tale**: *Star*, October 8, 1894; *Mail*, October 9, 1894; and *Empire*, October 9, 1894.

54 **Priestman's death and the arrest of Constable Smith**: *Globe*, June 13, 15, and 16, 1888.

55 **Rachael Smith … reported to be seriously ill**: *Globe*, July 28, 1888.

55 **By 1894, when the Priestman case**: *Telegram*, May 4, 1895.

55 **"a peculiar chain of suspicions"**: *Globe*, June 16, 1888.

56 **low rate of pay for constables**: *Globe*, November 8, 1888

56 **who signed himself "Justice"**: *Globe*, June 20, 1888.

56 **"Please, good kind mister policeman"**: *Globe*, June 18, 1888.

FOUR: THE BAD HAT

58 **Bad Hat**: I learned of this term from Ludwig Bemelmans' *Madeline and the Bad Hat* (New York: Viking, 1956).

59 **"is in the cooler"**: *Globe*, October 30, 1894.

59–60 **controlled through the Orange Order**: Gregory Kealey, "Orangemen and the Corporation," in *Forging a Consensus: Historical Essays on Toronto*, ed. Victor Russell (Toronto: University of Toronto Press, 1984), 46.

60–61 **John Clark's biography**: John Clark's profession is listed as inspector at the Customs house in the Toronto Street Directories from 1873 to 1883. From 1875 onward, his residence is listed in "West York" (Parkdale was part of West York until it was incorporated as a village in 1879), and from 1879 onward in "Parkdale": Toronto Reference Library. He is listed as working for the customs house in the 1861, 1871, and 1881 censuses. He is listed in Parkdale's assessment records, found in Toronto City Archives, from 1879 to 1889 – from 1885 onward as a "gentleman."

60 **donated money to . . . first primary school**: *Globe*, January 16, 1879.

60 **"aroused and indignant"**: *Globe*, December 12, 1877.

60 **"a circus"**: *Globe*, December 29, 1885.

60 **rich through land speculation**: Parkdale, assessment records, 1879–89.

61 **Temperance Colonization Society**: lawsuit, *Globe*, April 2, 1884; and J.H. Archer, "The History of Saskatoon to 1914" (master's thesis, University of Saskatoon, 1947).

61 **servant who lived in a separate "stables"**: Census of Canada 1881, Library and Archives Canada.

61 **John Clark died**: death, John Clark, 1889, "Ontario Deaths, 1869–1937 and Overseas Deaths, 1939–1947," obtained through *FamilySearch*, March 9, 2018, citing York, Ontario, Canada, Pg 332 CN 016238, Registrar General, Archives of Ontario, Toronto, FHL microfilm 1,853,493.

61 **"a refuge and home for young girls"**: *Globe*, June 17, 1893.

61–62 **Catherine Clark's movements and purchase of CPR Hotel**: *Might's Directory*, 1892–95.

62 **Gus Clark's first arrest**: *Globe*, April 14, 1888.

62 **"admitted his name was Gus Clark"**: *Globe*, January 1, 1892.

62 **"Paris Hair Works"**: G.P. Mulvaney, *Toronto Past and Present: A Handbook of the City* (Toronto: W.E. Craiger, 1884), 282; see also K. Taylor, "Of Barbers, Hair Dressers and the Dorenwends," *One Gal's Toronto*, January 17, 2016, https://onegalstoronto.wordpress.com/2016/01/17/of-barbers-hair-dressers-and-the-dorenwends/.

62–63 **"seminal weakness" and history of vibrators**: Lori Loeb, "Consumerism and Commercial Electrotherapy: The Medical Battery Company in Nineteenth-Century London," *Journal of Victorian Culture* 4, 2 (1999): 252–75; Lauren Young, "The Victorian Tool for Everything from Hernias to Sex: A Vibrating Electric Belt," *Atlas Obscura*, July 12, 2016, https://www.atlasobscura.com/

articles/the-victorian-tool-for-everything-from-hernias-to-sexa-vibrating
-electric-belt; and Chris Bateman, "A Brief History of the First Electricity
Company in Toronto," *BlogTO*, September 7, 2013, https://www.blogto.com/
city/2013/09/a_brief_history_of_the_first_electricity_company_in_toronto/.

63 **"boy burglars"**: *Star*, July 4, 1895.

63 **drunkenly insensate and half-frozen**: *Star*, February 6, 1895.

63 **Slemin, who asked Frank about Clark**: *Globe*, November 6, 1894.

63 **Slemin wasn't an objective actor**: "Mr. Charles Slemin Dead," *Globe*, August
27, 1900.

64 **According to Coombes, Frank seemed**: *Globe*, October 30, 1894.

64 **David Low's residence**: *Might's Directory*, 1894.

64 **David Low Sr.'s death**: *Globe*, July 14, 1894.

64 **David Low Jr.'s death**: *Globe*, July 12, 1906.

64 **"desperate and unscrupulous man"**: *Empire*, October 8, 1894.

64 **"incurred the enmity" and Benjamin Westwood denial**: *Empire*, October 9,
1894.

65 **police had detained "a young man"**: *Star*, October 8, 1894.

65–66 **David Low's, Gus Clark's, and David Boyd's testimony**: *Globe*, November 13,
1894; and *Mail*, November 13, 1894.

65 **Percy, aged seven, had died**: death, Percy Z. Clark, October 4, 1894, "Ontario
Deaths, 1869–1937 and Overseas Deaths, 1939–1947," obtained through
FamilySearch, citing Toronto, York, Ontario, yr 1894, cn 23014, Registrar
General, Archives of Ontario, Toronto, FHL microfilm 1,853,697.

65 **he was found in Parry Sound**: *Star*, November 6, 1894; and O. Lavalee, "The
Ottawa, Arnprior and Parry Sound Railway," *Canadian Rail* 156 (1964): 131–37.

66 **"took a boat that was lying"**: *World*, November 13, 1894.

66 **"not welcome in Parkdale"**: *Mail*, October 13, 1894.

66 **he changed his story**: *Globe*, November 6, 1894.

67 **"questioned minutely"**: *Globe*, November 22, 1894.

67 **"had a 'good time' with the cash"**: *Mail*, November 21, 1894.

FIVE: FROM WHENCE SHE CAME

72 **"plump infant so dark"**: *Star*, November 24, 1894.

72 **"baby farmer"**: *Mail*, November 22, 1894.

72 **"half Spaniard"**: Inspector Stark's testimony at Clara's trial, *Globe*, May 2,
1895.

73 **Flora's testimony at the preliminary hearing**: *Globe*, November 28, 1894.

73 **"good-natured, hardworking woman"**: *Globe*, November 22, 1894; Jessie is
noted as illiterate in the 1861 Census.

73 **"loss of reputation"**: Constance Backhouse, *Petticoats and Prejudice: Women
and Law in Nineteenth-Century Canada* (Toronto: Women's Press/Osgoode
Society for Canadian Legal History, 1991), 136.

73 **poisonous screed**: *Globe*, February 11, 1884.

74 **"Blacks in Canada lived in a state of paradox"**: Barrington Walker, *Race on Trial: Black Defendants in Ontario's Criminal Courts, 1858–1958* (Toronto: University of Toronto Press, 2010), 3.

74 **Marriages between Black men and white women**: Barrington Walker, "Killing the Black Female Body: Black Womanhood, Black Patriarchy, and Spousal Murder in Two Ontario Criminal Trials, 1892–1894," in *Sisters or Strangers? Immigrant, Ethnic, and Racialized Women in Canadian History*, ed. Marlene Epp, Franca Iacovetta, and Francis Swyripa (Toronto: University of Toronto Press, 2004), 89–107.

74 **Martha Ford**: Census of Canada 1861, Library and Archives Canada.

74 **Chloe Dorsey was personally acquainted**: *Mail*, November 23, 1894.

75 **Jessie McKay's death certificate**: Ontario Archives, record 021534, 1894; and burial certificate, Toronto Necropolis, record 25065, 1894.

75 **Her family was from the Scottish Highlands**: *Globe*, November 21, 1894.

75 **half of the wealthiest businessmen in Canada were Scots**: J.M. Bumsted and Maude-Emmanuelle Lambert, "Scottish Canadians," *Canadian Encyclopedia*, December 20, 2021, https://www.thecanadianencyclopedia.ca/en/article/scots.

75 **She worked as a nursemaid with a family in Sydney**: *Mail*, November 26, 1894.

75 **nursemaid to the three children of**: 1861 Census; and *Hutchinson's Directory*, 1862.

75 **Yonge Street**: J.M.S. Careless, *Toronto to 1918: An Illustrated History* (Toronto: James Lorimer, 1984), 94.

75 **Tory Ford**: 1861 Census.

76 **Little Trinity**: John Lorinc, "Introduction," in *The Ward: Life and Loss of Toronto's First Immigrant Neighbourhood*, ed. John Lorinc, Michael McClelland, Ellen Scheinberg, and Tatum Taylor (Toronto: Coach House Press, 2015), 11–26.

76 **William Hickman**: listed as Anglican in 1861 Census.

76 **date of Clara's birth**: There is no record of Clara's, Flora's, or Annie's births. Clara testified that she was thirty-three years old at the time of her arrest in November 1894 and was reported as being the same age at her trial, in May 1895.

76 **Protestant Girls' Home and Nursery**: *Globe*, January 4, 1865.

76 **Jessie is not listed in a street directory**: *Hutchinson's Directory*, 1862; the next listing is *Chewett's Directory*, 1867. *Mitchell's Directory*, 1864, shows Jessie's former address as an empty lot.

76 **Clara moved a lot during her childhood ...** : City of Toronto, St. John's Ward, assessment records, 1867.

77 **"a comfortable living"**: *Mail*, November 23, 1894.

77 **"Bertha Brusk"**: *Globe*, December 26, 1868.

77 **"little dark-skinned girl"**: *Mail*, November 26, 1894.

77 **Rebecca Alexander**: *Mail*, November 21, 1894.

78 **St. John's Ward**: Barrie Dyster, "Captain Bob and the Noble Ward," in *Forging a Consensus: Historical Essays on Toronto*, ed. Victor Russell (Toronto: University of Toronto Press, 1984), 85–115.

78 **Macaulaytown had a distinct Black community**: ibid. See also Stephen Otto, "Before the Ward: Macaulaytown," in Lorinc et al., *The Ward*, 32–35; and Karolyn Smardz Frost, "A Fresh Start: Black Toronto in the 19th Century," in ibid., 66–70.

78 **"bought, sold and compelled"**: Walker, *Race on Trial*, 5.

78 **American Loyalists were lured**: ibid., 26.

78 **384 slaves in 1794**: ibid., 28.

79 **Chloe Cooley and Simcoe's "compromise"**: Afua Cooper, "Acts of Resistance: Black Men and Women Engage Slavery in Upper Canada, 1793–1803," *Ontario History* 99, 1 (2007): 3–17; see also Robin Winks, *The Blacks in Canada: A History* (Montreal/Kingston: McGill-Queens University Press, 1971), 96; and Adrienne Shadd, Afua Cooper, and Karolyn Smardz Frost, *The Underground Railroad: Next Stop, Toronto!* (Toronto: Natural Heritage Press, 2002), 17.

79 **"black men in red coats"**: Karolyn Smardz Frost, *I've Got a Home in Glory Land* (New York: Farrar, Straus and Giroux, 2007), 196.

79 **In 1834, the newly named City of Toronto**: Shadd, Cooper, and Smardz Frost, *The Underground Railroad*, 15.

79 **William Hickman**: ibid., 66–67.

79 **John Gallego**: John Lorinc, "First Census of Toronto's Black Population in 1840 Counted 525 People," *Toronto Star*, February 1, 2018.

80 **"a black family [could] ... keep white men"**: Smardz Frost, *I've Got a Home in Glory Land*, 262.

80 **John Butler, a successful barber**: Shadd, Cooper, Smardz Frost, *The Underground Railroad*, 14.

80 **US Fugitive Slave Act**: Winks, *The Blacks in Canada*, 253.

80 **Lucie and Thornton Blackburn**: Smardz Frost, *I've Got a Home in Glory Land*.

80–81 **Underground Railroad**: Shadd, Cooper, and Smardz Frost, *The Underground Railroad*.

81 **In 1854, another independent census**: Michael Wayne, "The Black Population of Canada West on the Eve of the American Civil War: A Reassessment Based on the Manuscript Census of 1861," *Social History* 28, 5–6 (1995): 465–85.

81 **Seaton Village**: Shadd, Cooper, and Smardz Frost, *The Underground Railroad*, 5.

81 **Attitudes hardened toward Black Torontonians**: Winks, *The Blacks in Canada*; Robyn Maynard, *Policing Black Lives: State Violence in Canada from Slavery to the Present* (Winnipeg: Fernwood, 2017); see also Sarah-Jane Mathieu, *North of the Colour Line: Migration and Black Resistance in Canada, 1870–1955* (Chapel Hill: University of North Carolina Press, 2010).

81 **Tory Ford moved back to Peoria**: US Census, 1870, 1880, 1900, and 1910.

81 **excluded from white-dominated public schools**: Walker, *The Blacks in Canada*, 36–37.

81 **integrated into one of the three large "common schools"**: *Mail*, November 21, 1894.

81 **"the innocent [are] preserved, the vicious reclaimed"**: "Visit to Our Common Schools," *Globe*, November 14, 1853.

82 **a sense of the curriculum**: *Report of the Past History and Present Condition of the Common or Public Schools of the City of Toronto* (Toronto: Lovell and Gibson, 1859).

82 **17 James Street**: Canada Census, 1871; *Robertson and Cook Directory*, 1871; and St. John's Ward, assessment records, 1871.

83 **"inexpensive housing"**: Richard Harris, "The End Justified the Means: Boarding and Rooming in a City of Homes, 1880–1951," *Journal of Social History* 26, 2 (1993): 331.

83 **House of Industry**: "Our Destitute Poor," *Globe*, January 5, 1875.

83 **"day relief"**: D.C. Masters, *The Rise of Toronto, 1850–1890* (Toronto: University of Toronto Press, 1947), 155.

83 **Clara's school days were over**: *Mail*, November 23, 1894.

SIX: GO WEST, YOUNG MAN

85 **earn her own living from the age of twelve**: *Mail and Empire*, May 4, 1895; on Roach's Tavern, *1874 Fisher and Taylor Street Directory*; and for John Roach's numerous appearances in Magistrates' Court, see, for example, *Globe*, November 20, 1863; March 28, 1865; January 26, 1869; and September 4, 1873.

85 **she was convicted**: *Globe*, August 11 and 19, 1874.

85 **Vagrancy was a catch-all**: "An Act," *Globe*, January 24, 1845; vagrancy and social control, Helen Boritch and John Hogan, "Crime and the Changing Forms of Class Control: Policing Public Order in 'Toronto the Good,' 1859–1955," *Social Forces* 66, 2 (1987): 307–35; Mariana Valverde, *The Age of Light, Soap and Water: Moral Reform in English Canada, 1885–1925* (Toronto: McClelland and Stewart, 1991); and Constance Backhouse, *Petticoats and Prejudice: Women and Law in Nineteenth-Century Canada* (Toronto: Women's Press/Osgoode Society for Canadian Legal History, 1991).

85 **"children whose heads barely reach above the dock"**: Ted Dunlop, "Toronto's First Street Kids and the Origins of the Child Welfare System in Canada, Part 1: The Early Years," *Scottish Journal of Residential Child Care* 16, 3 (2017): 27.

86 **costs of the court**: K. Cohl, S. Lightstone, and G. Thomson, *Ontario Court of Justice: A History* (Toronto: Ontario Court of Justice, 2015).

86 **"Arabs of the street"**: *Globe*, January 4, 1866.

86 **"Once again we would desire"**: *12th Report of the Commission on Prisons and Public Charities* (Toronto: Office of the Inspector of Prisons and Public Charities, 1882).

86–87 **Central Prison statistics**: *Globe*, January 8, 1875.

87 **By 1874, the Girls' Home had moved**: *Globe*, August 7, 1873.

87 **"under the management of Auntie Jane"**: *Globe*, January 30, 1882.

87 **Magdalen Asylum**: *Globe*, August 7, 1873.

88 **"was born in Toronto"**: *Globe*, November 21, 1894.

88 **"She never talked of her affairs" and "with evident amusement"**: *Mail*, November 21, 1894.

88 **Ingles had known Clara for fifteen years**: *Mail*, November 22, 1894.

88 **Ingles was twenty-three years old**: death, Charles Leycester Ingles, January 25, 1930, "Ontario Deaths, 1869–1937 and Overseas Deaths, 1939–1947," obtained through *FamilySearch*, March 8, 2018, citing Toronto, York, Ontario, Canada, 001302, Registrar General, Archives of Ontario, Toronto, FHL microfilm 2,313,286.

88 **in training at Clara's church**: *Globe*, July 31, 1882.

88 **visited her regularly during her time in jail**: *Telegram*, November 23, 1894.

88 **had only good things to say to the newspapers**: *Mail*, November 26, 1894; and character witnesses at the trial, *Mail and Empire*, May 6, 1894.

89 **Mary Crosier's age and children**: Census of Canada 1891, Library and Archives Canada.

89 **two dinner shifts ... and testimony at preliminary hearing**: *Mail*, November 29, 1894.

89 **Temperance Coffee House**: *Empire*, November 24, 1894.

89 **The Crosiers were working-class**: *Might's Directories*, 1894, 1895.

90–91 **Eliza Reed**: 1881, 1891 Census; and *Might's Directories*, 1890, 1891.

91 **"who from the kindness of her heart"**: *Mail*, November 26, 1894.

91 **"a gentleman who is an active worker"**: *Mail*, November 22, 1894.

91 **Burnside Lying-In Hospital**: *Mail*, November 23, 1894.

91 **The global Long Depression**: Matthew Lynn, "The Long Depression," *History Today*, February 29, 2012; and impact on Canada, Bryan Palmer and Gaetan Heroux, *Toronto's Poor: A Rebellious History* (Toronto: Between the Lines, 2016), 42–56.

91 **one in five Canadians**: Elijah Alperin and Jeanne Batalova, "Canadian Immigrants in the United States," *Migration Policy Institute*, June 7, 2018, https://www.migrationpolicy.org/article/canadian-immigrants-united-states-2016.

92 **combined population of the Twin Cities**: 1870 and 1880 US Census; and Toronto population, 1871 and 1881 Census.

92 **African Americans moved from the south and east**: Tina Burnside, "African Americans in Minnesota," *MNopedia*, July 25, 2017, https://www.mnopedia.org/african-americans-minnesota.

92 "found it easier to obtain employment" and "zealous boy": *Mail*, November 26, 1894.

92–93 Clara moving to Syracuse ... and Rochester: *Telegram*, November 28, 1894.

93 taxi driver and hostler: *Buffalo Evening News*, November 23, 1894; *Star*, November 24, 1894; and *Telegram*, November 22, 1894.

93 "secured work in a drug store": *Globe*, November 22, 1894. On African American doctors, see Karen Jordan, "The Struggle and Triumph of America's First Black Doctors," *The Atlantic*, October 16, 2016.

93 "By great industry and careful economy": *Mail*, November 26, 1894.

94 Both women and men relished the opportunity to reinvent themselves: Peter Boag, *Re-dressing America's Frontier Past* (Berkeley: University of California Press, 2011), "Go West, young man," 1; on Mary Johnston/Frank Woodhull, "walk, talk and work," 39; and on Georgie McRae, 34.

94 posing as a detective: *Empire*, November 24, 1894.

94 Black police: "History," Chicago Police Department website.

94 "They had all heard her stories": *Mail*, November 23, 1894.

95 remarkably blithe about cross-dressing: *Chicago Tribune*, September 18, 1888.

95 Annie Hindle, the celebrated male impersonator: *Chicago Tribune*, July 18, 1892.

95 Fedora: "History of Fedora Hats," *History of Hats*, 2018 online database.

95 Vic Steinberg: *Globe*, May 4, 1895; and for a YA biography of Vic Steinberg, see Christine Welldon, *Reporter in Disguise* (Markham, ON: Fitzhenry and Whiteside, 2013).

96 On lack of discourse on transgender identity and the "progress narrative": Boag, *Re-dressing America's Frontier Past*, 19.

96 "soon to be 15": *Empire*, November 25, 1894.

96 birthday was December 24, 1879: *Telegram*, November 22, 1894.

96 "to get her to admit to Flora's parentage": *Mail*, November 24, 1894.

96 wasn't "dissipated": *Mail*, November 21, 1894.

96–97 "a bright, good looking girl" and "olive complexioned": *Globe*, November 28, 1894; and *Mail*, November 21 1894.

97 23 Gloucester Street: Toronto Street Directories, 1879–87; 1881 Census; and City of Toronto Assessment, 1881.

98 two dismissed charges of drunkenness: *Globe*, April 5, 1880, and August 23, 1883.

98 she worked as a servant: *Might's Directory*, 1882; *Polk's Directory*, 1883; and 1881 Census, Rolph household.

98 "a quiet, well-behaved girl": *Globe*, November 24, 1894.

98 "temperate": Samuel Barnett, *Mail*, November 21, 1894; and Chloe Dorsey, *Mail*, November 23, 1894.

98 "her demeanour [race] attracting no special notice": *Globe*, November 22, 1894.

98 **St. Luke's Anglican Church**: "St. Luke's Bay Street," *Lost Anglican Churches* (blog), September 28, 2012, https://lostanglicanchurches.wordpress.com/2012/09/28/st-lukes-bay-street/.

99 **Christmas tree presentation**: *Globe*, January 6, 1873.

99 **unpleasant realities of working as a servant**: Backhouse, *Petticoats and Prejudice*, 69–71.

99 **60 percent of prostitutes in that city**: Carolyn Strange, *Toronto's Girl Problem: The Perils and Pleasures of the City, 1880–1930* (Toronto: University of Toronto Press, 1995), 36.

99 **"one lad of 18"**: C.S. Clark, *Of Toronto the Good* (Montreal: Toronto Publishing Company, 1898), 104.

100 **married in Chicago in 1885**: *Globe*, May 4, 1895.

100 **husband had been a white man**: *Telegram*, November 23, 1894.

100 **between 1870 and 1900, Chicago's Black population**: Bureau of the [US] Census, "Negro Population of Fifty Cities, 1880 to 1930," 1930; and Christopher Manning, "African Americans," *Encyclopedia of Chicago*, 2005, http://www.encyclopedia.chicagohistory.org/pages/27.html.

100 **Sarah Crosier testified**: *Mail and Empire*, May 3, 1894.

100 **"The child spoken of has no relation"**: *Mail*, November 26, 1894.

100 **"who answers exactly to Clara Ford's description"**: ibid.

101 **"her adopted mother and her child[ren]"**: *Mail*, November 22, 1894.

101 **"Many a time when I have suggested to her"**: *Mail*, November 26, 1894.

SEVEN: BAD FENCES

103–4 **Samuel Barnett**: "a very positive character," *Globe*, November 22, 1894, and *Mail*, November 21, 1894; "all day without exchanging," *Telegram*, November 22, 1894; "her habits are temperate," *Globe*, May 4, 1895; "she had a temper," *Telegram*, May 3, 1894; and "Clara something," *Globe*, November 22, 1894.

105 **"race suicide" and gender imbalance**: Carolyn Strange, *Toronto's Girl Problem: The Perils and Pleasures of the City, 1880–1930* (Toronto: University of Toronto Press, 1995), 9, 24.

105 **"After paying her board out of that amount"**: C.S. Clark, *Of Toronto the Good* (Montreal: Toronto Publishing Company, 1898), 62.

105 **Knights of Labour and the Royal Commission**: Strange, *Toronto's Girl Problem*, 26–32.

105 **exposé on this practice**: *Star*, January 3, 1894.

106 **Palmer House Hotel**: *Globe*, November 21, 1894.

106 **St. Lawrence Temperance Hotel**: *Empire*, November 24, 1894.

106 **Gladstone Hotel**: *World*, November 24, 1894.

106 **Rossin House Hotel**: *Globe*, November 22, 1894.

106 **Pearson Avenue**: St. Albans Ward, assessment records, 1892.

107 **Fern Avenue**: St. Albans Ward, assessment records, 1894.

107 **"she was not afraid of any man"**: *Globe*, November 21, 1894.

107   **Flora seems to have worked with the Phyalls**: Harriet Phyall said Flora had worked for her before: *Globe*, November 28, 1894.

107   **Then she worked for the Lansells**: *Empire*, November 24, 1894.

107   **keep a close eye on Flora**: *Globe*, November 28, 1894.

108   **often went to the theatre with her mother**: *Telegram*, November 23, 1894.

108   **"her mother always acted kindly"**: *Telegram*, November 22, 1894.

108   **"Like Clara Ford, Flora possesses considerable temper"**: ibid.

108   **"ignorant and helpless female"**: *News*, November 24, 1894.

109   **"liked to sit on the steps from the boardwalk"**: *Mail*, November 21, 1894.

109   **Frank had thrown her down at the waterfront**: *Globe*, May 2, 1895.

109   **"exchanged a bit of 'chaff'"**: *Mail*, November 22, 1894.

109   **Frank "tantalising" Clara**: *World*, November 22, 1894.

109   **Gus Clark contended that Frank told The Telegram**: *Mail*, November 21, 1894.

110   **"Westwood's Frank" ... was twenty-eight-year-old Clara's informant**: *Globe*, May 3, 1894.

110   **Westwood boys had insulted the Clark girls**: *World*, November 23, 1894; and *Empire*, November 23, 1894.

110   **"That night [Clara] vowed revenge"**: *Star*, November 24, 1894.

110   **Clara and Frank were lovers**: *World*, November 21, 1894.

110   **Frank didn't return her affections**: *World*, November 23, 1894.

110   **Clara and Gus Clark were having an affair**: *Globe*, May 3, 1895.

111   **Gus Clark provided the following story**: *Mail*, November 24, 1894.

112   **"as good as a man"**: *World*, November 23, 1894.

112   **Catherine Clark's four stepchildren**: *Might's Directory*, 1889; and Census of Canada 1891, Library and Achives Canada.

112   **"heard a noise"**: *Mail*, November 26, 1894.

113   **"a few friends had gathered"**: *Mail*, November 24, 1894.

113   **excerpts were obtained and published in The World**: *World*, May 3, 1895.

114   **Judge Boyd's trial notes**: Patrick Brode, *Death in the Queen City: Clara Ford on Trial* (Toronto: Natural Heritage Books, 2005), 107.

114   **"Poor Clara. I cannot tell you"**: *Mail*, November 26, 1894.

115   **"nothing but the most pleasant relations"**: *Empire*, November 22, 1894.

115   **"When [the McKay-Fords] first moved"**: *Star*, November 28, 1894.

115   **In Parkdale's first assessment**: Parkdale, assessment records, 1879, 1884, 1885; and St. Albans Ward, assessment records, 1891, 1892.

115   **"lived behind Mr. Westwood's house"**: *Telegram*, November 28, 1894.

116   **Frank Jones of the** Toronto Star: "Scene of 1894 Jameson Avenue Shooting," *Star*, February 26, 1989.

117   **"Clara arrived ... drenched"**: *Empire*, November 24, 1894.

117   **"In Parkdale, there is a story"**: *Star*, November 24, 1894.

117   **Dixie Rice was the younger sister**: *Mail*, November 21, 1894.

117–18   **in the same article, John Harvey Hall**: ibid.

118 **"Dressed in Male Attire"**: *Telegram,* August 27, 1894.

118 **"dusky skin and wild pranks" and "It's easy enough"**: *Globe,* November 22, 1894.

119 **C.S. Clark had much to say about living in a boarding house**: C.S. Clark, *Of Toronto the Good*: rooms, 75; and food, 137.

119 **Chinese laundryman**: 1891 Census; and *Might's Directory,* 1894.

119 **Vic Steinberg, pioneering female journalist**: *News,* January 26, 1895.

120 **"not to enter her room"**: *Empire,* November 24, 1894.

120 **"protection against insult or assault"**: *Mail,* November 23, 1894.

120 **The Dorseys were at the centre of the Ward**: 1842, 1861, 1871, 1881, 1891 censuses.

120 **first wife died in childbirth**: *Globe,* April 17, 1862.

120 **married Chloe Hickman**: marriage, John Dorsey and C.A. Hickman, February 5, 1863, "Ontario, County Marriage Registers, 1858–1869," obtained from *FamilySearch,* March 17, 2018, citing Toronto, Ontario, Canada, Archives of Ontario, Toronto, FHL microfilm 1,030,065.

120 **taught Black immigrants from America**: *Telegram,* May 6, 1895; and night schools for Black refugees, from Adrienne Shadd, Afua Cooper, and Karolyn Smardz Frost, *The Underground Railroad: Next Stop, Toronto!* (Toronto: Natural Heritage Press, 2002), 45.

121 **frequent run-ins with the law**: *Globe,* January 17, 1874; October 9, 1874; July 24, 1879; and July 11, 1882.

122 **"stirring speech"**: *Globe,* October 31, 1874.

122 **Delos Rogers Davis**: *Globe,* November 16, 1882.

122 **"a very large number of colored citizens"**: *Globe,* August 2, 1894.

122–23 **Adam Samuel Morse case**: *Globe,* May 8, 9, 19, and 25, 1888, and June 4, 6, 7, 12, 13, and 16, 1888.

123 **A massive public celebration was held**: *Globe,* June 26, 1888.

124 **Reverend Robinson tried to check into the Queen's Hotel**: *Globe,* August 22, 1888; and Clark, *Of Toronto the Good*, 68.

125 **"never stayed out late"**: *Mail,* November 21, 1894.

125 **still attended St. Mark's**: *Telegram,* November 23, 1894.

125 **"extraordinary passion for the lake"**: *Mail,* November 26, 1894.

125 **"caught her round the waist"**: *Mail and Empire,* May 3, 1894.

125 **didn't visit Parkdale after mid-August**: *Globe,* May 4, 1894.

EIGHT: EIGHT HOURS

127 **"You may ask a man a question"**: T.E. St. Johnston, "Judges' Rules and Police Interrogation Today," *Journal of Criminal Law and Criminology* 57, 1 (1966): 85–92.

128 **right to counsel**: Albert Currie, *Riding the Third Wave: Rethinking Criminal Legal Aid within an Access to Justice Framework* (Ottawa: Department of Justice, 2004).

128 **James Bailey**: C.S. Clark, *Of Toronto the Good* (Montreal: Toronto Publishing Company, 1898), 17–26.

128–29 **"I was informed by one of the police"**: *News*, November 24, 1894.

130 **"The system of closeting a prisoner"**: *World*, November 27, 1894.

130–35 **Slemin's and Porter's testimony about their questioning at the preliminary hearing**: *Globe*, November 28, 1894.

132–37 **Reburn's testimony at the preliminary hearing**: *Globe*, November 28, 1894.

137 **Clara was – finally – formally arrested**: *Mail and Empire*, May 3, 1895.

NINE: MONSTER

140 **"My time is short" and plea**: *Globe*, November 28, 1894.

141 **"mulatto man-woman"**: *Globe*, November 24, 1894.

142 **The Brute and the Pitiable Colonized Subject**: Barrington Walker, *Race on Trial: Black Defendants in Ontario's Criminal Courts, 1858–1958* (Toronto: University of Toronto Press, 2010).

143 **"on account of the frequency of rape"**: Constance Backhouse, *Petticoats and Prejudice: Women and Law in Nineteenth-Century Canada* (Toronto: Women's Press/Osgoode Society for Canadian Legal History, 1991), 98.

143 **"a child of nature … docile" and "stupid ignorant mulatto"**: Walker, *Race on Trial*, 49, 52.

144 **"her heart was pure"**: David Pilgrim, "The Tragic Mulatto Myth," Jim Crow Museum, Ferris State University, 2012, https://www.ferris.edu/HTMLS/news/jimcrow/mulatto/homepage.htm.

144 **sensitive and highly strung**: *Telegram*, November 22, 1894.

144–45 **"Ushered into the world"**: *World*, November 29, 1894.

145 **The Tragic Mulatto Girl trope was subverted**: P. Gabrielle Foreman, *Activist Sentiments: Reading Black Women in the Nineteenth Century* (Urbana: University of Illinois Press, 2009).

145 **"strain of negro blood precluded her"**: *Star*, November 21, 1894.

146 **"She is a tall, fine-looking woman"**: *Globe*, November 21, 1894.

146 **Flora was Clara's daughter**: *Globe*, November 22, 1894; and *Telegram*, November 22, 1894.

146 **"One Fall evening Frank had seen her"**: *Globe*, November 24, 1894.

147 **"We made an error in commenting"**: *Globe*, November 27, 1894.

148 **"aggressive, unfeminine …"**: Wendy Ashley, "The Angry Black Woman: The Impact of Pejorative Stereotypes on Psychotherapy with Black Women," *Social Work and Public Health* 29, 1 (2014): 28.

148 **the Jezebel**: Patricia Hill Collins, *Black Feminist Thought: Knowledge, Consciousness, and the Politics of Empowerment* (New York: Routledge, 2000).

148 **"true pugilistic style"**: *Mail*, November 21, 1894.

148 **"Clara Ford is an immensely strong woman"**: *Star*, November 21, 1894.

148 **"at times has exhibited terrible ebullitions"**: *Empire*, November 24, 1894.

149 **"Much has said about her threatening"**: *Telegram,* November 28, 1894.

149 **"Clara worked 5 years ago as a tailor"**: *Mail,* November 21, 1894.

149 attacking **"a man at the Palmer House"**: *Mail,* November 22, 1894.

149 **Clara had tried to strangle one of the Clark sisters**: *Empire,* November 22, 1894.

149 **"hide a difficulty [pregnancy] caused by Frank"**: *Star,* November 22, 1894; and *Empire,* November 22, 1894.

150 **"the girl deliberately killed young Westwood"**: *World,* November 21, 1894.

150 **"Enamoured of his good looks"**: Hector Charlesworth, *Candid Chronicles: Leaves from the Note Book of a Canadian Journalist* (Toronto: MacMillan, 1925), 89.

150 **"Police say she became infatuated"**: *Empire,* November 23, 1894.

150 **"confident his dead son"**: *Globe,* November 22, 1894.

150–51 **"not intimately acquainted"** and **"had no reason to believe"**: *Globe,* November 21, 1894.

151 the Monster trope: Harry Benshoff, *Monsters in the Closet: Homosexuality and the Horror Film* (Manchester: Manchester University Press, 1997).

151 **"The accused is rather stoutly built"**: *Mail,* November 21, 1894.

151 **"Two pairs of men's suits"**: *Star,* November 21, 1894

152 **"an abnormal tendency to indulge"**: *Mail,* November 22, 1894.

153 **"the real motive"**: *World,* November 22 and 23, 1894.

153 **"complaints [were] made to the police"**: *World,* November 21, 1894.

154 **"With this perverted condition"**: *World,* November 22, 1894.

154–55 **"alienists and those who are the highest"**: *World,* November 23, 1894.

156 **"If it's so it's in** The World": *World,* November 29, 1894.

156 **"There is a story that Frank made slighting remarks"**: *Star,* November 24, 1894; and *World,* November 27, 1894.

156 **Chatelle case**: *Globe,* October 24, 1894.

156 **"resting on their oars"**: *Globe,* November 24, 1894.

157 **"revulsion of feeling"**: *Mail,* November 26, 1894.

157–58 **"What is the strong motive?"** and **"reserved and lady-like"**: *Telegram,* November 21, 1894.

158 **"It seems rather a curious idea"**: *Telegram,* November 22, 1894.

158 **"Fair Play, Gentlemen"**: *Telegram,* November 23, 1894.

158–59 **"She is an exemplary prisoner"**: ibid.

159 **"The flexible minds of some detectives"**: *News,* November 22, 1894.

160 paled in comparison to the scene at Magistrates' Court: *Globe,* November 29, 1894.

160 **"Stray flakes of snow"**: *Telegram,* November 28, 1894.

160–61 **"supported on the bench"** and **"the accused came up to the steps"**: *Mail,* November 29, 1894.

161 **"but the greater part of the time she sat with half-closed eyes"**: *Star,* November 28, 1894.

161 **"weird, tragic and almost pathetic recital"**: *Globe*, November 29, 1894.

161 **"As Reburn spoke, Miss Ford's lips tightened"**: *Telegram*, November 29, 1894.

TEN: THE FORCES OF THE LAW

166 **a *Star* reporter looked on**: *Star*, December 8, 1894; and Flora being "let go," *Globe*, April 18, 1894.

166 **"All winter the dusky woman remained"**: Albert Richard Hassard, *Not Guilty and Other Trials* (Toronto: Lee Collins, 1926), 8.

167 **Of the 750 executions between 1860 and 1962**: Richard Clark, "Executions in Canada from 1860 to Abolition," *Capital Punishment UK*, http://www.capitalpunishmentuk.org/canada.html.

168 **Elizabeth Workman's case had elements**: Scott Gaffield, "Justice Not Done: The Hanging of Elizabeth Workman," *Canadian Journal of Law and Society* 20, 1 (2005): 171–92.

168 **George Bennett**: Jeff Gray, "The Forgotten 15," *Globe and Mail*, August 27, 2017.

169 **Mary Aylward**: Desmond Morton, "Murder in Hastings County," *Canada's History*, May 7, 2015.

170 **John Radclive was packing his ropes**: Patrick Cain, "The Agony of the Executioner," *Toronto Star*, May 20, 2007; and Hector Charlesworth, *Candid Chronicles: Leaves from the Note Book of a Canadian Journalist* (Toronto: MacMillan, 1925), 81.

170 **"remarkable astuteness in giving hints"**: *Mail*, November 26, 1894.

170–73 ***The Telegram* began its campaign to prove Clara's innocence**: *Telegram*, December 1, 1894.

173–74 **"hysterical utterances"**: *Star*, December 8, 1894.

174 **"crazed about Clara"**: *Star*, December 17, 1894

174 **"Clara Ford's Head"**: *Globe*, December 1, 1894.

174–76 **"African blood"**: *Empire*, January 21, 1894.

176 **"white slavery"**: Carolyn Strange, *Toronto's Girl Problem: The Perils and Pleasures of the City, 1880–1930* (Toronto: University of Toronto Press, 1995), 14.

177 ***The Black Crook* is considered the first**: John Kenrick, "History of the Musical Stage: 1860s – The Black Crook," Musicals101.com, 2020, https://www.musicals101.com/1860to79.htm.

177–78 **In the play, the evil ...** : Douglas Reside, "Musical of the Month: *The Black Crook*," New York Public Library (blog), June 2, 2011, https://www.nypl.org/blog/2011/06/02/musical-month-black-crook.

178 **"code of chivalry had a revival"**: Strange, *Toronto's Girl Problem*, 152.

179 **E.F.B. Johnston**: G. Mercer Adam, *Toronto, Old and New* (Toronto: Mail Printing Company, 1891), 66.

179 **Harvey case**: Edward Butts, "Murders in 1889 Almost 'Unmanned' Guelph Police Chief," *Guelph Mercury*, October 13, 2015.

179 **"Counsel must prevent a witness from leading him off"**: J. Kristin Bryson, "Johnston, Ebenezer Forsythe Blackie," in *Dictionary of Canadian Biography*, vol. 14, University of Toronto/Université of Laval, 2003–, http://www. biographi.ca/en/bio/johnston_ebenezer_forsyth_blackie_14F.html.

180 **technique was to never meet with his clients**: Charlesworth, *Candid Chronicles*, 92.

181 **"every person charged with an offence"**: Ed Ratushny, "Is There a Right against Self-Incrimination in Canada?," *McGill Law Journal* 19, 1 (1969): 29.

181 **Born near Detroit in 1852 ...** : *Globe*, July 3, 1897.

182 **"harassed [by the police] to the extent"**: *Star*, January 17, 1895.

182 **Johnson had been brought in to lead Clara's defence**: *Globe*, January 21 and 22, 1895.

183 **"In the 1890s, the man who dominated the Canadian scene"**: Charlesworth, *Candid Chronicles*, 80.

183 **Osler came from a distinguished family**: Adam, *Toronto, Old and New*, 91.

183 **huge billings**: Patrick Brode, "Osler, Britton Bath," in *Dictionary of Canadian Biography*, vol. 13, http://www.biographi.ca/en/bio/osler_britton_bath_13F.html.

183–84 **her eventual cause of death**: death, May 2, 1895: "Canada, Ontario Deaths, 1869–1937 and Overseas Deaths, 1939-1947," obtained from *FamilySearch*, March 2, 2021, citing Toronto, York, Ontario, yr 1895 cn 21564, Registrar General; Archives of Ontario, Toronto; FHL microfilm 1,853,574.

184 **"a prisoner had little change of acquittal"**: ibid.

184 **"unfolded to the jury in a lengthy series of questions"**: Charlesworth, *Candid Chronicles*, 80.

185 **Birchall, a wastrel and confidence man**: Edward Butts, "John Reginald Birchall," *The Canadian Encyclopedia*, March 10, 2016, https://www. thecanadianencyclopedia.ca/en/article/john-reginald-birchall; and *Globe*, October 1, 1890.

185 **"When 'e's on the case"**: Charlesworth, *Candid Chronicles*, 81.

185 **Dewart was considerably younger**: Carolyn Strange, "Dewart, Herbert Hartley," in *Dictionary of Canadian Biography*, vol. 15, http://www.biographi.ca/en/bio/dewart_herbert_hartley_15E.html.

185–87 **Boyd was similar in background and character ... referred to himself as "The Chancellor"**: Peter G. Barton, "Boyd, Sir John Alexander," in *Dictionary of Canadian Biography*, vol. 14, http://www.biographi.ca/en/bio/boyd_john_alexander_14E.html. The National Club, where the magistrate and Denison spent their afternoons, still thrives in central Toronto.

187 **"her lower face had been swollen"**: *Globe*, March 20, 1895.

187 **"the supposed daughter of Clara Ford is being kept in hiding"**: *Globe*, April 18, 1895; location of shelter, *Might's Directory*, 1895; and Susan Houston, "McIntyre, Agnes Buchanan (Whiddon)," *Dictionary of Canadian*

Biography, vol. 14, http://www.biographi.ca/en/bio/mcintyre_agnes_
buchanan_14E.html.

187 **Hyams case**: Charlesworth, *Candid Chronicles*, 31–36; and W. Stewart
Wallace, "The Hyams Twins Case," *Maclean's*, June 13, 1931.

189 "**battle royal**": *Star*, April 21, 1894.

189 "**case was ready**": *Star*, April 29, 1894.

ELEVEN: WITNESS FOR THE PROSECUTION

191 **occupied desks with inkwells**: *Globe*, May 1, 1895.

191 "**Jail life seems to have agreed with her**": *World*, May 1, 1895.

191 "**neatly dressed**": *Globe*, May 1, 1895.

192 "**jurors' patience**": *Globe*, May 6, 1894.

193 **She rejected the first of twenty-two**: *Globe*, May 1, 1895.

193 "**jury is composed entirely of farmers**": *Star*, April 30, 1895.

193 **Judging from their names ... and their professions**: *Globe* May 1, 1895.

193 "**The famous QC's 25-minute opening statement**": ibid.

194 "**much interest in court**": *Mail and Empire*, May 1, 1895.

194 "**in no [sexual] complication**": *Star*, April 30, 1895.

194 **Benjamin Westwood's and Dr. Lynd's testimony**: *Mail and Empire*, May 1,
1895.

195 **Murdoch did ask Temple Cooper and Ed Lennox**: *Star*, May 1, 1895.

195 **the testimony of Flora McKay**: ibid.

195 "**it was evident that she was suffering severe mental distress**": *Mail and
Empire*, May 2, 1895.

196 "**They have not got the thing down correct!**": ibid.

196 **Harriet Phyall and the Crosiers' testimony**: *Globe*, May 2, 1895.

197 **Chancellor Boyd once again ruled**: *Mail and Empire*, May 2, 1895.

197 **hostile cross-examination of Slemin**: ibid.

198 "**debauched looking female**": *News*, May 3, 1895.

198 "**Lizzie Smith**": *Star*, May 2, 1895.

198 **long and distressing Magistrates' Court record**: *Globe*, August 12, 1875;
June 30, 1876; July 23, 1876; November 12, 1880; July 23, 1884; October 29,
1886; and August 24, 1887.

199 **Infanticide cases were common**: Constance Backhouse, *Petticoats and
Prejudice: Women and Law in Nineteenth-Century Canada* (Toronto: Women's
Press/Osgoode Society for Canadian Legal History, 1991), 136.

200 **Libbie Black testified**: *Mail and Empire*, May 2, 1895.

200 "**witness, who was expected to give evidence**" and "**story of a mulatto
girl**": *Globe*, May 2, 1895; and *World*, May 1 and 2, 1895.

200 "**proved an intimacy**": *Star*, May 2, 1895.

201 "**Perhaps he has escaped!**" and "**there did not appear to be any point**":
Mail and Empire, May 3, 1895.

201 "**the Crown needs to show beyond all doubt**": *Star*, May 2, 1895.

202 **"he did not see why criminals"**: *Globe*, May 3, 1895.

202 **"sweatbox" and a cross-examination called both "sharp" and "harsh"**: ibid.

202 **"wanted to get at the facts"**: *Mail and Empire*, May 3, 1895.

203 **"had frequently declared that if insulted by a man"**: *Mail and Empire*, May 4, 1895.

203 **"Samuel Barnett, the shrewd" and "a man tried to assault her"**: *Star*, May 3, 1895.

203 **"buggy riding every night"**: *Telegram*, May 3, 1895.

203–4 **Ballistics**: Lisa Steele, "Ballistics," in *Science for Lawyers*, ed. Eric York Drogan (Chicago: American Bar Association, 2008), 1–20.

204 **"Clara's revolver was of a very cheap iron," "animosity towards detectives," and "This is the case for the Crown"**: *Star*, May 3, 1895.

TWELVE: THE PERFORMANCE OF HER LIFE

206 **Clara took the stage**: *Globe*, May 4, 1895.

206 **"happy to join the noble work"**: *Globe*, October 4, 1893.

207 **the Trickster**: A.R. Leslie, "*Brer Rabbit*, a Play of the Human Spirit: Recreating Black Culture through Brer Rabbit Stories," *International Journal of Sociology and Social Policy* 17, 6 (1997): 59.

207–8 **"second person charged with murder to avail herself"**: *Star*, May 3, 1894.

208 **Luckey was charged with the triple murder**: *Globe*, April 18, 1893.

208 **Lizzie Borden, the axe-wielding**: Joseph Conforti, "Why 19th-Century Axe Murderer Lizzie Borden Was Found Not Guilty," *The Smithsonian*, July 23, 2019.

208–9 **Clara started by setting the scene ...**: *Globe*, May 4, 1895; and *Star*, May 3, 1895.

210 **"fired at two ducks"**: *Globe*, May 4, 1895.

211–15 **"In the Toils"**: *Mail and Empire*, May 4, 1895; and testimony from *Globe*, May 4, 1895.

216–18 **"Forcing the Confession"**: *Mail and Empire*, May 4, 1895; and testimony from *Globe*, May 4, 1895.

218 **the cross-examination**: *News*, May 4, 1895; and *Globe*, May 4, 1895.

219 **"From 4.10 to 5.25, Crown Attorney Dewart"**: *Mail and Empire*, May 4, 1895.

219 **"the woman showed surprising cunning"**: *Star*, May 3, 1895.

219 **"feckless demeanor on the stand"**: *Globe*, May 4, 1895.

THIRTEEN: TWELVE HUNGRY MEN

221 **"standing in a masculine attitude"**: *World*, May 4, 1895.

221 **charged with contempt**: *Globe*, May 6, 1895; and *Star*, May 6, 1895.

221 **suffering from gastrointestinal distress**: *Telegram*, May 3, 1895.

221–22 **Charles Clark and George Barnett of *The Telegram* testified**: *Globe*, May 6, 1895.

222 **"truthful and industrious"**: *Mail and Empire*, May 6, 1895.

222 "steadiness, truth and industry were good": *Globe,* May 6, 1895.

223 "Mrs. Dorsey, a very stout": *Star,* May 4, 1895.

223–24 Dewart took Dorsey through an extensive cross-examination: *Telegram,* May 4, 1895.

224 summoned back to court: *World,* May 6, 1895; and *Mail and Empire,* May 6, 1895.

224 the Opera House witnesses: *Globe,* May 6, 1895.

224–5 the Crown recalled several people: ibid.

225 "sit it out": *Globe,* May 6, 1895.

225–29 In his closing argument for the defence, Johnston: *Mail and Empire,* May 6, 1895; except "sin where there is no sin," *Star,* May 4, 1895; and "Czar-like actions," *Globe,* May 6, 1895.

229–30 Dewart ... laid out the Crown's case: *Mail and Empire,* May 6, 1895; except "flatly contradicted," *Globe,* May 6, 1895.

231 "The judicially stern yet kindly face": *Globe,* May 6, 1895.

231–34 Boyd's summation: *Mail and Empire,* May 6, 1895; except "skin for skin" and "four, eight, ten, twenty," *Globe,* May 6, 1895.

234 might want to recall the jury: *Globe,* May 6, 1895.

234 "The audience settled down for a long wait": ibid.

234–35 "retired from the courtroom": *Telegram,* May 6, 1895.

235–36 "ominous hush" and response to verdict: *Globe,* May 6, 1895; except "be kind to the little girl," *Mail and Empire,* May 6, 1895; and "well known bookmaker," *Telegram,* May 6, 1895.

237 "Set Free!": *Star,* May 6, 1895.

237 "Hundreds of people filled the street": *Telegram,* May 6, 1895.

237 "boys of Toronto": *World,* May 6, 1895.

FOURTEEN: WHAT CLARA DID NEXT

239 defence fund: *Globe,* May 6, 1895.

239 "the mental strain had been terrible": *Mail and Empire,* May 6, 1895.

239 "been offered work by several people": *News,* May 6, 1895.

240 "Walker is an entertaining youth": *Star,* March 13, 1895.

240 "I don't approve of that": *News,* May 6, 1895.

240 Flora McKay also visited her mother: *World,* May 6, 1895.

240 Two front-page editorials: "Jurors Forget Themselves" and "Abusing Detectives," *Star,* May 6, 1895.

241 "This crime, which has created such widespread interest": *World,* May 6, 1895.

241 "will meet with general approval": *News,* May 6, 1895.

241–42 credited E.F.B. Johnston with saving Clara's life: *Star,* May 6, 1895; *Globe,* December 5, 1895; Albert Richard Hassard, *Not Guilty and Other Trials* (Toronto: Lee Collins, 1926), 9; W. Stewart Wallace, *Murders and Mysteries: A Canadian Series* (Toronto: Macmillan, 1931), 79; and Carolyn Strange,

"Wounded Womanhood and Dead Men: Chivalry and the Trials of Clara Ford and Carrie Davies," in *Gender Conflicts: New Essays in Women's History,* ed. Franca Iacovetta and Mariana Valverde (Toronto: University of Toronto Press, 1992), 153.

242 **"Between the detectives and the accused"**: *Globe,* May 6, 1895.

242 **greater vigilance by constables against overcrowding**: *Globe,* May 9, 1895.

242 **an American "fixer"**: W. Stewart Wallace, "The Hyams Twins Case," *Maclean's,* June 13, 1931; and Hector Charlesworth, *Candid Chronicles: Leaves from the Note Book of a Canadian Journalist* (Toronto: MacMillan, 1925), 82.

243 **a police detective named Harrison was sued**: *Star,* June 12, 1895.

243 **"I knew if I was kept in the police cells"**: *Globe,* December 9, 1895.

243 **Boyd allowed another confession**: *Star,* June 12, 1899.

244 **"adding to the odors for which the Police Court"**: *Globe,* February 8, 1897.

244 **Stark refused to release Clara's suit**: *Telegram,* May 22, 1895.

244 **public lecture at the Temperance Hall**: ibid.

245 **"displayed the ability"**: ibid.

245 **advising "the audience never to make confessions"**: *Winnipeg Free Press,* May 23, 1895.

245 **"paid tribute to *The Telegram*"**: "Clara on the Platform," *Telegram,* May 22, 1895.

245 **"told her that but for him she would be facing the gallows"**: Charlesworth, *Candid Chronicles,* 92.

245 **"due to inferior companies under the title Creole"**: Lynn Abbott and Doug Seroff, *Out of Sight: The Rise of African-American Popular Music* (Jackson: University Press of Mississippi, 2009), 201.

245 **not one but three travelling shows**: *Chicago Tribune,* July 14, 1895.

246 **"Young, well-dressed, live, energetic up-to-date women"**: *Chicago Tribune,* October 27, 1895.

246 **the new season of *The Creole Show* premiered**: *Chicago Tribune,* August 27, 1895.

246 **In the show's chorus ... was Clara Ford**: Abbott and Seroff, *Out of Sight,* 202.

246 **"Clara Ford, the heroine of a recent Toronto murder trial"**: *Buffalo Evening News,* September 25, 1895. See also *Globe,* September 20, 1895.

246 **"erring girls"**: *Mail and Empire,* May 6, 1895.

247 **"Coloured society circles"**: *Massillon Independent,* November 12, 1896.

247 **Crawford owned a tavern**: *Cleveland Directory,* 1898.

247 **he remarried in 1906**: marriage, Charles J. Crawford and Meta Henderson, April 21, 1906, "Ohio, County Marriages, 1789–2016," obtained through *FamilySearch,* March 8, 2021, citing Marriage, Cuyahoga, Ohio, United States, V63, Appl. 46348, Franklin County Genealogical & Historical Society, Columbus, FHL microfilm.

248 **"Clara Ford's Hard Luck"**: *Star,* May 8, 1898.

FINALE: CLARA, ARMED

250 **King ... wrote a two-part feature**: Philip Gordon Mackintosh, *Newspaper City: Toronto's Street Surfaces and the Liberal Press, 1860–1935* (Toronto: University of Toronto Press, 2017), 58.

250–51 **"The Foreigners of Toronto"**: *Mail and Empire*, September 25, 1897, and October 2, 1897.

252 **social cleansing of the Ward**: Richard Dennis, "Private Landlords and Redevelopment: 'The Ward' in Toronto, 1890–1920," *Urban History Review* 24, 1 (1995): 21–35.

252 **Parkdale, too, was losing its lustre**: Carolyn Whitzman, *Suburb, Slum, Urban Village: Neighbourhood Transition in a Toronto Suburb, 1875–2002* (Vancouver: UBC Press, 2008).

252–53 **William Murdoch was the first actor to take his bow**: *Globe,* July 3, 1897.

253 **Lizzie Smith ... met with a noteworthy end**: *Globe,* June 28, 1899.

253 **Gus Clark continued his slow slide**: *Star,* July 4, 1895.

253 **dose of strychnine**: *Globe,* January 12, 1897.

253 **again stole from the tavern**: *Star,* December 2, 1897.

253 **once again in Central Prison**: 1901 Census.

253 **vibrator emporium failed**: The Dorenwends are in the 1901 Census but then disappear. See also K. Taylor, "Of Barbers, Hair Dressers and the Dorenwends," *One Gal's Toronto,* January 17, 2016, https://onegalstoronto.wordpress.com/2016/01/17/of-barbers-hair-dressers-and-the-dorenwends/.

253 **Clark's mother, Catherine, had a happier fate**: *Globe,* April 30, 1906; sells tavern to her son Casper, *Globe,* July 28, 1906; and death, Catherine Clark, July 24, 1911, "Ontario Deaths, 1869–1937 and Overseas Deaths, 1939–1947," obtained from *FamilySearch,* March 9, 2018, citing Toronto, York, Ontario, yr 1911, cn 4436, Registrar General, Archives of Ontario, Toronto, FHL microfilm 1,854,634.

254 **Chloe Dorsey lived ten more years**: death, Chloe Dorsey, November 30, 1906, "Ontario Deaths, 1869–1937 and Overseas Deaths, 1939–1947," obtained from *FamilySearch,* March 9, 2018, citing Toronto, York, Ontario, yr 1906, cn 4650, Registrar General, Archives of Ontario, Toronto, FHL microfilm 1,854,399.

254 **Mary Crosier also lived a long life**: death, Mary Crosier, December 4, 1931, "Ontario Deaths, 1869–1937 and Overseas Deaths, 1939–1947," obtained from *FamilySearch,* March 8, 2018, citing Toronto, York, Ontario, Canada, 7917, Registrar General, Archives of Ontario, Toronto, FHL microfilm 2,295,638.

254 **Charles Ingles as St. Mark's pastor**: death, Charles Leycester Ingles, January 25, 1930, "Ontario Deaths, 1869–1937 and Overseas Deaths, 1939–1947," obtained from *FamilySearch,* March 8, 2018, citing Toronto, York, Ontario, Canada, 001302, Registrar General, Archives of Ontario, Toronto, FHL microfilm 2,313,286.

254 **Benjamin Westwood died**: death, Benjamin Westwood, January 4, 1935, "Ontario Deaths, 1869–1937 and Overseas Deaths, 1939–1947," obtained from *FamilySearch*, March 11, 2018, citing Toronto, Ontario, 001631, Registrar General, Archives of Ontario, Toronto, FHL microfilm 2,413,411.

254 **Clara Westwood died**: death, Clara Bonnick Westwood, 1937, obtained from *FamilySearch*, March 16, 2018; Burial, Toronto, Toronto Municipality, Ontario, Canada, Mount Pleasant Cemetery, citing record ID 177633699, *Find a Grave*, http://www.findagrave.com.

254 **Bert Westwood, a successful businessman**: "C.H. Westwood," *Globe and Mail*, May 7, 1964.

254 **Emily Westwood Kennedy**: death, Emily Westwood in entry for Kennedy, September 3, 1918, "Ontario Deaths, 1869–1937 and Overseas Deaths, 1939–1947," obtained from *FamilySearch*, March 10, 2018, citing Toronto, York, Ontario, Canada, 005385, Registrar General, Archives of Ontario, Toronto, FHL microfilm 1,862,693.

254 **William Westwood**: marriage, William Augustus Westwood and Georgina Hill, April 8, 1912, "Ontario Marriages, 1869–1927," *FamilySearch*, March 11, 2018, citing registration, Toronto, York, Ontario, Canada, Archives of Ontario, Toronto, FHL microfilm 1,906,147.

254 **moved to St. Petersburg, Florida**: William Westwood, Saint Petersburg, Election Precinct 16, Pinellas, Florida, "United States Census, 1940," database with images, obtained from *FamilySearch*, March 14, 2018, citing enumeration district (ED) 52-17, sheet 4B, line 68, family 133, Sixteenth Census of the United States, 1940, National Archives and Records Administration, digital publication T627; Records of the Bureau of the Census, 1790–2007, RG 29, Washington, DC, National Archives and Records Administration, 2012, roll 609.

254 **estranged with his family**: William is not mentioned in his father's 1935 obituary.

254 **when they died, all between 1919 and 1922**: Reburn, *Globe*, November 28, 1921; Johnston, *Globe*, January 30, 1919; and Dewart, *Globe*, July 8, 1924.

254 **Carrie Davies**: Carolyn Strange, "Wounded Womanhood and Dead Men: Chivalry and the Trials of Clara Ford and Carrie Davies," in *Gender Conflicts: New Essays in Women's History*, ed. Franca Iacovetta and Mariana Valverde (Toronto: University of Toronto Press, 1992), 149–88.

254 **Slemin eventually became a police chief**: *Globe*, May 9, 1904.

255 **David Hawes**: Carolyn Strange, "Patriarchy Modified: The Criminal Prosecution of Rape in York County, Ontario, 1880–1930," in *Essays in the History of Canadian Law: Crime and Criminal Justice in Canadian History*, ed. Susan Lewthwaite, Tina Loo, and Jim Phillips (Toronto: University of Toronto Press, 1994), 207–51. See also *Globe*, November 12, 1901; and *Star*, November 11, 1901.

255 **Arthur Simonski:** *Globe,* August 7, October 6, and October 16, 1902; and May 26, 1909.

256 **"the negro element":** George T. Denison, *Recollections of a Police Magistrate* (Toronto: Musson, 1926), 39, 157–62 (Ford case).

256 **Hector Charlesworth's memoir:** Hector Charlesworth, *Candid Chronicles: Leaves from the Note Book of a Canadian Journalist* (Toronto: MacMillan, 1925), 89–92.

257 **The third account:** Albert Richard Hassard, *Not Guilty and Other Trials* (Toronto: Lee Collins, 1926), 5–28.

257 **Stewart Wallace published a similar account:** W. Stewart Wallace, *Murders and Mysteries: A Canadian Series* (Toronto: Macmillan, 1931), 72–91.

257 **Edwin C. Guillet:** *The Shooting of Frank Westwood* (Toronto: Edwin C. Guillet, 1945), folio available at Toronto Reference Library.

257 **legal pundit named J.V. McAree:** *Globe and Mail,* March 6, 1942.

258 **Conan Doyle and Clara:** Peter Costello, *Conan Doyle, Detective: True Crimes Investigated by the Creator of Sherlock Holmes* (New York: Carroll and Graf, 1991), 177–78.

258 **columnist Frank Jones:** *Toronto Star,* February 19, 1989, and August 5, 1996.

258 **online account by local historian and genealogist:** Bill Gladstone "A Sensational Murder Mystery from 1894," *Bill Gladstone Genealogy,* December 4, 2011, http://www.billgladstone.ca/?p=3216.

258 **Richard Fiennes-Clinton:** Richard Fiennes-Clinston, "The Strange Case of the Parkdale Mystery," *Toronto Then and Now* (blog), May 14, 2015, http://torontothenandnow.blogspot.com/2015/05/57-strange-case-of-parkdale-mystery.html.

259 **A book about Clara's trial was published in 2005:** Patrick Brode, *Death in the Queen City: Clara Ford on Trial* (Toronto: Natural Heritage Books, 2005): Gus Clark as a "peculiar" low-life friend, 13; Clara's family living behind the Salvation Army refuge, 11 and 25; arrest by 9:00 p.m. and statement taken down by Stark, 32; rapport between Clara and Reburn and her "pride" in turning down counsel, 32; and motive, 156.

259 **A 1980 play *Clara* by francophone writer Marcelle McGibbon:** reviewed in Katherine Gilday, "*Clara* Lacks the Colour of Woman Swashbuckler," *Toronto Star,* February 18, 1980; and Carole Corbeil, "*Clara* Asks Burning Questions of 1895," *Globe and Mail,* February 16, 1980.

259 **Carolyn Strange wrote an article:** Carolyn Strange, "Wounded Womanhood and Dead Men: Chivalry and the Trials of Clara Ford and Carrie Davies," in *Gender Conflicts: New Essays in Women's History,* ed. Franca Iacovetta and Mariana Valverde (Toronto: University of Toronto Press, 1992), 149–88.

259–61 **Artist Anique Jordan:** "arming by clara," Anique Jordan, https://www.aniquejjordan.com/arming-by-clara-2017.

IMAGE CREDITS

172 *The Telegram*, December 1, 1894.

180 *The Globe*, May 2, 1895.

184 G. Mercer Adam, *Toronto, Old and New* (Toronto: Mail Print Co., 1891), 92.

186 *The Globe*, May 2, 1895.

190 *Toronto News*, May 2, 1895.

195 *Toronto Evening Star*, November 28, 1894.

205 *The Globe*, May 2, 1895.

220 *The Globe*, May 2, 1895.

238 Scene from The Octoroons by John W. Isham, Wikimedia Commons.

249 Photo by C. Whitzman. Used with the permission of the artist, Anique Jordan.

INDEX

Printed and bound in Canada by Friesens
Set in Copperplate and Tundra by Artegraphica Design Co.
Editor: Lesley Erickson
Proofreader: Kristy Lynn Hankewitz
Indexer: Celia Braves
Cover designer: Jessica Sullivan